The Protestant Movement in Italy

PIEMONTE
LOMBARDIA
ALTO ADIGE
VAL D'AOSTA
TRENTINO
FRIULI-VENEZIA GIULIA
VENETO
LIGURIA
EMILIA-ROMAGNA
TOSCANA
MARCHE
UMBRIA
ABRUZZI EMOLISE
LAZIO
PUGLIA
SARDEGNA
CAMPANIA
BASILICATA
CALABRIA
SICILIA

THE PROTESTANT MOVEMENT IN ITALY

Its Progress, Problems and Prospects

Roger E. Hedlund

William Carey Library
South Pasadena, California

International Standard Book Number: 0-87808-307-3
Library of Congress Catalog Number: 71-131302

Published by the William Carey Library
533 Hermosa Street
South Pasadena, Calif. 91030
Telephone 213-682-2047

PRINTED IN THE UNITED STATES OF AMERICA

Dedicated to

Raymond Buker who first taught me the Science of Missions, and to all my missionary colleagues who serve the Evangelical cause in Italy

Contents

Figures

Foreword

Italy is not just another country in Europe. From that oddly shaped piece of land jutting out into the Mediterranean streamed disciplined legions that held the world at bay for half a millenium. Then for another thousand years disciples of a new faith streamed forth from that same piece of land to supervise the faith of most of Europe and much of the entire world.

Evangelicals well recall the great breakaway of the northern part of Europe in the Protestant Reformation and the new emphasis of the Reformers which, in effect, declared once and for all that you don't have to be Roman to be Christian. In this emphasis the Reformers borrowed from the Apostle, whose letters had made it crystal clear that in his day the Greeks did not have to be Jewish to be Christian. But in Italy today the situation is reversed, and evangelicals back home may not readily see that present-day Italians do not have to be Americanized in order to be Christian. Missionaries sense that they cannot get very far in Italy "protesting" as good Protestants that the Gospel is capable of being accommodated to German or English tongues and cultures. Evangelical missionaries in Italy have to be very careful lest they find themselves preaching a "Protestant Catholicism." They face the spectacle of immense commitment of mission funds apparently accomplishing less than a single nationalized movement that came from the United States but is now startlingly more "Italian" than the other Protestant churches. Thus one question is, "How Italian can you be and still be evangelical?"

Though not so extensively treated in this book, a quite different question is, "How evangelical can you be and still be Roman Catholic?" We easily forget that in the early period of the Reformation "everywhere in Italy there were people who felt, even more keenly and intimately than the Germans, the Swiss, or the English, the abuses that were demoralizing the church," (see p. 5). Perhaps this can be true again, and if so, then hopefully politics will not swing the weight of the Roman church against evangelical reform, as happened in the Reformation.

Thus, while this book is for those who are far more excited about where Italy is going than where Italy has been, it does effectively show the continuing significance of the past upon the present. It pulls together many threads in the situation in readable, brief compass. It performs a great service to those who are serious about Europe's ailing faith and the perplexing impasse of evangelism and church renewal in Italy in particular, but it does much more than that.

Italy is the heart of the enigma of Christian renewal. Given the continuing cohesiveness of the Roman world church and its persisting center in Italy, it is quite possible that attempts to evangelize Catholics outside Italy might be successful when they would fail at the hub; it is less likely that solutions developed in Italy will fail to shed light on the evangelical encounter with Catholics in the many nations on the periphery. In this sense this issue--and this book--is for all Christians everywhere.

RALPH D. WINTER
School of World Mission
Fuller Theological Seminary
Pasadena, California

Introduction

Several histories have been written covering aspects of Protestantism in Italy. This study is not primarily a history although it deals with historical data. Nor is it an anthropological or sociological treatment even though anthropology and sociology are brought to bear. Rather this is a religious study, specifically devoted to church growth.

It has not been possible to treat exhaustively any of the groups of Evangelicals (Protestants) in Italy. An attempt is made to recognize each church or mission of significance, but this is limited to the information available to me at this moment. A section is devoted to each of the major denominations, but a case study is devoted to the Brethren and the Pentecostals, two of the groups most relevant to the question of present church growth in Italy. These two were chosen rather than the Waldenses. Much has been written about the Waldensian Church. From a historical viewpoint the Waldenses are the most important Protestant Church of Italy. From the perspective of contemporary church growth, however, the Pentecostals and the Brethren are of greater interest. Each group is to be treated separately. Special attention will be given to areas of the country where there seems to be special response. Where meaningful, comparisons will be made utilizing graphs and charts.

The present study has limitations. There is by no means an excessive amount of recent literature on a number of branches of the Protestant Church in Italy. I have consulted those materials which were known and available to me. Undoubtedly I missed some, and others were not available to me in the United States. This study is not exhaustive, nor is it "the final word." My knowledge of the subject is limited. Others, including missionaries of many more years of experience and broader adquaintance with the field, will be able to make a number of corrections and additions. I hope they will feel inspired to write their contributions.

This subject was chosen because of a need. To my knowledge no church growth study has been previously made of Italy. This is written to show that there has been Evangelical Church expansion in Italy, to indicate where and when growth has occurred, to discover under what conditions it takes place, and to point out some of the obstacles it has encountered. It speaks to the present, trying to find a better way in the task of Italian evangelism. Of the 53 million residents of

Italy, only a few thousand have become Evangelical Christians. There are today some 53 Evangelical groups at work in the country with several hundred workers - national as well as foreign. Most of these are seeing small numberical increase. Yet growth is taking place. It is the purpose of this study to describe this growth and to help the Missions and Churches to achieve yet greater growth for the Glory of God. The task is to bring Italians to an encounter with Jesus Christ which will result in both commitment to Him as Lord and also fellowship in His Church. (The Church into which evangelism brings converts, unless otherwise stated, is assumed to be the Evangelical Church in its various branches). Such is the understanding of evangelism in this study. Through research I have endeavored to discover the ways in which the Holy Spirit is best able to accomplish His purposes in Italy.

The preparation of this project involved consulting reports, questionnaires, private correspondence, books and articles in Italian and in English. The Italian section of the Research Library of the University of California at Los Angeles was especially useful to me. The Honnold Library at the University Center of the Claremont Colleges and the Fuller Theological Seminary Library were also of great help.

Books were inadequate, however, for the essential statistics which church growth research requires. Finding some reliable figures was the most difficult part of the survey. Memberships reported in books tended to be vague and contradictory. The definition of "member" was unclear. Therefore it was necessary to look elsewhere for membership statistics. For this the reports of persons near the actual situation were invaluable. In some cases it was necessary to be content with book figures which were, however, refined according to all the available date. In no case was it necessary to rely on a wild guess. While it was difficult to obtain statistics, the number of churches and their locations were available for nearly every denomination and group. Despite precautions gaps can be found. Further work needs to be done and corrections made.

I am indebted to my colleagues of the Conservative Baptist Mission in Italy for graciously sending materials direct from Italy and for supplying much of the inspiration for this study. I acknowledge with gratitude the guidance of Dr. Ralph Winter in this project and the contributions in various ways by the faculty of the School of World Missions and Institute of Church Growth of Fuller Theological Seminary in Pasadena, California.

PART ONE
The Setting

1

History

In some ways the history of Italy is the history of Western Civilization. Many volumes describe that history. Will Durant devotes over 700 pages to a treatment of the history of civilization in Italy during the period 1304 to 1576 A.D. (Durant 1953).

Since I am not writing primarily a historical study, the history of Italy will not be reproduced here. The information is readily available in encyclopedias and books such as *A Short History of Italy* (Herder and Waley 1963). The classical Italian work by Guicciardini is also available in an English translation (1969).

Nor is it possible here to review the ecclesiastical history of the country. Aspects of that history are touched upon in the rather lengthy section dealing with the Catholic Church. The Italian Protestant Reform provides some light for the present study, and is included in this chapter. A large part of Protestant history is treated in relation to the Waldensian Church (chapter three).

This study is concerned with church growth. Italian history is herein considered as it seems to bear on the growth of the Church. Figure one (the time line) provides a backdrop of some significant names and events of secular and sacred history.

SECULAR	A.D.	SACRED
Pompei and Ercolano destroyed (79)	100	Christian community in Rome Paul beheaded (64)
	200	
Decius Valerian / Joths invade	300	1st persecution 2nd persecution
Diocletian Constantine (324) Empire divided east and west (395)	400	Edict of Milan 3rd persecution / Arianism
Attila retires Western Emperor vandals sack Rome abdicates Rome Theodoric invades	500	
Justinian Lombard invasion	600	Benedictines Gregory the Great
	700	
Pepin Charlemagne crowned Holy Roman Emperor	800	
Arabs hold Moslems take Sicily	900	
Sicily	1000	
Normans invade S. Italy Normans	1100	Split with Greek Orthodox Church Hildebrand (Pope Gregory VII)
in Italy Barbarosa	1200	Francis of Assisi/ Peter Waldo Innocent III
French Marco Polo Crusades	1300	Pope Boniface VIII
dominion Dante Petrarca Boccaccio	1400	
Michelangelo, Leonardo, Raphaelo	1500	Savonarola Julius II
Michiavelli Spanish Sacking of Rome Galileo	1600	Italian reform: Bernard Ochino, U. Valdez P. Martyr, Vergerio
Dominance	1700	
Napoleon invades	1800	
Unification: Garibaldi, Cavour, Mazzini, Victor Emmanuel II	1900	End of temporal power/ Brethren Methodists and Baptists enter
Fascism: Mussolini		Laterau Agreements/ Pent. Vatican II - Pope John / Faith missions

FIGURE 1 TIME LINE

2

The Reformation in Italy

INITIATIVE FOR REFORM

Will Durant, in his own inimitable style, begins his treatment of Italian Protestant reformers with this potent statement:

> In climatically pagan Italy, constitutionally polytheistic, favoring a genial and artistic faith, populated with undying saints whose awesome or beloved effigies moved annually through the streets, and enriched by the gold that came to the Church from a dozen subject lands, one should not have expected to find men and women dedicated, sometimes at mortal risk, to the replacement of that picturesque and hallowed faith by a somber creed whose political support was the reluctance of northern nations to fatten Italy with the proceeds of their piety. Yet everywhere in Italy there were people who felt, even more keenly and intimately than the Germans, the Swiss, or the English, the abuses that were demoralizing the Church (1957:891).

In Italy pressures for reform came from the educated classes. The writings of German reformers were popular, and helped stir desires for intellectual freedom. In 1535 Lutherans claimed 30,000 adherents among the clergy and laity of Italy (Durant 1957:891).

Huguenot ideas were for a time fostered at Ferrara by Princess Renee, daughter of Louis XII.

But is was, as Durant states, "impossible that Italy should go Protestant" (1957:894). There was too much to lose: the wealth and art of the Church. Besides, the accommodating air of Italy was not congenial to the puritanical ideas of the reformers. Also the presence of Spain assured continual loyalty to Catholicism.

Italian reform efforts were therefore largely directed within the Church. The sack of Rome in the 16th Century gave incentive. A corrupt clergy was reformed. Social reforms were enacted. Cardinals and bishops acted with a sense of urgency: either "the Church must reform of die" (Durant 1957:896). Pope Paul III was unwilling to make radical changes in a time of political and national crises, but he did accept graciously the report of a reform conference. His appointments were of some of the leading lights of the Counter Reformation. Its leader, Caraffa, was to become Paul's successor. As Paul IV -- he carried the reform to its triumph.

Simultaneously monastic reform brought into existence the Capuchins. Their austere emulation of the ideals of Francis of Assisi served to retain the loyalty of Vittoria Colonna "and other incipient Protestants" to the Catholic Church. After all, "a Church that could still produce such ardent Christians" (Durant 1957:900) could not be all bad.

Much of the reform was superficial, imposed from above by high ecclesiastical authorities. It did not penetrate the soul of the Italian Church. Rather it stultified the true religion of Italian genius. Gebhart feels that in the early Middle Ages Italy enjoyed an "astonishing freedom of thought" which found religious expression in her greatest artists, poets, and saints (n.d.:27). Francis of Assisi was the apex of a period which found its end in the institution of Roman Catholicism. The instrument in forming Roman Catholicism was, according to Gebhart, the creation of the Jesuit Order and the Council of Trent:

> The Council of Trent, aided by the Inquisition, imposed upon Christendom a moral rule, a devotion and a religious method of an absolute uniformity, at the same time that, repairing the breaches made in the pontifical power by the councils of the fifteenth century, it assigned to the Church of Rome an uncontrolled and unlimited disciplinary authority over the episcopate, and monastic orders, the secular clergy, and the simple believer. (Gebhart n.d.:28).

Roman Catholicism, partly in reaction, was experiencing change. Yet there was a Protestant Reform in Italy. In fact it was a Reform pre-dating the protests in Germany, Switzerland and France. This is Waldensianism, whose story is told in the following chapter, and need not be detailed here.

Outside of the Waldensian Valleys the Reformation movement was carried on during the sixteenth century by some of Italy's greatest churchmen. Whether some of these men had any connection with the Waldenses *per se* is not clear. Some of them tried to operate entirely from within the Catholic Church. In this they were often apparently successful - for a time. But their views and efforts usually brought them into conflict with Rome. Many of them were forced to flee for their lives.

The Reformation arose out of the crises of the sixteenth century. In its background was the reforming crusade of a charismatic preacher who called for repentance in an age of moral decadence and religious corruption. "Girolamo Savonarola stands as a great prophetic figure on the eve of the religious crisis of the sixteenth century" (Olin 1969:1).

The Reform was also in reaction to a revival of paganism which was taking place as indicated by the great men of the day. Perugino, it is said, did not believe in the immortality of the soul. Leonardo doubted the truth of Roman Catholicism. A notoriously lustful woman was apparently the model for Raphael's beautiful Madonnas (Luzzi 1913:55). Michelangelo stands alone as a destroyer of idols, his art "the cries of a restive genius" (Luzzi 1913:64).

The Reform movement was the continuation of the best of Savonarola's spirit. Its causes were three: religious corruption, the influence of the Bible which seems to have been studied more than is generally believed, (a translation printed in Venice is said to have gone through nine editions in the last part of the fifteenth century and twenty more in the sixteenth), and the presence of German students in Italian universities and Italian students in German universities.

Reformers were found throughout Italy.

PROGRESS OF THE REFORM IN ITALY

(1) Ferrara

More than any other, Ferrara protected the friends of the Reformation. Princess Renata, from the court of Margaret of France, encouraged Reform opinion. As early as 1528 several Protestant preachers labored in Ferrara (MeCrie 1842:82). Calvin once visited there.

(2) Modena

Everyone was quoting the Scriptures in Modena at the height of Gospel preaching in 1540. The learned, the illiterate, and even women "all promiscuously tortured the sacred Scriptures" (McCrie 1842:86). The Academy was thought to be the center of "heresy". Citizens were in correspondence with Luther and other heretics.

(3) Florence

The Medici opposed the Reformation. Nevertheless by 1525 young Antonio Brucioli had become an aggressive Protestant. Accused, tried and banished, he translated the Bible and became influencial in his writings. "So far as the influence of the press is concerned, Brucioli is entitled to the name of the reformer of Italy" (McCrie 1842:93). Other Florentines were also important Protestants.

(4) Bologna

In 1545 a nobleman of Bologna "was ready to raise six thousand soldiers in favour of the evangelical party, if it was found necessary to make war against the Pope" (McCrie 1842:98). Bologna formed part of the Papel States. The University favored Liberal opinion. Protestants in Bologna were numerous.

(5) Venice

The many printing presses of this rich and powerful Catholic republic produced versions of the Bible and other religious books in the vernacular. Venetian merchants circulated the German and Swiss Protestant books to the different parts of Italy. "Among those who contributed most to the propagation of reformed opinions at Venice, were Pietro Carnesecchi, Baldo Lupetino, and Baldassare Altieri" (McCrie 1842:105). Great progress took place between 1530 and 1542. The city could easily have moved to the Protestant side. In the surrounding territories Vicentino and Trevisana had the greatest number of Protestants. There were numerous converts at Padua and some at Verona, Brescia and Vicenza.

(6) Milan

Influenced by bordering Piedmont and Switzerland, Milan contained adherents to reformed doctrine as early as 1542 (McCrie 1842:110). The name of Celio Curione (or Curio) is associated with reform opinion in Milan.

(7) Naples and Sicily

The southern part of the peninsula and the island of Sicily were under Spanish rule. Reformed teachings spread widely in this territory. The Waldenses still existed in Calabria around 1536. The city of Naples especially was to see many great reformers. Among them were Juan Valdes, Bernardino Ochino and Pietro Martire Vermigli. Through their labors a reformed Church was established in Naples.

(8) Lucca

Peter Martyr labored here upon leaving Naples. Lucca is said to have had "among its inhabitants a greater number of converts to the reformed faith than perhaps any other city in Italy" (McCric 1842:129).

(9) Pisa

In 1543 a Protestant church was formed here.

(10) Sienna

The Gospel was preached in Sienna by Ochino and by Paleario. The reform apparently had many followers.

(11) Mantua

A Benedictine and a Cardinal introduced extensive reforms within the Church at Mantua.

Other cities where there were persons holding reform convictions include Locarna, Istria, Faenza, Imola, Ancona, Geneva, Cittadella, Cremona, Brescia, Cevita di Friuli, and Rome.

In each the Reform movement was suppressed by the Inquisition.

LEADERS OF REFORM

Naples became the beacon of the South from which the Reformation light beamed throughout Italy.

Juan de Valdes. From a palace at Chiaia this Spanish gentleman became in eight years "the most constructive force for spiritual religion in Italy" (Church 1932:50). Until his death in 1542 he attracted the "flower of Italian piety". The list of followers include some illustrious names (Luzzi 1913: 78-79):

Pier Martire Vermigli
Bernardino Ochino
Marco Antonio Flaminio
Pietro Carnesecchi
Jacopo Bonfadio the historian
Lattanzio Ragnoni of Sienna
Bartolomeo Spatafora, a nobleman of Messina
Donato Rulla from Puglia
Mario Galeata from Naples
Placido di Sangro (or de Sanguine) the head of the Academy of de'Sereni
Giovan Galeazzo Caracciolo, son of the Marquiz of Vico
Vittoria Soranzo and
Giovanni Buzio from Montalcino (Mollio)
Vittoria Colonna, Marchioness of Pescara, a literary star of her century and twin soul of the great Michelangelo,
Giulia Gonzaga, Duchess of Trajetto and Countess of Fondi, a woman of exquisite piety and famous for her misfortunes not less than her fascinating beauty, and
Donna Isabella Brisegna, the wife of Don Gorzia Manriquez, the Governor of Piacenza.

Valdes taught justification by faith. His disciples developed this doctrine. The three most influential of his followers were Vergerio, Vermigli, and Ochino (Church 1932:50).

A flourishing evangelical church developed at Naples with Valdes as pastor (Standridge 1968:5), although he may have remained unordained.

Bernardino Ochino. The influence of Valdes upon Ochino was significant. Ochino came from Sienna. A member first of the Observantist monks, he left them for the more severe Capuchins. He became the Order's fourth Vicar General. His fame was as a preacher. Valdes influenced large audiences through the preaching of Bernardino Ochino. It is said that Valdes furnished Ochino with the themes for his tremendous sermons. The night before Ochino was to preach Valdes would send suggested topics to him written on slips of paper (Church 1932:53). He was popular. As a great preacher he "swept from city to city"(Church 1932:56). Four times he was in Naples - in 1536, 1539, 1540, and 1541 (Church 1932:58). When Ochino separated from the Catholic Church and fled to Geneva the event was a shock which nearly destroyed the Capuchin Order (Olin 1969:151). It is unfortunate that in his reaction he became antitrinitarian.

Vermigli. Ochino associated with Pier Martire Vermigli and Curione. Vermigli, commonly known to us as Peter Martyr, was born in 1499, destined to become a leader of the Reform in Italy. The work by McNair (1967) not only is a significant study of this man's life and influence upon the Italian Reformation, but is a commentary on Ochino and Valdes and others of Vermigli's associates. His father may have been an admirer of Savonarola. Pietro Martire did not become a Dominican, but at around the age of sixteen he did enter the religious life as an Augustinian (McNair 1967:63, 69).

Vermigli like Ochino was to be a preacher. More than Ochino he was to become the scholar, and doctor of theology. Studies, teaching, and preaching caused him to go beyond scholasticism. "From the Schoolmen he turned to the Fathers, from the Fathers to the Vulgate, and from the Vulgate to the Source itself" - the original Greek and Hebrew (McNair 1967: 124). Peter Martyr Vermigli was to be a scholarly voice for reform within the Church.

In 1537 Vermigli was elected Abbot of S. Pietro ad Aram in Naples. The three years he spent there changed his life. It is said he came as a reformer in the style of Ximenez but left as a reformer after the order of Zwingli (McNair 1967:142). It is possible that the abuse of indulgences at S. Pietro ad Aram produced in him an effect similar to that of St. Peter's in Rome upon Luther. Through Valdes Peter Martyr imbibed Protestant literature and ideas.

Peter Martyr had come to Naples a Catholic reformer. He left a Protestant. In his preaching he had denied the doctrine of Purgatory. This was but the expression of his Calvinistic theology, the cornerstone of which was "the doctrine of Justification by Faith alone in a crucified yet living Christ" (McNair 1967:179).

Still Martyr continued as a reformer within the Church. As Prior at Lucca he set about seriously putting his Order's House in order. The reform was moral, educational, and doctrinal (McNair 1967:219). The result was nearly revolutionary, and it all centered on the Word of God and was reenforced by the exemplary life of the Reformer.

Many factors may have caused him to decide to flee. Basically it was a crisis of conscience no doubt centered upon the celebration of the Mass (McNair 1967:268). In 1542 he quietly fled beyond the Alps.

Vergerio. The circle at Naples at one time must have included the Bishop of Capodistina. Vergerio fitted among the followers of Luther (as Vermigli followed Calvin). Many shared his Protestant views. Vergerio himself, convinced of the truth of Justification by Faith, proceeded to preach it throughout his diocese. His brother Giambattista, bishop of Pola, joined with him. Their efforts "made the whole peninsula, in the years following his return from the diet of Worms, seethe with rebellion against the Church" (Church 1932:73).

THE FAILURE OF THE ITALIAN REFORMATION

In spite of transformed lives, in spite of outstanding leaders and a popular following the Italian Reformation failed. Why? Many possible explanations come to mind: Pope Paul III, the Jesuits, the Inquisition, Julius III, Trent, Paul IV, Pius IV, Pius V. The presence of the Vatican is a unique problem for Italy, and is one reason for the failure of the Reform.

Other valid explanations have been offered. At the time Italy lacked a national spirit. The princes did not sympathize with the Reform. The thought of foreign invasions brought terror. The form of Protestantism from beyond the Alps was not congenial. The reform had a deficient organization; there were too many leaders. Conversely too few followers meant a lack of energy (Luzzi 1913:87-88).

Luzzi, however, feels that more profound answers include the following. (1) The Renaissance in Italy made religious reform impossible. Its doubt and indifference and revived paganism undermined religious sentiment. (2) The Papacy made religion an external thing without faith. (3) The aspirations of Italy clashed with German conceptions of the Church of Rome and the Papacy. The Papacy was practical for national pride and "unity". (4) Egoism: the Papacy attracted wealth; indulgences were a source of revenue for Italians as well as "interest in the Bank of Heaven". (5) The reform began among the elite, not among the masses. The people did not long for truth and righteousness, and the reform lacked the good-will of the princes (Luzzi 1913:88-96). Given these facts, the Reformation could not have succeeded.

3

Roman Catholicism

The story of Western civilization may be said to be somewhat synonymous with the history of Italy, and the intricacies of the Roman Catholic Church are woven into its fabric. At times the Church completely overshadows the country. When the Pope retired within the walls of the Vatican in self-imposed "imprisonment", it was to prepare to emerge in greater prestige. Politicians and economists must reckon with the power of the Vatican. The Papacy, for all practical purposes, has for some 600 years been an Italian institution. Therefore any study of Evangelicalism in Italy must be made in light of Rome.

DEGREES OF CATHOLIC RELIGIOSITY

How Catholic is Italy? The 1931 census reported Italy as 99.6% Roman Catholic. What if anything does this show? The Communist vote has been increasing. Religious observance is down. The birth rate has increased, but the number of marriages has decreased. There is a growing tendency to ignore the Church. Therefore, in some respects, the census figures seem meaningless. They do indicate the fact that in Italy everyone is normally considered Catholic, exceptions being some 50,000 Jews and 100,000 Protestants. Apparently no provision is made in the census for conversions. That is, once a Catholic, always a Catholic so far as the census bureau is concerned. Census reports do not show recent Protestant growth. Nor do they indicate the degree of nominality.

The sociological studies of Silvano Burgalassi

indicate some of the variations in degree of Italian Catholic religiosity. Burgalassi writes as a Roman Catholic religious sociologist. Hence religious observance is considered in terms of participation in the Roman Catholic Church. I have relied heavily upon Burgalassi for the following information. Quotations are my own translations of the original Italian.

(1) As seen in the cities. Research conducted in several cities indicates a higher percentage of religious participation in the city centers than in the peripheral areas that surround the cities. Even when allowance has been made for those who prefer attending mass in the larger central churches outside their own parishes, there is still more participation in the centers. On an average the inhabitants of the centers are more religious than those of the suburbs. People in the larger cities are less religious than those of the smaller cities. Religious practice is particularly intense in cities under 50,000 as indicated in figure 2 (Burgalassi 1968:19).

Further examination reveals that women are considerably more faithful in attending mass than are the men. This is even more true in the smaller cities. Generally people under 21 years of age are more religious than those over 21. Again the central city appears more intensely religious than does the surrounding area (Burgalassi 1968:20-21). Figure 3 shows these facts.

(2) As seen in the country. Turning from the city to the country we find a slightly higher degree of faithfulness as indicated in figure 4 (Burgalassi 1968:22).

In the rural areas the women are much more actively religious than the men, and younger people than those over 21 (see figure 5).

(3) According to geography. Catholicity may be determined by comparing sections of the country. The extreme northern regions of Trentnio-Alto Adige and Veneto have the highest degree of religious observance. Next are Lombardia, Calabria, Marche and Puglie. Regions with a lower degree are Sicilia, Toscana, Lazio and Emilia (Burgalassi 1968:27). This is an oversimplification, however, as pockets of religious intensity, or the lack of it, are to be found in most sections. The South is especially full of sharp contrasts with their many implications making generalizations unwise.

> The areas with the highest religious practice seem to be those of Abruzzi and Calabria with a striking richness of traditional religiosity; nevertheless the strong

CITIES	CASES STUDIED	RELIGIOUS PARTICIP. (in Center)	RELIGIOUS PARTICIP. (in Periphery)	DIFFERENCE
over 300,000	6	27%	16%	11%
100,000 - 300,000	8	33%	18%	15%
50,000 - 100,000	9	33%	29%	13%
under 50,000	21	72%	25% .	47%

FIGURE 2 RELIGIOUS PRACTICE IN CITIES

	Males over 21	Males 7-21	Average Male rate	Females over 21	Females 7-21	Average Femalo Rate
CENTRAL CITY	23%	31%	29%	48%	45%	47%
PERIPHERY	12%	23%	18%	26%	38%	30%

FIGURE 3 RELIGIOUS PRACTICE BY MEN AND WOMEN

PARTICIPATION IN SUNDAY MASS			TAKING EASTER COMMUNION		
CITY	COUNTRY	DIFFERENCE	CITY	COUNTRY	DIFFERENCE
36%	41%	5%	50%	58%	8%

FIGURE 4 SUNDAY MASS, EASTER COMMUNION

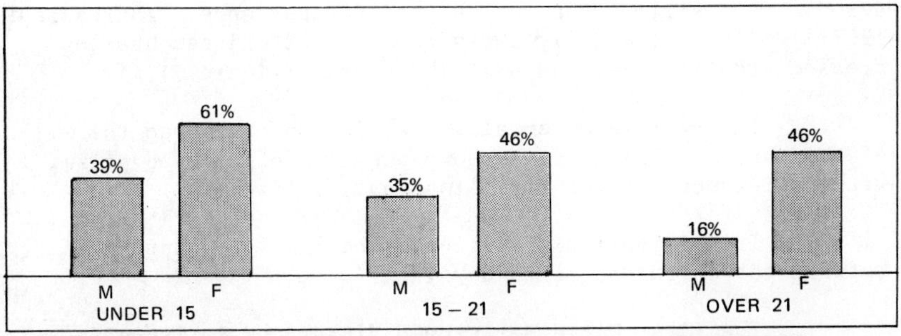

FIGURE 5 RURAL RELIGIOUS PARTICIPATION BY SEX AND AGE

Sunday presence is accompanied by other acts of a heavily pagan nature (superstitious rites) or by acts of religious and social pathology (legal separations, homicides, lewd conduct) especially in areas of Calabria (Burgalassi 1968:57-59).

Sicily is especially low with an average of 25% practicing religion - 12% below the national mean.

Study needs to be made to determine the relationship of Southern religious mentality to evangelistic response. Sicily has proven a fertile field for Pentecostals in spite of its strong traditions and Mafia. It is poverty-stricken and low on the religion scale. Calabria and Abruzzi too are poverty areas and have many traditions, but they are considered actively Catholic. Yet here too the Evangelical message has found good response. What are the factors which cause these areas to be receptive? Someone needs to explore the unique facets of the religious isolation of the South.

There is also a relationship between the terrain where a municipality is located and the amount of religious practice. In Northern Italy communities located in the internal mountains show the highest religiosity, followed by the coastal mountains and inland hills, and by the coastal hills and plains. The South shows the highest practice in the hill communities. Hill municipalities in Central Italy score the lowest (Burgalassi 1968:72-73). Figure 6 shows the relationship between terrain and religiosity according to geographical area.

(4) <u>According to baptismal practice</u>. How much of the participation in the life of the Church is based on religious conviction? Religious activity, including attendance at Mass, may have a superficial base. Catholic researchers feel that an index of religious vitality is delay in baptism. Catholic parents are expected to baptize the newborn at the earliest possible moment. Therefore postponement of baptism is considered a very serious test of Christian conscience. (Burgalassi 1967:112-115). The chart shows that the time lapse has increased steadily over the past 100 years (Figure 7).

The year 1870 reveals a people conforming to the will of the church. There is a strong practice of early baptism, with preference for the first two days after birth.

In 1910 variation begins. The time for baptism is between the third and fifth days.

The First World War proved disastrous in its effect

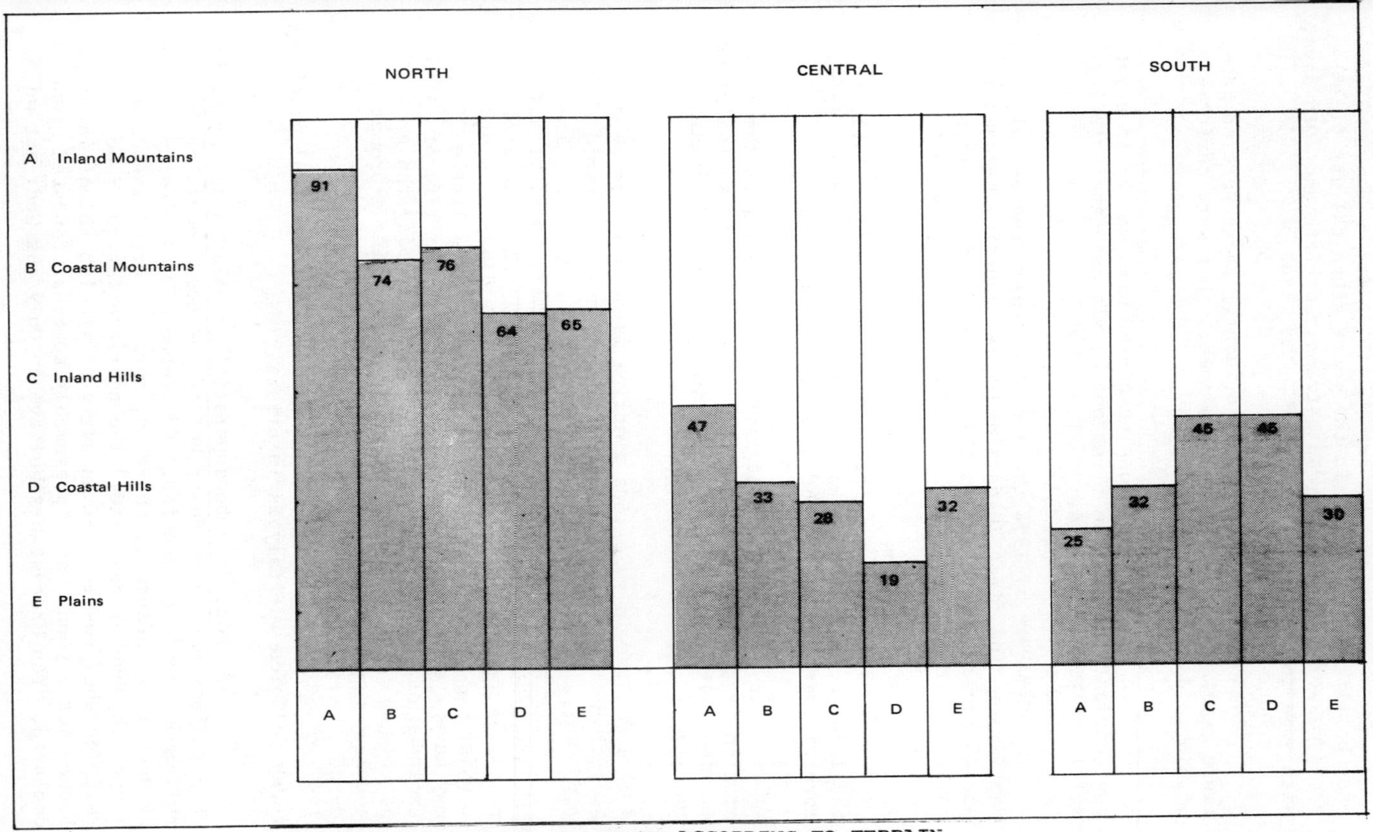

FIGURE 6 RELIGIOUS PRACTICE ACCORDING TO TERRAIN

upon baptismal practice. In the years after the war (1924) baptisms were being performed between the fifth and 20th days, with some coming after a month.

In 1934 correction was evident. There were no baptisms registered past the 30 day mark. Most were performed within 10 days.

In 1944 the tensions connected with war again create postponements beyond the first month, although the majority still are within 10 days.

However by 1954 the situation has worsened, with fewer baptisms in the first 10 days and more occurring between 10 and 20 days. The record in the German-speaking regions indicates that there was a higher Catholic conscience in that area in this regard.

An interesting point which appears, particularly in the 1964 record, is that rural parishes instead of remaining more diligent have come the more delinquent.

To a Roman Catholic student of these facts the conclusion is that postponement of baptism accompanies religious decline, although there may be several causes (Burgalassi 1967:126).

> A decline in religious practice is accompanied by a diminishing sensibility of parents toward a rapid babtism; we have, then, witnessed a progressive infiltration of lay mentality, of indifference, of anti-Christian ideologies and the logical consequence of what has been the abandonment of the "fear of sin," that no longer frightens parents who have little religion. Only those who really live the life of Grace with its delicate shades, value today the profound motives of the Church in prescribing a prompt baptism.

According to the trend in Catholic baptismal practice, today religion in Italy is in crisis.

(5) <u>According to superstitious beliefs and practices.</u> The Italians have been described as the descendants of the most religious people of mankind. Evidences of religiosity are to be seen in abundance at churches, shrines, crucifixes and images throughout the land. The characteristics of popular religion show vestiges of an early polytheism (Blunt 1823:4). I once met a young man - presumably somewhat educated - who declared, "You Protestants believe in Only one God: but we

YEAR	WITHIN 24 HOURS	WITHIN 5 DAYS	WITHIN 10 DAYS	WITHIN 20 DAYS	WITHIN 30 DAYS	OVER 30 DAYS
1870	Rural: ALL (in "good" parishes)	-20% of rural parishes	city: 53% of cases rural: 10% of parishes			
1900	"Alt' Italia" same as in 1870	Rural: 15% of cases in "best parishes"	city: 10-15 (as above) rural: 10%			
1910	Rural: 15% of cases	Rural: 12% of cases	Rural: 10% of cases	City: majority of cases All other cases.		
1924			30% of parishes	26% of parishes		10-20% of cases
1934			majority of cases	12% of parishes have majority bptms. 10-20 days	city: majority of cases	
1944			50% of parishes (majority baptized here)	1.8% of parishes	15% of parishes	15-25% of cases
1954			20% of parishes (Alta Italia - better:	6-20 days pref.) 33% of parishes	2% of parishes (15% of cases)	15% of cases
1964				"Best" parishes : 15-20 days Alta Italia 15-20 days	city: 25-30 days	rural: over 30 days

FIGURE 7 BAPTISMAL POSTPONEMENT

Catholics have many gods". He was referring to the Madonnas and the Saints.

John Blunt of Cambridge University made a study of the relationship between Catholic practice in Italy and pre-Christian religion. Concerning the Saints he says: "If we consider their numbers, their reputed lives, the places and objects over which they preside, then miraculous powers, together with some other circumstances relating to them, we shall find in them a wonderful resemblance to the gods of Rome (1823:7). At Viterbo Blunt discovered this Latin inscription on a church altar:

"But ah! what powers of tongue can paint,
The virtues of this virgin saint?
For whom, a chaste, celestial bride,
The ruler of Olympus sigh'd." (1823:12).

The confusion of paganism with Catholicism is not surprising when one considers that pagan temples which were converted into Christian churches are still standing and in use today. The writer has personally visited several: the Parthenon in Rome, the Temple of Minerva in Assisi and the Temple of Saint Michael the Archangel in Perugia.

In the home as much as in the church the same pattern is seen. Every bedroom has its saint or Madonna over the head of the great matrimonial bed. Pictures or images of saints and Madonnas are found throughout. These objects are considered necessary for protection. For similar reasons a crucifix or picture may be worn. This is similar to the practices of the Romans whose idols decorated the rooms (Blunt 1823:27).

In the hospitals of Southern Italy large images of the Madonna, of Saint Anthony and other saints are conspicuous even though clean lives may be lacking. The relatives of patients frequently are seen caressing the image while praying to the saint. Lighted candles may be found nearby at anytime.

Electricity has made it possible for tiny lights to burn continually before the pictures and images in homes, hospitals, shops and cemeteries. Sometimes these are placed every night beside the beds of children. The idea of protection is more than implicit in such cases.

The functions of the saints are divided. Thus there are patron saints for fishing, for travel, for fertility, etc., just as there once was a godess of fertility, the god of the sea, etc. Patron saints serve as "guardians" of persons, cities, countries and areas.

Someone has said concerning the superstitious Italian farmer: "To better his frugal life he is a weekday Communist. For the safety of his soul he is a Sunday Roman Catholic. At heart he remains a pagan" (Evans 1963b:9).

Locally superstition takes various forms. It may be the wearing of charms, belief in the efficacy of love potions, or consulting diviners.

Some superstitions are held to quite apart from religious teachings. That is, the person who believes in and practices religion to some degree according to the teachings of the Church, may also resort to magic or superstitious acts for additional advantage. For instance an infant is baptized for the salvation of its soul according to the teachings of the Church. The parents may also, however, place a charm on or near the child for further protection from evil influences. Most commonly this is a religious medal, worn not only by small children but by persons of all ages. It has been noted that beliefs may be very different from actual Church teachings, (i.e.: a child who is unbaptized will grow up without a soul).

It is not surprising that people holding such views also have a fear of werewolves and other superstitious creatures. There are tales of persons who turn into animals at night, who fly through the air, etc. Certain persons are thought to be witches, to have mysterious powers. These are all views held alongside religious beliefs.

Similarly it is believed by members of the lower classes in some areas that spells can be cast by manipulating in a prescribed manner. A young man declares he can have any woman he wants by saying certain magical (Latin) words while performing certain rites involving certain objects. Or the acts may involve either curing or causing illness and trouble. The objects used vary according to the purpose.

Such acts are either considered illegitimate, if evil, or acceptable, if for good purpose. There seems to be little or no religious scruple against practicing "white magic". To place an egg outside the window during the night so that the fairy may turn it into a beautiful flower for Easter morning is an acceptable practice.

Going to Mass for the purpose of receiving the priest's blessing upon some object which is later to be used in evil rites is unacceptable as related to black magic.

Inasmuch as similar rites, practices and beliefs are common in certain localities, they must be known to the Church which apparently chooses to ignore their existence.

Other acts are so obvious that they can only be said to be condoned by the Church. A most common animistic practice is for the "worshiper" in a Catholic shrine, chapel or church to make some form of physical contact with the object of veneration. This may be to fondle the feet of an image, or to caress the heart in a painting. If the supplicant is concerned for a physical need, there appears to be some practice of touching the part of the "Saint" corresponding to the ailing member of the body.

The preceding has been observed as a very common procedure in the magnificient Gesu Church of the Jesuits in Naples. This church contains a chapel which is a very popular healing shrine. The walls are covered with thousands of silver trinkets brought by the devotees (miniture arms, legs, hearts - "tokens for grace received").

A cruder form of the practice may be observed at S. Pietro ad Arum Church, also in Naples. The basement of this church contains cases of human bones believed to be the relics of early Christian martyrs. Here the faithful purchase plugs (nails driven into a wooden handle) which they insert into sockets before the bones, lighting the adjoining light bulbs. This form of "devotion" is said to be especially helpful for winning at totocalcio (the lottery)! Taboos are also observed. For a pregnant woman to gaze at the bones in St. Peter's basement may cause the unborn baby to be disfigured.

The most common superstition in all of Italy is belief in the evil eye. Naples is known as the home par escellence of this concept, but it is found throughout the country under various names. In Southern Italy it is *jettatura*. In Tuscarry the terms are *affascinamento* or *mol d' occlio*. It has several different names in the North. Each refers to the power of the evil eye.

Various persons are suspected of possessing this evil power. Since the establishing of religious orders, the monks are said to have had a reputation for its possession (Elworthy 1958:23). It is amazing that one of the Popes, Pius IX, was accused of being a *jettatore* (person possessing power of evil eye). "Everything he blessed made *fiasco*" (Elworthy 1958:25)! Those who came to him to be blessed were said to point two fingers at him. This favorite symbol (pointing with the first and last fingers) represents the *corne* (horns) and has many connotations. In this instance, as an amulet, it is protective.

Protection is important as the influence is believed to be deadly. The most universal amulet in Italy is a common cow's horn. Often painted red, it can be seen mounted on a farmer's cart or dangling under a large truck on the autostrada.

The images of Saints are believed to possess power. This has been noted in relation to healing practices. Women visitors of relatives in hospitals frequently light candles and pray before the Saints found in the corridors.

On feast days appropriate images are carried in procession through the streets. During the month of May, which is dedicated to Mary, the various Madonnas are carried through the streets. The Madonna of Casa Luce is each year brought to Aversa where she is paraded and then deposited for a time so that she might bless the city.

In Aversa there is also a day when all of the saints are removed from the churches and carried through the main streets in elaborate procession. In these activities the curative powers of the images are not so much in view as their protective powers.

It is impossible not to feel that Catholicism is very mixed with paganism in its Italian expression. The judgement of Malinowski on the Roman Catholicism of Europe seems to apply to Italy (1965:105):

> The saints of the Roman Catholic Church become in popular practice passive accomplices of magic. They are beaten, cajoled and carried about. They can... stop flows of lava by confronting them and stop the progress of a disease, of a blight or of a plague of insects.

The purpose for honoring the saint seems to be to secure the general blessings of health, wealth and good fortune.

The wide diffusion of superstitious beliefs and practices which are a contradiction to Church teaching indicate the degree of spiritual illiteracy. One of the most knowledgeable persons of Italian rural religious life is G. D'Ascenzi. He admits that religious behavior is very much mixed with superstition and based upon habit and fear as much as conviction (Burgalassi 1967:93).

> In several areas and not rarely, one still encounters superstitious practices and rites that make one suspect residues of pagan cults. Today they are disappearing

> more due to the influence of civil progress than to evangelism. Religion is often in the conscience a mixture of sentiment and fear that makes it bitter and heavy.

(6) Some implications. Burgalassi deduces that around 50% of all Italians meet the bare minimum requirement of attending mass at Easter and that 37% is a national mean for participation in Sunday mass (1968:24). This figure seems high, however.

Several factors stand out in these findings. One is the lack of religious participation by the men. They have traditionally been anti-clerical, particularly in the South.

Another factor is the sharp contrast between dwellers in the periphery of the cities as opposed to inhabitants of either the central city or the country. One plausible explanation lies in the fact that in the periphery are found those who have migrated and are less settled. Not having put down roots they are less attached to tradition.

Both of these factors have implications for evangelism. In a society which is strongly family oriented missionaries recognize the value of a family-group approach. The aim is ot win entire families to Christ rather than individuals in isolation. There is a feeling that in order to win the family we must win the father who is the head of the household. We recognize that Italy is very much a man's world. But the soundness of this assumption may be questioned when considering the religious aspect. As Barzini humorously points out, it may be a man's world, but women run the men (1967:201-202).

> The man is the titular head of the household but by no means the absolute monarch...the wife is officially a subordinate figure, in charge of humbler duties, but the sphere is largely undetermined and wideranging.
>
> The arrangement gives no overwhelming authority to either. It gives the woman the greater moral responsibility...She usually manages things in a subtle, almost imperceptible, way...Men run the country, but women run men. Italy is, in reality a crypto-matriorchy.

Nowhere is this more evident than in religion. The woman is protectress and preserver of religious tradition, and the evangelist must reckon with this as he seeks to win families to Christ.

The laxity with which religious tradition is maintained in the areas on the edge of the cities indicates that these may be the areas of greatest potential. People who have been uprooted are less attached to traditions, often are searching. They are prepared to be responsive. However they must be reached before the transition period is passed. Once they have become settled into their new surroundings they will have once more developed traditions and the opportunity will be past.

Often these migrants have proven themselves bright new lights in their new surroundings. They become active in the organizations of the church. Priests have found them favorable to "new traditions." In his old surroundings he was a conformist. As an immigrant he must acculturate, though his move has been a relatively short one. In the process he can easily drop old habits. New types of conduct easily lead to religious indifference (Burgalassi 1967:50-51).

The priest sees as many difficulties as he does opportunities in this type of situation. The Evangelical must see in it an opportunity for the Gospel. The failure on the part of the Roman Catholic Church to evangelize the superstitious (animistic) peoples of Italy stands as a challenge to Evangelicals. It seems that Pentecostals in some sections have risen to this need with considerable success.

Timing is important if they are to be reached. At this moment they appear to be open. This readiness may soon be past. As materialism in the name of progress takes over, these people will discard the superstitions of the past. Therefore they are open to change. Before them are several possibilities. They may become mere materialists or Marxists. They may turn to a renewed, purified and progressive Catholicism. Or they may become Evangelical Christians - if they are given that opportunity.

CATEGORIES OF CATHOLICS

Nominally all the people of Italy are considered Roman Catholic (Protestants, Jews and others are negligable). One must not make the mistake, however, of treating all alike. The preceding examination of the degree to which these Catholics feel and practice their religion reveals great variations. It is possible to put these people into several categories. This has significance in that persons in different categories will react differently. A person in category one will require a different approach from the one in category five or category two. Category three people are distinct from category four persons.

(1) Those without religion. Sixty years ago one writer described Italy as "the land of no religion." (Clark & Clark 1909:36). The people, surrounded by beautiful churches and cathedrals, were said to have broken with the Church. Not having found refuge in Protestantism, they were largely adrift.

The Italian was admittedly difficult to convert to Protestantism. Some declared the Italian to be "deficient" religiously. Persons with this attitude felt that Italians were lacking in moral character, in discipline, in conscience, etc., and were too easy going (today we recognize that such opinions sometimes tell more about the person making the statements than about the people being judged). The lack of religious consciousness was said to be reflected in Italian art, literature and thought.

However the presence of any or all, of these traits does not necessarily indicate a deficient personality. It may, in fact, be the product of a deficient Church. That is the opinion of Rose who states that there is evidence of "the utter spiritual and moral inefficiency of Roman Catholicism upon the national life of Italy" (1922:47).

It is not surprising, then, that in the 1915 census a million persons stated themselves as without religion.

There are definite, historical antecedants for this fact. The second half of the 18th century had seen the struggle for political unity in Italy. The Papacy fought unity and the loss of its territory. Continued opposition caused a reaction on the part of Italian people (Rose 1922:42).

Today there is some carry-over of this spirit. The Vatican is very unpopular. Most people do profess religion (99.6%). But a growing number professes no religion. There are atheists and agnostics, some of whom are Marxist. Most are merely indifferent "materialists". This problem of the Church has traditionally been with the working men in the cities and with professional people. Estimates are not always reliable, but it is possible that Catholics (as those who obey the Church in religious and secular areas) are a minority group in Italy of between one third and two fifths of the population, with the bulk of the rest being the indifferent, Agnostic and Atheist, non-religious (Salvasoi 1965:13).

(2) The Anti-clericals. The second category is different from the first. The first consists of those who profess no religious faith. Those of the second definitely do.

Southern Italy is traditionally anti-clerical. It has

been said that anti-clerics in the South make up one half of the population - the male half. Their relationship to the Church varies. I have known men who were completely loyal to the Church and active in the Church but who openly criticized the priests and corrupt practices in the Church. Then on the other side are the multitudes who pride themselves on complete aloofness to the Catholic Church. They refer to the Church as "the Mother of thieves" and to the priests as "parasites." They say, "Why should I confess my sins to a man who is a worse sinner than I?" The Sacraments are meaningful to them, but they despise the professionals who administer the sacraments. Yet these same individuals are quick to affirm their belief in God and in Jesus Christ. One of them in conversation the day following the national election in 1967 raised his eyes heaven-ward as he said, "God forgive me, but I voted Communist".

A leading Italian religious sociologist, G. Bonicelli, in his work, *Situazione religiosa nel mondo del lavoro*, summarizes, as quoted by Burgalassi (1967:92) "For the mass of laborers and workmen the priests are cut off completely from life and become considered necessary beaurocrats, even though detested".

(3) Those having the minimal external marks of religion. There are many who vigorously proclaim that they are Catholics. They make the sign of the Cross and see that their children are baptized and receive first communion. They may attend mass either fairly regularly or very irregularly. But there is little understanding of the Faith. There is an amount of external observance, but little or no internal reality.

Outward observance may be based on superstition. Twenty miles from Naples in the town of Aversa there are people who baptize their children "because unless baptized the child will have no soul". Religious rites in that section are valued by many as magical.

Because they maintain the external observances these people are Roman Catholics. But in dealing with them one is confronted with practices and view points that are more pagan than Christian. They are not necessarily anti-clerical. Some of them live in fear of the priests and the power of the Church.

(4) Catholics without external markings. In the South there is a common belief in "destino." Peasants and professional people alike believe that things are predetermined. Sometimes this is a quasi-fatalistic view reminiscent of Islam. The Arab Moslem invasions of the Southern peninsula and islands centuries ago must have left an imprint in the Southern Italian

world-view.

In some sense these people are Catholics. Some beliefs may be alien to the Catholic Church. External observances may be lacking. They do not care that the Church disapproves, for they disapprove of the Church. These independent thinkers consider themselves Christians. But they are non-Church Catholics or "non-Catholic Catholics" - if that is possible. Such persons have shown a ready interest in the Bible and in Evangelical beliefs. Though anti-clerical they call themselves Catholics. They are relatively unconcerned that their views are not those of the Church. The Church in their estimation is powerless anyway; all is the result of fate (Schacter 1965:66).

(5) The devout. The total number in this class would be impossible to determine. The estimate that between a third and two fifths only of the population really professes Catholicism means that the number of devout is relatively small. The term "devout" describes the Catholic who not only professes but who is zealous in his devotion. It applies to fervent women and laymen and supposedly the most of the clergy.

It is not uncommon to hear anti-clerical people complain that "there is no such thing as a good priest". While such a statement does reflect the attitude of many, it does an injustice to those who are sincere Churchmen. Unfortunately many priests, at least in the South, are ignorant, dishonest and immoral. However there also are sincere priests with a spiritual concern.

If it can be said that the men comprise the anti-clerics of Southern Italy, then it can be said that the women are the devout. That may be an over-simplification, but generally it is the women who are fervent Catholics.

There are exceptions. Noteworthy is the Society of the Madonna of the Ark. This is an organization of laymen with chapters scattered throughout Naples and the South. They are noted for their extreme forms of devotion to the Virgin Mary. In the months preceding Easter the members are especially active soliciting offerings for the Madonna. The poor people give sacrificially hoping thus to secure the blessing of the Virgin for crops, business, home, child-bearing, health and happiness. On Easter Monday the chapter members carry these gifts in procession as they make the pilgrimmage to the Shrine of this particular Madonna on the slopes of Vesuvius.

Let me give the impressions received from personal

observation during an Easter Monday. The little village was overflowing with the uniformed pilgrims and the spectators who had come. A patriotic or civic overtone was mixed with the religious. Several chapters participated in the town square in a program of songs which were sung and speeches given lauding the virtues of the Madonna as Protectress of the village from the dangers of war and the volcano. There was a holiday atmosphere with fireworks and a carnival along the road to the Shrine. Nearer the basillica the crowds, of "human wave" proportion, made it difficult to progress. State police were present to control, somewhat, the traffic. They kept a clear corridor in the street leading to the basilica. Here the various chapters would group and prance, then run as t their turn came to enter the church. Inside the crowd was even more dense. Human bodies packed against human bodies making it extremely difficult to move and to breath. It was stiffling. TV cameras and lights were trained upon the altar and space at the front of the aisle. Here was the center of devotion - a tattered, grotesque painting of the Madonna and Child. At this altar continuous mass was being said. The devotees as they came down the aisle of the church expressed their fervour in great emotion. There were groans and shrieks. For some it was an ecstacy of joy. Others were overcome and fainted. Some kissed the altar. The large banners which they carried (pinned with offerings) were dipped in homage before the altar, then removed to the treasury. Several who had been overcome were carried out in a rigid position into recovery rooms at the rear of the church. Later they left these rooms, supported on the shoulders of friends, apparently worn out by the experience which has been described by observers as a kind of possession.

These are the devout, fanatical in their worship of the Virgin. Members of the Society are men, but women also participate in the exercise.

Are such persons responsive to the Gospel? We must recognize that these people have a deep religious consciousness. They are seeking religious reality. They are vitally interested. Therefore such persons are likely to have a greater degree of religious concern than does the typical anti-clerical person. That concern may express itself in fanatical reaction. But genuine spiritual hunger can also lead to conversion when a meaningful witness is offered, as illustrated by the following account (Rohrbaugh 1969:3).

> Antonio was tired of being crippled. He wanted to be able to walk down the street and not have people notice his limp. Surely if the Madonna saw his devotion to her in making the pilgrimage she would heal his withered foot.

Antonio made his way to the altar to present his offering to the Madonna of the Arch. He fully expected to experience something that would help him in his life, perhaps even a complete healing of his crippled condition. But the confusion of the moment and the emotional situation brought him no peace or joy.

About this time he met some members of the Bagnoli Baptist Church. These people witnessed of their faith in Jesus Christ. They had experience a change in their lives since receiving Christ as Savior. Antonio wondered if this might be the peace he had been seeking.

In Christ Antonio found spiritual life and strength to bear the problems of life as a cripple. He often reflected upon his teen years when he was so desperately seeking meaning to life. He thought of the years when he had looked in vain for help from the Madonna of the Arch. He thought of all those who continued to go to the shrine looking for something to give meaning to their lives.

And he was grateful to those who had told him about Christ.

It is not only the lower class devout who can respond to the right kind of witness, however. There are fervent Catholic individuals at all levels of society. One such is Fernando Naiola. A leading attorney of Southern Italy, practicing in Salerno, Fernando was also a devoted Catholic. His piety was expressed publicly by kneeling in the streets as a procession passed, despite the derision of the crowds. He was an intelligent, satisfied Catholic. Therefore he had no reason to be in the least interested when a missionary, coming to him for professional advice, spoke to him concerning the "Evangelical" Gospel. But the utter simplicity - and sincerity - of a humble missionary, who could not even speak Italian correctly, drove Fernando to examine the Scriptures. There he was convinced of the truth of what he had heard. As a result he was converted and baptized, in opposition to all he had been taught and had practiced, and against the wishes of his wife and family.

MARY

Roman Catholic piety in Italy is to a great extent centered in the Virgin Mary. The extreme form which such devotion may take has been illustrated in the case of the Society of the Madonna of the Ark. In popular piety it is crass worship.

(1) Madonna Cults. In Italy, as in other Roman Catholic countries, there are many Madonna cults. Near Naples, for instance, there are the Madonna of Pompei and the Madonna of Casa Luce. Powers of healing, of protection, and of fertility are assigned these Madonnas. In the minds of the people these Madonnas seem to be confused as separate beings, rather than manifestations of one Virgin. The common people - and possibly their leaders - seem to leave no idea of theological distinctions between devotion and adoration (hyperdulia as worship reserved for God verses or veneration as applied to the Saints and including Mary).

There are many interesting results of this confusion. On one occasion a relative stranger, upon learning my identity, stated, "You Protestants have only one God, but we Catholics worship many gods." He was referring to the "pantheon" of Saints and Madonnas.

On another occasion an old woman entered our Evangelical meeting hall in Aversa, looked around, and then told of having used the cavern in the ground under the hall as a bomb shelter during the war. "And because we had the Madonna of Casa Luce as our Protectress, we were never bombed," she informed us.

(2) The Position of Mary. Among educated people too the position and person of Mary is peculiar. They are emotional at this point. It is possible to reason with people about almost any other subject. But in regard to Mary they seem prejudiced and refuse to reason or to consider the statements of Scripture. Priests and people alike decline to discuss the subject of Mary. Protestants are attacked as "not believing in the Virgin Mary."

Nida confirms to us that a similar attitude exists in Latin America. "Protestant missionaries have found...that almost any doctrine of the Roman Church can be challenged with comparatively greater impunity than can the dogma concerning the Virgin Mary" (Nida 1960:130).

Why are even anti-clerical and anti-church people so hypersensitive on this issue? Nida gives the answer..."the reason of course, is that the Virgin Mary is not merely a religious symbol, but a social one as well, and as such a focus of Latin life" (1960:130). Nida's reasoning, although drawn from the Latin American context, fits Italian social structure perfectly.

For a while Italy is overtly male-dominated, it is also female-oriented. The Virgin Mary, in this setting, becomes a symbolic "mother." And who would criticize motherhood? The father may be criticized, yes, even condemned for his philanderings. He is almost expected to be unfaithful. But mother is loyal. Father is domineering, sometimes abusive. Mother stands in a mediation position, acts as protectress, the one to whom children turn to obtain desired things.

In religion, Nida points out, "God is cast largely in the role of the substitute father, as the judge and ruler of the universe" (1960:131). Mary becomes the mediator of good, a kind of substitute mother, and symbol of life and beauty and the good things of life. Jesus Christ is not a mediator or intercessor as in Protestant teaching, but is portrayed in Catholicism as dying and suffering. He is the symbol of death. And who wants to identify with a death figure? (Wolf 1965:229). Mary is more than His equal. He pales before the manifestations and miracles attributed to His mother. She is an official protectress of Italy. The month of May is hers, and at least one day is dedicated to her each month.

Mary is upheld as protectress of the home and family. It is logical that she be idolized in this social country. She is the symbol of the matron's welfare. Because of her meaning to home, motherhood, and family, her position must be preserved.

This has deep significance for evangelism. Because of the emotional connotations, communication is virtually impossible on this subject. Rather, the Catholic must be brought to know the unique person of Jesus Christ as Lord.

> Then and only the, will the Virgin assume her rightful place in the thinking and emotional structure of the believer's personality. In other words, Mary connot be driven from her place, but Christ can be so reinterpreted to Roman Catholics that He takes His rightful place as the "only mediator between God and man." Only when such an interpretation is accepted will Mary reassume her rightful, Biblical role (Nida 1960:132).

That the position of Mary in the Church grew out of a pagan context is without doubt. The earliest Christian documents show no cult of the Virgin Mary. Dogmas and rites related to the Virgin and accretions to Christianity which have gathered through the centuries. The Madonna of popular piety seems "heiress" to the cult of the Mother Goddess which spread from Asia Minor. The interesting book *The Cult of the Mother*

Goddess by E. O. James (1959) should be read in this connection. Additional research needs to be done on the actual origins of individual Madonna cults in Italy.

To the Christian observor it appears that in many ways in Italy the Virgin Mary has taken the place of Jesus Christ. James states that in the fourth century the first feasts were dedicated to Mary and that they were really festivals belonging to Christ (The Armunciation and the Presentation). At that time also churches began to be dedicated to Mary in Rome (Santa Maria Maggiore, Santa Maria Trastevere and Santa Maria Antigua). This helped promote the worship of the Madonna (1959:254-255).

Sir James Frazer feels that there is a connection between Egyptian worship of Isis which spread to Asia Minor and throughout the Mediterranean world and the development of devotion to Mary (1935:118-119).

> Indeed a stately ritual, with its shaven and tonsured priests, its matins and vespers, its tinkling music, its baptisms and aspersions of holy water, its solemn processions, its jewelled images to the Mother of God, presented many points of similarity to the pomps and ceremonies of Catholicism. The resemblances need not be purely accidental. Ancient Egypt may have contributed its share to the gorgeous symbolism of the Catholic Church as well as to the pole abstraction of her theology. Certainly in art the figure of Isis sucking the infant Hours is so like that of the Madonna and Child that it has sometimes received the adoration of ignorant Christians.

(3) Mary worship. Roman pagan religion was thus reflected in Mary worship. The rites and reverences which had been attached to various female deities were applied to the Madonna. When the term *theotokos* was accepted by the Church it is easily seen how it could have become confused with the pagan female deity.

Is all this changing? The Second Vatican Council which has brought winds of change to the Catholic Church has also brought a renewed interest in the Person of Christ and in the Bible. This seems to offer hope for correctives. However some changes move slowly. It must be remembered that Scripture is treated as part of tradition, and tradition also includes much about Mary. In conservative Italy tradition runs deep and change arrives slowly.

Doctrinally Mary is proclaimed as having shared in

Christ's sufferings for the sins of mankind. She is promoted as co-Redeemer. To Protestant Biblicists such a suggestion is not only objectionable but heretical.

It is hoped that the influence of Vatican II will correct much of this excess. While certain currents seem to be moving in the opposite direction, especially on the popular level, voices are being raised in protest. The liberal German Catholic theologian, Hans Kung, recognizes the problem (1965: 64).:

> The dangers of Mariolatry, or at least of unhealthy excesses in isolated, emotional, unscriptural Mariology and Marian devotion, obscuring the one Mediator, Jesus Christ, were pointed out to the Council...A Mariology that is more Scriptural, ecumenical, soundly pastoral and integrated into ecclesiology is happily becoming more and more established in the Church.

Protestants can only rejoice in the enlightened views of this Catholic ecumenical leader. When similar views spread in Italy many present practices may be modified and abuses corrected.

ROMAN CATHOLIC ATTITUDES

Attitude toward women. Italy is a man's world. Women have rights, but their purpose is largely to serve men. Nevertheless, womanhood is elevated. Great Italian men have often had an idealized love, a woman on a pedestal where she remained untouched and undefiled. Dante had his Beatrice and Michelangelo his Vittoria Colonna.

Great liberties may be taken with other women. Keeping a mistress is considered normal. The sexual exploitation of other women is expected. Yet sex, which is so freely indulged in, is looked upon as something bad - a necessary evil. The idealized lover therfore remains outside the realm of sexual contact. Michelangelo's love for Vittoria Colonna is platonic. Dantes' affection finds only poetic expression.

Church attitude reenforces this antithesis. Womanhood is exalted in its Virgin state in the person of Mary. The perpetual virginity of Mary is held tenaciously. Any other suggestion horrifies. For Mary to have ever had sexual intercourse would destroy her sinlessness.

Women are the upholders of Marian tradition. But Mary

devotion has not found a correlary in improving the lot of the Italian woman. Wives are expected to be faithful and hard working. Failure in either may result in beating or worse. Women who commit adultery may be shot along with their lovers, and the slaying is not considered murder. Such a crime of honor is punishable by a relatively mild sentence. Until very recently divorce was completely denied. Remarriage for a divorced or separated woman is denied. Nor is there adequate legal protection for women in the form of financial redress.

Attitude toward morality. "The Church has expressed its attitude toward morality in a legalistic rather than a realistic fashion. Pope Paul remonstrates against birth control and divorce as the signs of an immoral nation, implying that Italy possesses a higher degree of morality by denying both. At the same time he ignores widespread though illegal practices of abortion and prostitution. This seems hypocritical.

The same might be said concerning his upholding of celibacy. True celibacy is not practiced in Italy. Every Italian understands perfectly the joke, "the cardinal virtue of the clergy is chastity; they pass it on from father to son."

Gambling is part of everyday life in Italy, being promoted by the government. Protestants frown upon gambling as a form of immorality. In Italy it is classed as a vice which is much different from a sin. The Church looks upon it as wrong only when abused by cheating and stealing or when it deprives the gambler's dependents of basic needs (White 1955: 140). In all fairness, however, the Church does tend to be suspicious of gambling as a possible means of wrong use.

Likewise obeying the law is pretty much identified with morality by Protestants. In Catholic Italy this is not so. Illegal acts are not necessarily considered wrong. There is little real respect for law and order. Obeying the law is not considered important. What is important is to not get caught. That is embarrassing. The pressure socially of the "bruta figura" is much more of a controling factor than is the law.

As a result lying is very common. It is assumed that everyone is dishonest in what he says as well as in what he does. No one is to be trusted. Perjured testimony is the norm. An attorney once warned me against seeking the aid of the law because of the fact that perjured witnesses made justice an impossibility. Italians commonly say of other Italians that they are 90 per cent thieves and not to be trusted. The postman is not to be trusted. Too many postmen have been arrested and sentenced for stealing from the mails. The lament of others who hear of his "failure" is not so much over his dishonesty as over the fact that "now he is worse off than ever, and his family will suffer because he is in prison."

There is a tendency to blame the Catholic Church for the dishonesty which is so prevalent. This is a bitter reaction to the monetary interests of the clergy. Priests perform the rites of the Church for a price. Cases are known - and widely reported - of parish priests who "managed" church funds for their own advantage. Thus one priest who had built a new church was also reported to have, in the process, constructed for himself two villas in the country.

Not all is rumor. In some cases the morals of certain priests are very low. Missionaries opening the work in Aversa were challenged to debate by the parish priest of that section of the city. Not only was this man found to be illiterate in terms of acquaintance with the Bible, but when he became insulting to the believers it was revealed that he was father of an illegitimate son. In the same community nuns are reputed to be the mistresses of the priests. Much may be mere gossip, but some, no doubt, is based on fact.

Dishonesty (lying, stealing, a double standard) must be understood in terms of a nation which has been down-trodden through the centuries. These people have had to live under foreign, negative domination, and with the Vatican. They have learned to survive. In the process they have adopted whatever practices necessary.

In spite of the pressures of the Vatican, for the first time in history it appears that a form of divorce is to be permitted in Italy for certain cases. The "*piccolo divorzio*" (little divorce) law passed the lower house on November 28, 1969, by a vote of 325 to 283. It provides for a divorce only after a separation of five years. There are three possible conditions: (1) in the event of imprisonment or insanity, (2) in the event of having obtained a divorce abroad as a foreign citizen, (3) in the event the marriage has not been consumated. Whether or not the bill will be placed in effect is yet to be seen. It is amazing that it has come this far. The Vatican considers the divorce law morally wrong as well as a violation of the Lateran Pacts of 1929. It comes at a time when possible revisions of the Pacts, are being studied. In any event the fact that such a law could make such headway today does dramatize the "declining control of the Roman Catholic Church over the policies of the nation" as well as the declining marital morality in Italy where the number of marriages has been declining while the population is expanding"

(Fleming 1969:4).

Attitude toward Protestants. All Protestant groups are considered "sects" by the Roman Catholic Church. The "proselyting activities" of the despised "sects" are deplored. Protestant groups have always been subjected to various pressures, controls and persecutions. In Reformation times Wasdensians were hunted down and killed. In the 19th Century the Brethren and other evangelicals were imprisoned or banished. Under Fascism the Pentecostals suffered savage persecution. After World War II missionaries of the Churches of Christ encountered difficulty in advertising meetings, and Evangelical literature was destroyed by a priest.

A writer describes the prevailing attitude towards conversions and Protestant activities in general in the post-war period of the 1940s (Jemelo 1960:316):

> The conversion of a Catholic to Protestantism today would be regarded as a challenge to the existing order. All activity outside the churches is repressed by the police, who resort to methods which in other countries would be unthinkable, intruding into private houses, where the Gospel is being expounded or hymns are being sung, closing down huts hired by sects for the purpose of holding services, confiscating devotional literature, the prosecution of any minister who is known to have conducted a baptism by immersion together with those attending the ceremony...

The Second Vatican Council was to soften this hostile attitude. Still today, however, conversion is considered an affront to Mother Church, a denial of all one's "beliefs". - That, in spite of the fact that the majority of so-called Catholics are, in fact, without religion. Pastoral care may be totally lacking, but when the lamb that is farthest from the Catholic fold strays to the Protestant cause, it is a reason for considerable attention. Overt persecution is largely unseen today, but opposition to Protestantism is very real. It may take the form of threatened ex-communication toward those who would rent a meeting place to an Evangelical group (this happened in Aversa in 1967). It may be the power of the bishop who, it is feared, may cut off all employment possibilities for the convert (this fear was still present in 1968 in Aversa). Disdain may be expressed in the contemptuous acts of a priest who enters a Protestant home and throws down water upon the floor in place of the customary blessing given in Catholic homes (this too happened in Aversa in 1968).

Much ground must still be covered before the ideals of

the Council will be realized in Italy, even though great advances have taken place. The larger cities have realized the changes to a much greater extent than have the smaller cities and towns.

Changing attitudes. The preceding paragraph indicates that some change, at least, is beginning. Protestants observe the abuses in the Church and are rightfully critical. So are Catholics. Hans Kung, perhaps the most influential of contemporary liberal European Catholic theologians, states that Pope John felt the need for a reform of the Italian Church so strongly that this was one of the main reasons why he called for the Ecumenical Council! Kung's judgment of the Church sounds like that of a very polemical Protestant.

> But how can a Church be equipped for positive confrontation with Communism when its masses suffer from appalling religious ignorance, from superstition and poverty of belief...when its clergy...are educated within a seminary system as insulated from the world as possible; when its theology...because of a fundamental look of intellectual freedom, has hardly produced one work of international importance; when its services...are unable to generate any sense of Christian community; when it has largely lost contact with the intellectuals and with the workers? (Kung 1965:11).

It is a picture of a Church desperately in need of renewal, of a Church that has lost its power. Yet the Catholic Church had emerges from the Mussolini decades "as the dominant intellectual and political force in Italy" (Salvadori 1965:54). The former non-Christian trend had stopped. The reversal was the result of a hundred years of reflection and change, of clarification and restatement. The 20th Century began with "a vigorous Catholic intellectual counter-offensive which has borne fruit in this post-war period" (Salvadori 1965:14).

It was a more popular Church, then, but one that had lost its soul that Pope John hoped to save. The instrument for bringing new religious life was to be the Council. Pope John was to be its Saint. "The Catholic Church, after John XXIII, can never be the same again. A new era of church history started with him, an era of new life, of new freedom, of new hope" (Kung 1965:18).

The Council was to bring new life to the Church because it was to be a Council of the Church concerned mainly wiht the Church. Rahner (1966:38) states it succinctly: "It was a Council concerned with eccesiology, the formal study of the Church - with a unity of theme that no previous Council ever had." And again (39), "---the Second Vatican Council was a Council of the Church reflecting on her very nature."

The purpose for renewing the Catholic Church was "preparation for reunion with separated Christians" (Kung 1965:13). *"Aggiornamento"* was not undertaken simply to make the Church appear more up-to-date, more attractive, more appealing to the world. It was "to prepare the Church in advance to deal with the questions of life and death which will confront her" (Rahner 1966:27).

Kung finds the Church very open as it considers its task (1965:138): "There is not a single question (birth control, celibacy not excluded) which cannot be discussed in the Catholic Church today." This openness is illustrated by key themes of the constitution *"On Ecumenism"* (Kung 1965: 140-141):

> Blame on both sides for schism, and request for pardon by other Christians; the Catholic Church as a church of sinners needs constant reform not only in practical church life, but also in doctrine; the Gospel as norm for renewal; non-Catholic Christian communities also called "Churches" or "eccesiastical communities;" the necessity of an ecumenical attitude, improvement of the knowledge of one another or both sides, dialogue, recognition of the good existing in others, learning from them, cooperation in all areas, common prayer with separated Christians.

The post-Vatican II Catholic Church is a Church committed to ecumenism. It is actively seeking to come together with other Christian communions. Protestants are divided in their feelings toward this embrace. By some it is welcomed as the signof true love. This has been the attitude of traditional Protestant denominations in Italy. To others, however, it appears to be planned seduction. Conservative Evangelicals fear the One World Church Monster. Many see it as a plan to make Protestants return to the fold of Rome. What is the Catholic view of ecumenism? Kung presents a view quite different from many popular conceptions (1964: 144-145):

> How can Catholics and Protestants come together? ...It does not mean playing down the truth, softpedalling our differences, making fake syntheses and easy compromises, but self-searching, self-criticism, self-reform...Reunion will then be neither a Protestant "return" nor a Catholic "capitulation," but a brotherly approach from both sides...

This is the Catholic Church of today. Such is its program. In conservative Italy there remains a great deal of catching-up. The ecumenical spirit is present. It finds expression. Locally, and away from the big cities, it has a long way to go. Sometimes the Church appears to be still under Vatican I or even under Trent. But the winds of change are blowing.

The changes are not so pronounced in Italy, perhaps, as outside. But the shifts are beginning. The Church as hierarchy is no longer exclusive. It is beginning to be the Church as people. Rahner stresses that the Church of tomorrow will be expressed in local community (1966:49). As such it will be "united with all other communities who will share their identity with the Church" (Rahner 1966:50).

The Italian Church today claims a Catholic population of 50,922,200 out of a total of 53,639,000 national citizens (1966 census). A total of 61,411 priests (43,328 diocesan and 18,083 religious) serve 27,450 parishes. There are 228 bishops in 209 dioceses (including suburban sees), 49 archbishops, 1 patriarch, and 34 cardinals. Seminarians comprise 8,768; men religious 24,659; and wome religious 148,041. There are 5,000 schools and 570,283 students (Foy 1969:440).

4

Church and State

THE ROMAN QUESTION

Essential reading for anyone interested in the relationship of the Roman Catholic Church to the Italian State during the past 100 years is the 340 page *Church and State in Italy, 1850-1950* by Arturo Jemelo (1960), in either English or Italian.

The shapers of Italian unity were not good Catholics. Guiseppe Garibaldi, the one best known outside Italy and the military unifier, was an opponent of the Church who did not hesitate to grant favors to non-Catholics at the expense of the Church. However, as a general of the 1860 campaign in which he conquered Sicily and the South, he also possessed a quantity of political intuition. Thus he went to pains to not offend the Catholic populace, and "offered prayers in church and sanctuaries, and witnessed the miracle of St. Januarius at Naples" (Jemelo 1960:15).

Another popular leader of the Revolution which made of Italy a unified nation was Guiseppe Mazzini. Convinced of the importance of religion in shaping a nation, Mazzini was, however, not a Catholic. He felt the Catholic Church to be inadequate for the task and did not concern himself with working out any system of relations between Church and State. He did believe in a personal God, and was convinced that men needed more than a code of ethics (Jemelo 1960:16).

The third important figure, and Prime Minister of the new Kingdom, was the Piedmontese count and statesman, Camillo Beuso Cavour. He has been called "the true artificer of national unification," and was said to be "devoted to the ideal of liberty" (Jemelo 1960:16). Little is known of this man's religious beliefs. At times he called himself a Catholic, but he probably did not accept the dogmas of Catholicism or believe in the sacraments of the Church. His mother was a Swiss Calvinist. He embraced rationalism. On his death-bed he sought reconciliation with the Church - possibly out of concern as a statesman rather than religious conviction. His concern was for freedom (a concern which seems to indicate his mother's influence). His belief found expression in the formula "a Free Church in a Free State." The source of Cavour's conception of separation of Church and State seems to have been an *Essay* published in 1842 by a Protestant pastor, Alexandre Vinet. The Essay maintained that a State religion was inadmissable because tbe acquisition of a religious faith was a spontaneous act. Jemelo comments (1960:17):

> From this source, as well as from his passionate belief in freedom, Cavour derived the idea that the State should renounce all control over the Church, which in its turn should not lay claim to any special privileges, but should be subject to the law of the land. Accordingly, all the fundamental institutions of civil life should be secularized, although the Church should be left free to expand, to win souls, to persuade an everincreasing number of people to submit their own free will to its discipline. But even an overwhelming majority of believers must never be allowed to impose its will on a minority or otherwise to embarrow it, just as a majority of unbelievers, must never transform the State into an instrument of atheistic propaganda or in any way weaken the position of the Faithful.

Here is the essence of Cavour's thought.

King Victor Emmanuel was the Savoyan monarch of the new State under which Cavour achieved Mazzini's dream of unification. The King's relations with the high clergy are described as "extremely frigid." He received Church dignitaries formally. He never attended the services of the Church. His children were cared for by Protestants - foreigners and Waldenses. He built no churches, although he did open the synagogue in Rome (Jemelo 1960:105). Twice under him, in 1901, the government proposed bills on divorce. Both were dropped. The fact that such a proposal could even be made indicates something of the liberalism and freedom of the Risorgimento.

Cavour's successor as head of the Italian government, Bettino Ricasoli, was a Catholic who wanted the reform of the Church. His proposals were radical, amounting to a revision, if not destruction, of the hierarchical structure. He wanted to place church properties and, possibly, the appointment of bishops and parish priests in the care of religious communities.

In 1867 he proposed a bill which was to separate Church and State completely. The State would no longer control the Church or participate in the appointment of clergy. Ecclesiastical privilege and immunity would be terminated. The Church was to be "governed exclusively by canon law," and would not be able to own immovable property. The inherited estates of the Church were to be sold and the procedes to be distributed by the bishops among the ecclesiastical organizations of the dioceses (Jemelo 1960:35). Ricasoli would have permitted the clergy to marry and the use of the vernacular at mass. He regarded the refom of the Church as <u>inevitable</u>, but wondered whether to await it passively or to take the lead in promoting it! But it was all illusion. Ricasoli deluded himself. Reform did not come.

Unification had eliminated the temporal power of the Pope. First there was the loss of the Papal States. Then the capitol of the new State was moved to Rome. The Pope was indignant, began a self-imposed "imprisonment" within the walls of the Vatican. In 1887 Pope Leo XIII declares "the fate of Rome has been linked, divinely and indessolubly, to that of the Vicar of Jesus Christ" (Jemelo 1960:78). It was protested that the temporal power was therefore an essential: "Hitherto the only effective means that Providence has devised in order to protect the freedom of the Papacy has been the temporal power" (Jemelo 1960:78).

A champion of the secular State was the philosopher and literary statesman, Benedetto Croce. He was anti-clerical in the old liberal tradition, critical of Catholic writers who falsified history of the Church. His philosophy is anti-religious, although he appreciates the ethical and social values of Christianity (Jemelo 1960:96-97).

The Roman Question remained unsettled for 70 years. With the loss of temporal power the relationship between Italy and the Vatican was broken. It remained so during the reign of three popes. Then at the death of Benedict XV, there came a change. The government declared a form of official mourning that was unprecedented. The new Pope, Pius XI, in his turn blessed the people on February 6, 1922, from the outer portico of St. Peter's, breaking tradition set by his three predecessors. He repeated the act six days later on the occasion of his enthronement. In the crowd were units of the Italian army that had come to present arms (Jemelo 1960:168). Thus the Roman Question was settled, terminating a conflict of 70 years between Church and State. This was hailed too as the peak point of Mussolini's career.

FASCISM

Catholics who had felt at odds with the "secular" state were to find a united voice in the foundation of the Italian Popular Party which had its beginning in 1919. The Party is associated with the name of Luigi Sturzo, an ascetic priest who was an administrative genius and became influential in the ministries of Rome. While not an official party of the Church, the Popular Party was Catholic. It succeeded because it joined the right and the left in one common political party. Non-Catholics were not able to join the Party. It was known as "non-confessional" because it was run by laymen. It was not part of the diocesan structure and did not officially represent the Church. In reality it upheld "Christian" values, sought the support of bishops at elections, and could never oppose the Church, its rulers, its morals. The Popular Party declared its support of the Pope and of the League of Nations. Protection was demanded for the family against alcoholism and prostitution. Schools and large families were promoted (Jemelo 1960:172-175).

The Fascist government at first included the Popular Party. Later the Party split, the left wing being expelled and Don Sturzo removed from his post.

Quasi religion. In Italy it has always been well-nigh impossible to extract religion from politics. The involvements of the Church with Fascism have been noted with the negative results from Protestants and other minorities. Actually at the time of its rise Fascism was in competition with Communism (which it later supressed) for the allegiance of the People. Fascism was apparently chosen as "the less of two evils" (Jemelo 1960:182). While The Fascist regime chose to cultivate friendwhip with the Church for its own ends, Fascism was really competitive to the Catholic religion. Jemelo expresses this antithesis (1960:190-191):

> Fascism, like Bolshevism was itself a Church, claiming the whole man, in all his waking moments and in all his activities....It had its uniforms, its epistolory style, its formulas, its gestures of solution, its rites that accompanied the partymember to the grave: the summons to the burial service, the Roman salute with which the Blackshirt greeted even funerals, even religious processions. (For many years the anti-Fascist was easily recognizable by the way he saluted a hearse and by his behaviour when passing a cemetery, by his recourse to the traditional forms of greeting and his refusal to adopt the Fascist salute). As the parish church and its pres-

> bytery are focal points of the activities of the good Catholic, so was the local party headquarters a place of meeting, recreation and meditation: a place where the new faithful gathered in the evenings and on feast days, when all initiatives, whatever their object, had to originate....The party was a Church that persuaded its zealots to renounce all other interests....

Brides were known to exhange the golden wedding band required in a Church ceremony for the plain iron cross of the Party. The conflict was resolved, in typical Italian style, by utilitarian compromise. Generally there was no clash between the two totalitarian systems. Similarly today knowledgeable Italians feel that a Communist regime would not come to blows with the Catholic Church but that compromise would find a path of accomodation to the advantage of both.

Masonic suppression. Mussolini also declared war on Masonry which he was determined to destroy as a "perversion" of spiritual and national life. With typical Mussolini vigor he denounced it:

> Its secret character throughout the twentieth century, its mysterious meetings, abhorrent to our beautiful communities with their sunlight and their love of truth, gave to the sect the character of corruption, a crooked concept of life, without programme, without soul, without moral value (Mussolini 1928:157).

The Masonic Order was virulently anti-clerical in Italy. Its supression was to the immense gratification of the *Curia* (Halperin 1937:87). A number of shapers of the Unified Italy had been Masons. Freemasonary, which has exercised a profound influence toward religious liberty in Latin America, was not to be permitted to operate in Mussolini's Italy.

The years of Fascist suppression, were the years of the "Anti-Risorgimento" (Jemelo 1960:224). In the 1930s the values of liberalism and democracy, which were the ideals of the Risorgimento, were "discarded forever" (Jemelo 1960:260). Fascism showed its alliance with Hitler.

Catholic rapport. This was also an era of new rapport with the Vatican. The relationship of the Church to Fascism is history. The effects of the Fascist era on religious life in Italy, however, are still felt today.

Mussolini made peace with the Pope. He needed the support of the Church (at least its non-interference). Thus he promised to support the Church. This arrangement was beneficial for both. Italian bitterness toward the Holy See because of opposition to political unity tended to subside. Mussolini on his side found in the Church an ally for his expansionist policies. Upon the completion of the Lateran Pacts the Pope says, "We express the belief that through it We have given God to Italy and Italy to God" (Jemelo 1960:232). Mussolini is hailed as the restorer of religious and moral values! Mussolini asserted the place of the State over Church. The Pope retorted by affirming the pre-eminence of the Church.

Mussolini, from an early negative religious attitude, had turned to a self-image of benefactor of the Catholic Church. "I have seen the religious spirit bloom again, churches once more are crowded, the ministers of God are themselves invested with new respect. Fascism has done and is doing its duty" (Mussolini 1928:306).

This had many ramifications. An absolutist State correlated an absolutist Church. Non-Fascist and non-Catholic parties and bodies were suppressed. This was to bring on a post-war Communist reaction and revival. The genius of Italian Communism, Antonio Gramshi, was to die in a Fascist prison and become the hero of the PCI and of Italian intellectuals.

Mussolini saw the Church and the State not as separate entities, but as moving together to the same end. His autobiography cannot but give the impression that the Church - religion - was but a tool for achieving the goals of Mussolini (1928:307):

> Today, with the highest loyalty, Fascism understands and values the Church and its strength: such is the duty of every Catholic citizen. But politics, the defense of national interests....must be the work of the modern Fascist Italians who want to see the immortal and irreplaceable Church of Saint Peter respected....Fascism gives impulse and vigor to the religion of the country.

This upholding and strengthening of the Catholic Church led, inevitably, to sanctions against non-Catholic religious groups. This was partly based on the psychology of absolutism which allows for no deviations. It was also due to the program of Fascism which required loyalty in order to reach the goal. Variations were suspect as disloyal.

Protestant repression. In the Senate a bill dealing with "permitted religions" provided that the appointment of ministers would have to be approved by the Government. Concern was expressed over Protestant propaganda which, it was feared, could harm both Fascism and Catholism through proselytism. Protestants were to be permitted the free practice and preaching of their religion in church or chapel. Outside, however, it was to be regarded as a possible source of public disorder. The Government Minister was to eliminate the menace of an "alien" propaganda.

All "sects" were required to ask permission for opening churches and chapels. Permission was granted only when the said places "were found to be essential to the needs of substantial bodies of believers." The decision was made by local officials. As a result Protestants often suffered under the police and the Criminal Courts. Evangelicals gathered for private worship in homes were fined or imprisoned. Bible distributers received similar treatment. "Being a Protestant meant in practice exclusion from political office and from all important posts" (Jemelo 1960:250).

Pentecostals were particularly the targets of persecution under Fascism. Others also suffered. No particular reason was given for individuals actions against Protestants. Priests apparently had the power to direct local police and often did so against Protestants. Thus one hears of the arrest of our independent Baptist pastor at his church in Pozzuoli. No reason is given. A Baptist layman in the same town is arrested and imprisoned for preaching in the street.

Protestantism in general was suspect because it was not "Roman". The fact that Italian Protestants received considerable financial support from outside the country no doubt greatly strengthened that feeling. Resources in men and money from America were unpopular in a country which was asserting its complete self-sufficiency. Also a Fascist imperialism was beginning to asset itself and America began to be seen as an enemy. Protestant ties with the West were eyed suspiciously.

Catholics also arose to the occasion. In a book in defense of Fascism, one churchman declared that the control of the press is good. Unity of religion is an essential condition for Italian expansion in the world, a "mission of civilization." Protestantism was declared to be the "enemy of Rome", and defined as "a free and personal faith with its sole authority being that which is within every individual, with neither worship nor dogma" - in essence, <u>mystical anarchy</u>. This denunciation includes a statement which gives the attitude of the time toward Protestant missionaries (Misciattelli 1924:90):

> The American evangelical missionaries perfect apostles of that hypocritically humanitarian religion that had its most authoritative pontif in President Wilson,

> frightened by the enormous progress that Catholicism makęs in the United States and in England, have believed to be able to combat it handily at Rome with the arm of the philanthropic dollar.

That Pentecostals felt the brunt of the attack was due not to missionary influence and subsidy (for they had little of either), but to the fact that the movement owed its origin to Italian-Americans and that individuals maintained close ties with relatives and believers in America. Therefore they were suspect as subject to outside (i.e. American) influence.

The Fascist State as well as the Roman Church apparently exploited the idea that to be Italian was to be Catholic. Therefore if a person was non-Catholic he was suspected of being non-Italian. Protestants who were aggressive in their witness and fervent in their worship were wrongly thought to be unpatriotic.

Eleven years after the signing of the Concordat, relations between Church and State were described as "extremely cordial" and "characterized by a spirit of compromise and co-operation" (Jemelo 1960:267).

During the War the "neutrality" of the Vatican "State" was declared, and pains were taken to see that it was observed. Pope Pius XII is today sometimes referred to contemptuously as the "Fascist" Pope.

Continuing effects. The effects of Mussolini's rule are still felt today. Basically Mussolini reinstated the Catholic Church in Italy.

> The curcifix was restored to all the classrooms of the land, the stipends of clergymen wer increased, religious instruction was made compulsory in the elementary schools, special precautions were taken to protect religious processions, and Catholic chaplains were once again assigned to the Italian army (Halperin 1937:87).

These and other results of the Fascist rule are in evidence in Italy today.

The Lateran Pacts, signed by Mussolini and the Pope, are the subject of continued debate. Basically they consisted of three documents: a political treaty, concordat, and financial convention. In the first the Pope recognized Italy. The second governs the relationship of Church and State. By the third the government paid a settlement to the papacy.

Communist resurgence may also be noted as a reaction to Fascism. The fall of the Fascist regime and the end of the War gave opportunity for the rise fo the Left. The Church, however, would not tolerate approachment with Communism. Communists were excommunicated. In Rome and some other cities there arose a group of persons who were Catholics but who accepted the basic principles of Communism. Since they denied dialectical materialism they were not Communists, and they tried to maintain themselves as a "Christian Left." But the Church refused even this bridge (Jemelo 1960:287). The first beginnings of an opening toward the Left had to wait for the coming of Good Pope John.

RELIGIOUS LIBERTY

Provisions. The 1947 Italian Constitution, which guarantees freedom of religion to every individual, is sometimes said to be in conflict with the Concordat with the Vatican signed by Mussolini in 1929. Italy today lives under both. The Concordat gives a preferred position to the Catholic Church and obligates the Italian State to protect that Church. "Protection" has been interpreted as covering almost anything at variance with the interest and teachings of the Catholic Church.

Circumstances surrounding the adoption of the Constitution are of interest in understanding how the Lateran Pacts came to be included. Following the War an anti-Communist coalition was formed largely through the influence of the Catholic Church. The Church was the only organization that had continued to operate somewhat independently under Fascism - with the possible exceptions of the army, the police, and the Communist underground. (Fried 1963:237). Fascist collapse left a vacuum. The Church stepped in to prevent revolution. Its instrument was the Christian Democrat Party, (which replaced the old Popular Party), "with the active support of the United States, the Catholic clergy, Catholic interested groups (such as Catholic Action, the Catholic trade unions, and the Catholic farmers' organization)" (Fried 1963:137). A coalition was formed with the Liberal Party, the Republicans and the Social Democrats - all secular democratic parties - and conservative interest groups.

Argument concerning the proposed inclusion of the Lateran Pacts in the new Constitution of the Republic of Italy illustrates the complexity of the relationship between religion and politics in Italy. The Christian Democrats proposed their inclusion. Opposition came chiefly from Socialists and

Communists. The debate was never heated. Opponents showed respect for the Church and religious values. Proponents expressed concern for religious minorities and for religious freedom (Jemelo 1960:292). Socialist leader, Pietro Nenni, declared that his group was vitally interested in preserving religious peace and saw little need to even consider revision of the Concordat, that agricultural reform was of greater interest. Fascist survivors defended the article which included the Pacts. The Communist leader, Palmero Togliatti, declared Communist support for the inclusion of the Pacts. The Communists "regarded the Lateran treaty as inviolable", he said (Jemelo 1960:303). Because of "heavy political responsibility," and so as to avoid "religious dissension," and to not divide Christian Democrat workers from Communist and Socialist workers "the Communists would vote in favor of the article" (Jemelo 1960:303).

Protests were heard. In September, 1947, the Federal Council of Evangelical Churches in Italy called for religious liberty - true democracy in Italy - for all people. On February 21, 1947, the Council pronounced against the Lateran Pacts. The Councils' Declaration on that date stated that the inclusion of the Pacts in the Constitution "cannot be reconciled with religious liberty" (Pettazzoni 1952:144).

Nevertheless, with the favorable Communist vote, the Pacts were included. Their inclusion has been the basis for continued controversy.

(1) The Concordat establishes Catholicism as the sole religion of the State. "The Church acquired sole jurisdiction in matrimonial courses....Catholic religious instruction was stipulated for all State schools....ex-priests and priests under ecclesiastical censure were barred from State employment" (Webb 1958:7).

(2) The Concordat still governs the relationship of Italy with the Catholic Church as stipulated by Article 7 of the Constitution of the Republic of Italy (Cappelletti, Merryman and Perillo 1967:282):

> The State and the Catholic Church shall be, each in its own sphere, independent and sovereign. Their relations shall be regulated by the Lateran Pacts. Modification of the Pacts, mutually agreed upon, will not require procedure analogous to that required for Constitutional revision.

(3) Their inclusion (Article 7) has subsequently been regarded as in conflict with the statement of religious freedom

of Article 8 (Cappelletti, Merryman, and Perillo 1967:282):

> All religious creeds are equally free before the law.
>
> Religious creeds other than the Catholic shall have the right to organize themselves according to their own statutes, so long as they do not conflict with the law of the land.
>
> Relations with the State shall be regulated by law on the basis of agreements between their respective representatives.

Thus the Constitution of the Land does provide for free religious expression on the part of all. "All religious creeds are equally free before the law". The non-established believers and groups cling to that. It is a guarantee

However Article 8 makes two stipulations. First, "so long as they do not conflict with the law of the land." How is that phrase to be interpreted in light of the establishment provided for by Article 7? The second is for regulations based on agreements between the State and the representatives of non-Catholic religions. This means that each non-Catholic religious group must enter into an agreement with the State. Such a group is recognized as having legal status.

Violations. The statement has been made that "Evangelical preachers who are not ministers of religions that have reached agreement with the State have sometimes been hampered in the performance of missionary work" (Cappelletti, Merryman and Perillo 1967:61). That is an understatement which obscures the truth. It hides the fact that some Protestants have encountered great difficulty in trying to obtain legal recognition. Nor does it explain the opposition, abuse and outright persecution sometimes encountered, not only by foreign missionaries but by the national Christians.

It would be more accurate to admit that Italy has not been that "free" in practice, and the the Constitution has been violated and ignored. The stipulation of Article 8 and the supposed conflict of Article 7 were the excuses for vitriolic expressions of hatred.

Webb, in his study of religious liberty in Italy (1958:27), is mild in his statement that -

> Non-Catholic religious groups have been subjected to discriminatory treatment by the central government and the prefectural authorities and that Protestant pastors

> have suffered grave disabilities in carrying out their functions.

Examples were given of cutting off the water supply to the houses of Protestant pastors to prevent them from functioning. There have no doubt been many such instances, and many worse, in the not distant past.

The Pentecostals have been mentioned as the special objects of persecution in the Fascist era. Following the War they, as well as other minority groups, were able to function under the government of the Allied Military Command (Evans 1963c:285). Until specific legal sanction was secured from the subsequent Italian government, however, they encountered difficulty.

The story of the bitter treatment of the Church of Christ evangelists is told in another chapter.

The right to religious liberty is further defined in Article 19 of the Constitution. We rely again on the translation of Cappelletti, Merryman and Perillo (1967:284):

> Everyone shall be the right freely to profess his own religious faith, in whatsoever form, individuals or collective, to propagate it, and to worship in private or in public, providing that the rites do not offend against public decency.

This seeming *magna carta* of individual religious liberty in Italy must be accepted cautiously. "Public decency" is easily offended. It is defined in terms of the teachings of the Catholic Church, because of the provision of the Concordat. Therefore it may be a crime to ridicule the Church in public or to give out birth-control information.

Something of the changes taking place and the difficulty in making changes may be seen in the following account, reported in the newspapers of Italy (Mammarella 1968:308):

> The bishop of Prato, Monsignor Pietro Fiordelli, had officially banded as "public sinners" and "concubines" a young couple from his diocese, who instead of celebrating their wedding with a religious ceremony had chosen to get married according to the civil procedure stipulated by Italian law. The case arose because the two statues governing marriage, the common law and the civil law, were in contradiction. According to the former, civil marriage is nonexistent and consequently Fiordelli's

> attitude was justified; following the civil law, according to which the marriage was perfectly valid, the bishop's statement amounted to an act of defamation. The case went to court and the bishop was convicted (March 14, 1958) and fined 40,000 lire by the Florence tribunal.
>
> The punishment was nominal, but the question of principle was serious --- the reaction of the Church was violent to the condemnation of the bishop, an unheard of event and therefore quite shocking. Newspapers, Catholic associations, bishops, cardinals and finally the Pope condemned the action of the Florentine court; its judges were menaced with excommunication....the debate was officially closed a year later with the annulment of the sentence by the Florence Court of Appeals.

Incidents such as this have led to increased agitation for a review of the Lateran Pacts. Added to this much publicized case are the scores of unknown incidents in which individuals have been intimidated and discriminated against.

The common people of certain areas of the South fear the power of the hierarchy. In some towns there are no jobs without the "raccomodazione" (recommendation) of the bishop. Some of these people do not attend Protestant services because of the feared reprisals of the priests. Though a Protestant church may open its doors freely in such a comminity, real religious liberty does not exist for the people. Change in the status quo is needed.

Sensitivities of non-Catholics may thus be freely violated. Yet Catholic priests and religious who have insulted and defamed the disseminaters of Protestant opinion, or who have "even seized and destroyed their stocks of tracts and pamphlets" have always been acquitted by the courts (Jemelo 1960:317).

Fortunately the climate has been changing during the last decade. Protestants are enjoying freedom in proclaiming their faith. There is less opposition, open attacks are rare. Little interference is met in opening meeting places and conducting services privately or in public. Street preaching is possible and actually enjoys the protection of the police. The study of Jemelo (1960) is excellent; however the final chapter in its treatment of Protestant persecution is no longer applicable. The study seems to accurately reflect the despicable treatment afforded various groups in the years following the war. Pentecostals and the Churches of Christ are prime examples. Fortunately those tragic years are past.

Possible Pact revision. The Constitution, drafted in 1947 and put into operation January 1, 1948, is "democratic and liberal in character"; yet by ratifying the Lateran Pacts it created "the confessional State" (Jemelo 1960:308). There is nothing reminiscent of Fascism. But the State is bound by the Concordat. While the Concordat stands the State cannot set up ecclesiastical legislation of its own. Nevertheless the Constitution "prescribes equality of status for all religious, Catholicism among them" (Jemelo 1960:309).

This contradiction is being called in question today. Study is now in progress and change can be expected.

Reform is needed....The State has fulfilled all its obligations towards the Catholic Church but not towards the other "communions" (Jemelo 1960:309). Prejudice is clear in the laws protecting the Catholic Church but providing no such protection for other communions.

The interests of the Vatican which are often in conflict with the best interests of the land of Italy have caused an Italian journalist and statesman to declare:

> There is no Italian Church. What exists in Italy is the Universal Church. The Primate of Italy is the Bishop of Rome, the Holy Pontif, whose divinely imposed duty is to promote the welfare of all Catholics and Church organizations in all parts of the world. Where there is a conflict with the aspirations and needs of the Italian people it is obvious that the Holy See take precedence (Barzini 1968:566).

Early in 1969 the Italian government set in motion a study of pact revisions. What the result will be is not yet known. It is anticipated that there will be agreement on some changes. The agreements must be mutual.

5

Spiritism

IMPORTANCE

Spiritist belief and practice is widespread in Italy. Yet to find information on the subject is difficult.

Leland's *Aradia or the Gospel of the Witches* (1899) pruports to be an ancient relic obtained for the author by an Italian sorceress. The book is thought by Leland to be proof of the origin of Italian witchcraft, which, he feels, is descended from Roman or Etruscan times. Aradia (or Herodius) was born of Diana, according to this *Gospel* (Vangelo), and is a female Messiah. Witchcraft is thus the old religion (*la vecchia religione*) of Italy.

The Italian witch (*strega*) is given a place of honor in such a system. The system itself must understandably be kept secret. Therefore its teachings, practices, and traditions are not well known. But the arts of witchcraft have been treasured and practiced generation after generation in certain families. If the construction (Leland 1899:*v*) is correct, the sorceress is really the honored high priestess of an ancient pagan cult.

Leland supports his contention that the *vecchia religione* was a high and noble post by reporting the similarities. He says that at the time of his writing there were many old people in Northern Italy who knew the Etruscan names of the Twelve Gods and could recite invocations to Bacchus, Jupiter, Venus, Mercury, and the ancestral spirits. Furthermore the women who prepared amulets muttered spells that were of Roman origin (Leland 1899:*vii*). Leland's study is apparently from Northern and Central Italy. He mentions specifically Florence and Milan, and refers to Romagna more than once.

He states as his own personal knowledge, supported by papers published in several magazines,

> That the witches even yet form a fragmentary secret society or sect, that they call it that of the Old Religion, and that there are in the Romagna entire villages in which the people are completely heathen (1899:116).

Regardless of its origins, witchcraft is still being practiced. Elliott Rose (1962) also finds a solitary clue to the recent history of European witchcraft in Leland's *Vaugelo*. But he finds Leland's "relic" suspect for several reasons. Was witchcraft the ancient religion of Italy? Rose's conclusion is safe: we do not know.

"Of course, the Italian common people have long memories for old gods, and nobody would be surprised to find pagan survivals there" (Rose 1962:217). However the saints and festivals of the Catholic Church have so exactly replaced those of the pagans that no one can tell the difference. Rose feels that Catholicism, as much as a Diana cult, a good candidate for representing ancient paganism (1962:217).

The pagan cult today finds expression, especially in the South, as spiritism. It is the secret religion of the common people. But one hears of it amoung the advanced as well. A few years ago the *Rome Daily American* carried a series of articles on spiritism in the cities.

Spiritism is not new to Italy. In the 1890's and 1900's the most famous Italian medium in history lived in Naples. She was Eusapia Polladino, born in the mountain village of Minervo-Murge, near Bari. She has been called "the princess of spiritism" (Carrington 1909:22).

At present the Catholic Church enjoys a much more prominent position than at the turn of the century. Spiritism is still a religion of the masses, but it is practiced privately. Officially the people are Catholics. In practice they consult mediums. The two religions are mixed. Many people are Catholic-Spiritists.

CHARACTERISTICS

Spiritism manifests a power unknown in the rites of Catholicism. The seance actually reenforces Catholic beliefs by the invocation of saints, etc. It is probably for this reason that spiritism is simply ignored by the Church.

Folk belief in *Destino* (fate) is part of the animistic world-view which leads credence to spiritistic phenomena. The peasants believe in a cruel fate which can only be manipulated by magic. Thus each village has its own sorceress "who induces fate to change its evil design" (Schachter 1965:67). In the animistic world of Southern Italy, religion as such has little meaning "since everything is seen to participate in divinity" (Schachter 1965:67). Magic, however, has a great deal of meaning. For in a view where no border exists between the human, animal, and supernature, "everything is bound by magic" (Schachter 1965:67).

Spiritism fits neatly into animistic thought patterns. If everything participates in divinity, what is unusual about making contact with the dead or even communicating with the Saints?

APPROACH

Church growth is greatly influenced by the presence of spiritism. In Italy the spiritistic phenomena must be recognized as animistic. The church planter needs to understand something of the philosophy of animism. He must not dismiss it as "primitive," but should recognize it as a developed system of thought. He should acknowledge that he is dealing with animistic Catholics. For the masses are people whose Catholicism is animistic.

The approach to the animist is not the same approach that is made to the Catholic. Here is a common mistake. Protestants have probably wasted many hours in polemics aimed at Roman Catholicism. Yet many times the hearers were already convinced of the failings of Catholicism. But this did not lead to conversion. Why? One possible reason is that we have used the wrong ammunition.

Almost all the evangelistic literature produced in Italy is aimed at the Catholic - and, obviously, at the literate one. But what if anything, has ever been geared toward the illiterate peasant with animistic beliefs? Probably the only treatment of "superstition" is denunciation. What about a tract to attract the spiritists? A spiritist once came to the Bible Center in Naples for information on spiritism, and he was converted to Christ. What is being done to reach the masses of people like him who could also be saved? There is a need for information to help the Christian worker to deal effectively with spiritistic, animistic, superstitions, semi-literates who form such a large part of the Italian social structure. This is where significant church growth could occur.

Spiritism means power. To the spiritist Catholicism alone is sterile. Empty rites of the Church are filled with power through spiritistic "reality". Protestantism as a philosophical, theological, or puritanical system offers nothing to the spiritist.

The spiritist is interested in action. He wants experience. The Gospel must be presented to him as a living option. The power of the Gospel must be announced, and for his conversion there must be power encounter. Tippett emphasizes the necessity of "coming 'to grips at the level of experience' rather than at 'the level of intellect'" (1967:6).

To animists the idea of encounter between Christ and Satan is very meaningful, says Tippett (1967:6). He bases this Gospel of power encounter upon the word of Christ himself in Luke 10:19 - "Behold I give you power (exousia)....over all the power (dunamis)..."

Since Italian spiritism has an aura of evil about it (spirit contact readily relates to black magic and devil invoking) the idea of contest between Christ and Satan is quite realistic. But in Catholicism Christ is dead, weak, or dying. The Christ of the Gospel, in contrast, is alive, powerful, and present.

Tippett's observations in *Solomon Islands Christianity* seems to speak to this Italian setting. All the missions there emphasized personal encounter in the struggle with Satan. The Anglicans were particularly strong on this point:

> The Anglican priests practiced exorcism in line with the apostalic commission. This power encounter is implied in two petitions and responses in the Litany...the Litany for Missions asks for salvation from the deceits of the devil...In Baptism and Confirmation the candidate answers the question: "Do ye here, in the presence of God, and of this congregation, renounce the devil and his works..?" The power encounter between Christ and Satan and the Christian's personal involvement in the encounter are continually brought before the Anglican people" (Tippett 1967:234).

Brazil is a Latin land with a veneer of Roman Catholicism where multitudes are practicing various forms of spiritism in several different spiritist denominations. Harmon Johnson, an independent Assemblies of God missionary, has made an excellent study of Brazilian spiritism (1969). In many ways the Brazilian situation is very different from that in Italy. Nevertheless Johnson gives some insights which apply. Particularly he stresses the absolute necessity of power encounter. Johnson states that in Brazil only the Pentacostals are winning the Spiritists, and they do so by direct encounter. He cites several examples.

In Italy spiritists will come to Christ when they can experience His transforming power in their lives.

Pentecostalists acknowledge the reality of the spirit world. "A part of Pentecostal worship services often takes the form of direct encounter with the world of demons" (Wold 1968:116). This goes far beyond preaching. Demons are cast out and the sick healed by the laying on of hands, anointing, and prayer. The Holy Spirit is recognized as more powerful than all other spirits. The Pentecostal message is of deliverance from and power over the spirits.

The same Holy Spirit is available to Baptists, Brethren, Methodists and Waldensians. Evangelism carried out under His anointing can demonstrate the Good News as the "power of God unto salvation from everyone who believes."

6

Communism

RISE

"The most Socialist and the most revolutionary of the authoritative leaders of the Russian Socialist parties," was the enthusiastic description of Lenin provided by the Turin Socialist newspaper, *Il Grido del Popolo*, on April 27, 1917 (Cammett 1967:59): Italian Socialists showed their support of the Russian Revolution which was exalted in a series of flyers distributed in Turin and the provinces.

In most contemporary usage "socialism" is distinguished from "communism." The two terms are often used interchangeable, however, in relation to early developments. Distinctions developed later.

Italian socialism began in the closing years of the 19th century. Although strong and active in various parts of the country, Piedmost became its center having the largest Socialist vote in Italy as early as 1897. It appears to have been a grassroots reaction. At first, the Turin workers appear to have been docile, but around 1900 they became militant. "The first urban general strike in Italian history occurred in Turin in February, 1902. Provoked by the use of soldiers as replacements for striking gas workers, it was unplanned and spontaneous" (Cammett 1967:24). Other spontaneous similar incidents indicate the mood.

The rise of socialism in Turin was related to the expanding metalworking industry. After 1904 the automobile industry grew rapidly there.

The enthusiasm for the Russian Revolution has been noted. At the same time local feelings of discontent and defeatism were exploited. Turin with its elite of specialized workers was to be the cradle and stronghold of the Italian Communist Party (Nammorella 1966:47). Its leader and hero, Antonio Gramsci from Sardinia, came to the forefront of the Socialist cause in Turin at this time.

Gramsci was instrumental in founding the P.C.I. (Partita Comunista Italiano) in the summer of 1920. Frequent and bloody conflicts between workers and police or army, and the occupation of factories in Turin and Milan provided the setting (Cammett 1967:111).

Communism was to be eclipsed by another sun. Mussolini came to power. His Italian Fascism was a different answer to the Socialist query. Communism was suppressed. Its genius Gramsci, earned a martyr's renown, by death in a Fascist prison.

STRATEGY

The Party emerged from the underground in 1943. The mantle of Gramsci fell on Palmiro Togliatti who led the Communists to victory after victory at the polls immediately following the War. In this he was aided by an excellent cadre of intellectuals and organizers. Togliatti eventually became Minister of Justice in the new Republic.

The genius of Italian Communism has been adaptability. This trait was imported by its new leader:

> "Togliatti was a scholar, philosopher and historian, a shrewd man who did not simply know his Marx and Lenin but also his Machiavelli and Gramsci and adapted the naive Soviet instructions he received from Moscow to the complex Italian historical reality (Borzini 1968:565).

Italian Communism under Togliatti has always been a deviant Communism.

Success is not to be achieved easily in Italy. The Vatican must be reckoned with. In the post-war years the Communists, respecting the tremendous power of the Vatican, adopted an attitude of religious tolerance:

> "The PCI statutes then adopted were unique in the Communist movement is specifying that any citizen, independent of race, religious faith, and philosophical conviction, might be accepted into the party so long as he accepted its political program (Blackmer 1968:219).

That was a departure from Marxist-Leninist orthodoxy.

The Communists participated in drawing up the Constitution of the Republic of Italy. The stratgey of compromise was evident. They voted to include the 1929 Lateran Pacts in the new Constitution. By voting to give the Catholic Church special status the Communists were, in effect, abondoning the traditional anti-clerical stance of the left-wing. It was a way of circumventing the barrier of Catholic hostility toward Communism in Italy (Blackmer 1968:14).

APPEAL

The appeal of Communism has traditionally been strong in North-Central Italy. Socialists and Communists have the majority of the votes in the regions of Emitia-Romagna, Toscana and Umbria (Mammarella 1966:187). The industrial North was the cradle of Italian Communism.

The depressed peoples of the South are increasingly being attracted by Communist propaganda. The Party is successfully exploiting a desperate situation. A prevalent attitude is that things could not be worse and might get better under the Communists. For many to vote Communist is to protest against corruption, misery, and the Church.

"Simple" people are susceptible. In the South it used to be common practice near election time for the various political parties to give free spaghetti in return for promised votes. The Communists used this ploy to advantage. More commonly today, though, a "boss" (person with prestige among the lower classes) secures promised loyalty from voters. If the man is held in esteem by the *poveri* (poor people), they will vote with him. To do otherwise would cause a *bruta figura* for the man. Loyalty is attached to his person.

Communism's greatest success today is among the poor migrant workers. To these the Party acts as employment agency, housing authority, and friend in a strange environment. Peck is correct in stating that "The Italian Communist Party is a huge service organization" (1968:165). The Party makes a practical difference in the lives of poor people. Through it they can secure coveted government jobs and a measure of material security.

For the PCI helps its own. That is the Italian way. "The Christian Democrats help the Catholics, and the PCI helps the Communists." I was once told, and that "Evangelicals should help Evangelicals."

The Party's appeal is successful. At the time of the 1968 general elections, I watched trainloads of migrant workers returning home to vote as they came and went at the Naples station (the government pays for their ticket home from other European countries to vote). In some cases long red banners were stretched from car to car the length of the train. There was no question as to which party would receive most of these votes. My middle-class neighbor was horrified as she exclaimed, "Rome pays their way home and look how they vote!"

IMPORTANCE

The Communist Party is looked upon by some non-Communists as essential "opposition" in the government. As the second largest party it certainly provides that. Only the Christian Democrats are larger. The DC refuses to form a coalition with the PCI. The Catholics turn instead to the Socialists and Republicans to form a government. The Communists are forced to oppose their Socialist cousins. It is a stand-off.

It is curious that the land of Fascism should also become a land of Communism. This is true in a certain sense:

> For more than 20 years the Partita Comunista Italiano (PCI) has been one of the largest, politically most influential, and intellectually most lively of the non-ruling Communist parties (Blakmer 1968:1).

Though not in power its influence is far reaching.

RELATIONSHIP TO THE CATHOLIC CHURCH

Hans Kung lays the blame for the increase in the Communist vote squarely on "the failure of the Italian Church to deal with the problems of the movement" (1965:10).

Pope John made a difference. Instead of condemming he was willing to listen. The encyclical *Pacem in Terris* opened the door. It seemed to Communists that the Pope was conceding that there could be a meeting on some points. The Party had insisted that Communists and Catholics could indeed colaborate to achieve "practical earthly goals" despite ideological differences. The encyclical was interpreted as agreement:

> Here was the Pope himself sanctioning the principle underlying the party's simple message to its potential allies among the Christian Democrats: let us maintain our doctrinal differences but not allow them to interfere with the work ther is to be accomplished in common (Blackmer 1968:230).

Agreement even to disagree is remarkable between these two dominant, mutually exclusive, opposing forces. They are opposite ideologies. But they are striking similarities between them as Blackmer points out (1968:218): (1) They are the only political movements in Italy attracting widespread support form the masses. (2) Both control powerful political organizations, social organizations, and trade unions that reach all levels of society. (3) Each articulates an ideology which claims univeral validity. (4) They belong to competing international power systems.

RELATIONSHIP WITH PROTESTANTISM

The PCI need not concern itself with Protestantism. In Italy Protestants are an insignificant minority. Protestants, however, must concern themselves with Communism.

Protestants have been accused of being Communists. In the case of Church of Christ missionaries (Gibbs 1958) this was deliberate false propaganda designed to force the workers out of Italy.

In the South Protestantism has had its greatest appeal among the depressed peasant population. This is the same sector from which Communism draws support. Consequently evangelicals are sometimes equated with communists. "Given the peculiar characteristics of the Italian social structure, such a confusion is in no way surprising" (Cassin 1959:168).

At the time of the 1968 election the local Communist Party hung a banner across the piazza adjoining the newly opened evangelical meeting hall in Aversa. This was construed by a politician of another party to indicate some relationship between the two. He remarked that the Communists had never done this before the Protestant church came to that quarter!

The strength of early socialism in the industrial North has been noted. Turin is also the center of Italian Protestantism.

Is there a relationship between Communism and evangelicals? Does one produce the other? Or, do Communist areas respond in a peculiar way to the evangelical message? Not necessarily. Superficially there may seem to be a relationship.

The industrial North is known as the Communistic part of Italy. Evangelical churches do exist in those areas (Milan, Turin, Venice and Bologna). I have talked with missionaries working in the North who stated that it was a very difficult field. Some have labored there for years without making a single convert. This has not been the experience of those working in the South. Brethren, Pentecostals, Baptists working in the South have all seen considerable response.

Communism has had a much smaller percentage of followers here than in the North. Should this be taken to imply, therefore, that Communists, or communistic areas, are hardened toward the Gospel? Not necessarily. We must remember that the North is a different Italy from the South. The Northerner even before he is a Communist, is a materialist in the sense that Americans are materialists. He is interested in the good life, here and now, and in the industrial North he is able to work hard at attaining that life and at enjoying it. These are his concerns. Therefore he is not very interested in the Church. Religion is superstition, and superstition is for the naive, for the ignorant and the foolish. And it is for the Southerner. For the Southerner is, in so many respects, the antithesis of the Northern Italian. Not only does he come from a different race and speak a different language, but he has different values. To him religion is important. He is superstitious. He is also poor. And he too may be a Communist. He apparently sees no great contradiction between Communism which is political and Christianity which is practiced on Sundays. This is the same Southerner who has been found more responsive to evangelism than his Northern counterpart. For Protestantism in Southern Italy has flourished "in just those strata of the peasant population which, because of the conditions of their existence, are most disposed to listen to socialist ideas" - i.e. Communism (Cassin 1959:168). It is not so much Communism, then, as the condition of the people that tends to make them responsive or non-responsive. This is but one factor, but the fact is that the South has been responsive despite a growing Communist element. I have talked to such persons and have found that they were ready to respond to Christ, having first had contact with the Gospel ouside of Italy. We need a Mission to the Communities of Southern Italians living outside the South - in Milan, in Turin, in Switzerland, in Germany - to reach them for Christ as Southerners.

In the South people are grasping for a way out of misery. Communism to them is a political straw. To vote Communist is to vote against corruption and against powers in office. The evangelical also offers hope - a spiritual hope, quite unrelated to the political. NO connection exists between the two. However the circumstances of human need tend to create receptivity for both.

Torino is another story. It was Protestant centuries before the birth of Communism. Does Protestantism lead to Communism? NO. The former is a religious heritage. Present Communism, on the other had, grows out of early Bolshevism centered in the industry of Turin. Gramsci long ago led bloody "demonstrations" among the workers of that area. There is thus a leftist political tradition.

Recent leftist Protestant publications should be judged in this light.

Missionaries laboring in socialist-oriented areas of the North have not found the people very responsive. Social factors which are very different from the South probably are a major factor.

Communism traps Protestants, according to some observers (Whitlock 1969:15). Protestant leaders have become involved in political and social concerns which were socialistic-communistic.

PRESENT EVALUATION

What is the significance of Communism for evangelism? Eugene Nida (1957) explains the differences between the Roman Catholic, the Protestant and the Communist approaches to social structure. The Catholic Church appeals to the elite and to the masses. The Protestant appeal is to the middle classes. Communism speaks of a "classless" society, but it creates of its leadership a new elite group. These facts have ramifications for church growth in Italy. Nida develops these points further.

The Roman Catholic approach is through the elite with the schools as a vehicle. The clergy is therefore politically conservative. This pattern fits the authoritarian structure of the Church. But the future is with the masses. And the masses are the anti-clericals of Italy.

Communism, like Catholicism, is authoritarian and

totalitarian. Society is seen as a strict pyramid composed of upper, middle and lower classes. The upper class must be removed by killing and brainwashing. The rulers are the new elite, from the lower class. Hence the appeal to the disadvantaged - the poverty stricken masses of Italy. The new leader is a dependent of the Party. He is not likely to push beyond second class status. His is an unquestioning loyalty.

Protestantism has infiltrated all classes. Its strenght is in the lower-middle and upper-lower segments. Its emphasis has started many "upward". Methodists in England, for instance, are now spread from the lower to the upper classes. The movement began in the lower classes. Protestantism demands too much from the wealthy in terms of stewardship and responsibility. Its congregational character creates an in-group awareness which tends toward segregation. There is more social prejudice and class consciousness than in Catholicism.

Roman Catholicism provides a ritual and makes few demands on its adherents. The ideal of Protestantism is reaching down as did Wesley, the incarnational approach to society. But denominations reach out to their fellows. Reaching down is excluded. The priesthood of believers is denied by a United Protestantism; therein lie the seeds of its own destruction.

Ecumenism is therefore in error in seeking an organizational unity when a spiritual unity is actually needed. The one light in the darkness for Italy, on the basis of Nida's insights, seems to me to be Pentecostalism. Pentecostal evangelism focuses on the masses. It reaches down. Traditional Protestantism has failed to do so. The lower classes have not yet given full allegiance to Communism. If the day arrives when that loyalty is given, the door of opportunity for evangelism may be closed.

The urgency of the situation is stressed by the militancy of the Marxists who clash with the more traditional Stalinists of Italy.

The masses who have passively obeyed the Church today are restive. They question. In Italy as in most of the world the bulk belong to the depressed classes. "The future is with the masses." They recognize the aloofness of the Church, her exploitation of the poor and illiterate.

Here enters the Communist as the "apostle to the poor." Hope is offered - not the "pie-in-the-sky" of religion, not a future millenium, but utopia - here and now. In this, he, the poor worker, the exploited, will have a part. He will rule! The exploiter will be excluded. The poor man will help destroy the inequality of the ages, and bring in the classless society (not the "spiritual" Kingdom). There are two alternatives, and most of the poor know which to choose. The Catholic Church has shown itself a villain and a deceiver. It is to be destroyed as a part of the evil establishment.

Yet, there is a third alternative. It is the preaching of the Gospel to the poor. It is the message of Jesus Christ as preached by Pentecostals. May their tribe increase! The hope of Italy is in the multiplication and growth of such Churches. Needed are Italian evangelists to go among their own kind, the exploited multitudes, with the call, "Workmen of Italy arise! Come, follow Christ." Italy can be saved as these people are won to a meaningful relationship to Christ in His Church.

PART TWO
An Overview of the Churches

7

Waldenses

ANTIQUITY

The origins of the people known today as Waldenses is lost in antiquity. Named for Peter Waldo, the movement's antecedants predated Waldo. The twelfth century saw several separatist movements. In southern France Peter di Bruys was burned in 1140, and Henry of Cluny died in prison in 1147. The two ex-priests held clearly "Protestant" views. The most of their followers joined the Poor Men of Lyons.

Simultaneously in Italy Arnold of Brescia led a similar movement. In 1155 he was burned in Rome and his ashes cast into the Tiber. His followers, known as Lombards, were dissidents insisting upon the purification of the Church.

Both Arnold of Brescia and Henry of Cluny were persecuted under Bernard of Clairvaux and the House of Cluny.

These protests and others such as the Humiliati and Patarini prepared the way for the mission of the Waldenses (Combe 1930:26).

Tradition has it that the Church in Lombardy and Piedmont had come down from apostolic days with little or no submission to Rome. According to this view the Bishop of Turin as late as the ninth century was independent of Rome, and the churches kept a purity of faith and worship which had come from their great leaders - Ambrose, Vigilantus, and Claude (Wylie n.d.:1). In the eleventh century the plains succombed to Rome's jurisdiction, but "not so the mountains" (Wylie n.d.:2). Regardless of how one interprets these traditions, it seems likely that the Poor Men of Lyons did have spiritual ancestors in the North of Italy.

That the Waldenses were Manichean dualists or Albigensian heretics is an unfair charge. They were orthodox Christians. Furthermore they were "Protestants" even though they pre-dated the Protestant Reformation by several centuries.

PETER WALDO

As Latourette says (1959:218), Waldensian history may be traced to the twelfth century. At that time several "anti-clerical" movements were taking place, the most celebrated being that derived from Peter Waldo of Lyons, a wealthy banker. Waldo was around 33 years of age at his conversion in 1173. His religious conscience was stirred one spring day when a companion without warning dropped dead at his side. Waldo thought, "And what would happen to me, if I should have to appear from one moment to the other before God?" (Comba 1930: 30). Seeking salvation for his soul he inquired of a theologian. The answer given was that of Jesus to the rich young ruler: "If you would be perfect, go and sell what you have and give it to the poor, and you will have treasure in heaven; then come and follow Me" (Matt. 19:21). This was taken as Christ's clear command to Peter Waldo, and he set out to obey (Comba 1930:32). This was the beginning of a life-long adventure. In many ways the experience of Waldo parallels that of Francis of Assisi. But for Waldo it led out of the Roman Church.

Waldo went from house to house teaching the Gospel which he had had translated into the vulgar tongue. His listeners became followers. Two by two they went teaching - and begging. Waldo had divested himself of all earthly belongings (including his wife - who got half his goods). In Lyons Waldo and his group were happily called the <u>Poor Men of Lyons</u> (Comba 1930:37). The way of perfection was to live without owning. Theirs was "a kind of penitential brotherhood vowed to practice poverty and to preach it" (Hughes 1952:336).

The Archbishop of Lyons was not impressed with the efforts of the revivalists. They were ordered to desist, and in 1176 expelled from the city. Three years later Waldo and a disciple are in Rome appealing before the Lateran Council. Finally the Pope blessed the poverty scheme, "but he would not allow them to preach where the bishops were opposed to it" (Hughes 1952:336). The Archbishop was opposed, but Pietro Waldo would not submit. From that time the community was considered rebellious, and in 1183 was condemned by the Council of Verona (Comba 1930:43).

What was the heresy of the followers of Waldo? It was merely their disobedience to the prohibition against preaching (Hughes 1952:337). Disobedience sprang from adherence to the Scriptural injunction to "obey God rather than men". The absolute authority of Scripture was the fundamental principle (Comba 1930:50).

Waldo and his disciples wished to remain loyal to the Catholic Church. But they tried to correct abuses. The efficacy of good works and masses for the dead were criticized. Sacramental acts were nullified when performed by priests in mortal sin. Bad priests were not to be obeyed. Laymen were permitted to say mass, in certain cases, and could hear confessions (Hughes 1952:337). Belief in purgatory was rejected as well the invocation of saints. The Madonna was to be imitated (and venerated?) but not worshiped (Comba 1930:46), the Waldenses of Italy were born. They were then known as the Poor Men of Milan. Numerous in Italy and France, they spread to Spain, Germany, Bohemia, Poland and Hungary (Latourette 1959:218). All of Central Europe is said to have been their field of activity, with Bohemia and Maravia proving especially fertile (Comba 1930:49). Peter Waldo himself died, probably in Bohemia, around 1217.

Meantime in Italy the inquisition began during the thirteenth century to search out the Waldenses of the North. In the following century the persecution became more ferocious and so continued in the fifteenth century.

BARBA

During this critical period spiritual life was nurtured by ministers called *barba* - a medieval northern Italian word meaning "uncle" used in contradistinction to the Roman Catholic *Padre* or "father" (Comba 1930:91). The *barba* studied, copied, taught, and memorized the Bible. Entire books were committed to memory. It was the text for training young people to be missionaries and evangelists. These youths were sent forth two by two, "concealing their real character under the guise of a secular profession" (Wylie n.d.:15). As pedlars or merchants they traversed Southern and Central Europe. The doors of both the rich and the poor were open to them. As the displayed their precious wares they were more intent upon selling "without money and without price" that jewel more rare and more valuable than the merchandize which gained them entrance. The portions of the Word of God which they concealed in their goods and on their person were often copies which they themselves had made (Wylie n.d.:16). The Holy Pedlars gave these portions to deeply interested persons who could not pay.

MISSION

Groups of Waldenses sprang up throughout Italy. In the South one hears of Manfredonia, Cambro, Aquila, Naples. It is Tuscany and Umbria in Central Italy. Did the pedlar missionaries play a founding role? We do not know.

A colony was transplanted to Calabria in the fourteenth century. Some years later a second migration took place, and in 1500 a third. Crowded conditions in Piedmont were thus relieved, and the colonies in the South thrived for about 200 years (Wylie n.d.:107). The *barba* who were sent in pairs to minister in Calabria for two year terms would on the return journey visit their fellow-believers in the Italian towns. "For at that time there were few cities in the peninsula in which the Vandois were not to be found" (Wylie n.d.:108). Ironically the kiss of death for the colonists was to be the Protestant Reformation from beyond the Alps. For when lines of battle were drawn the Waldenses were identified with the (Protestant) enemy and marked for persecution and death.

News of Luther and Zwingli created excitement among the Waldenses. Representatives were sent to Switzerland and Germany in 1526. Four years later two *barba*, George Morel and Peter Masson, went seeking to establish relations with the nearest reformers. At Basil they confered with Oecolampadius and at Strassbourg with Martin Bucer. They also encountered William Farel. Following these contacts the Waldenses established rapport with the Reformed Churches of Switzerland and were aligned with the Protestant Reformation.

The Protestant Reformation did not send out missionaries. They were preoccupied with other problems. The Waldenses of Italy however, managed to send out their ambassadors (disguised as pedlars and merchants) despite the persecution. In the Valleys the Waldenses multiplied to around 40 thousand faithful with over 30 pastors. If other areas are added the number rises to considerably over 50 thousand (Comba 1930:133), in spite of large losses in France where there was a renewed persecution.

Severe measures were taken against Protestantism in Italy. The Calabrian colony was liquidated in 1560-1561. Its brilliant young pastor, Giovanni Luigi Pascale, was martyred. The sixteenth century was filled with bloodshed.

WALDENSIAN PERSECUTIONS

Giovanni Jalla gives the account of the bloody sufferings of early Italian Protestants in his *Storia della Riforma in Piemonte* (1914) which covers the years 1517-1580. Piemonte (Piedmont) is defined as "the geographically Italian places in which the Reform was definitively suffocated under the government of the House of Savoy" (p.2).

Concerning the Catholic Church in Italy around the end of the fifteenth and beginning of the sixteenth centuries, it is said to have been common knowledge that it was the most corrupt that could be found in all the world. Machinelli is quoted as saying that together with the Church and priests the Italians were become "without religion and bad" (p.4). A cardinal wrote to the Pope that there were with ruffians nor soldiers more impudent and dishonest than the monks (p.4).

The Protestant Reform was long overdue in such an area. But in a sense there was no need to "introduce" the Reform. For the Waldensian Church was already present. The Reform of Luther was more radical than that of Waldo, and was largely accepted by the Waldenses (p.7). The protest was already present, however, in the ancient Waldensian Church whose *barba* "courageously pilgrimaged in all of Italy, thro' many dangers, spied upon by ferocious inquisitors...preparing the ground to receive and cause to grow the seed planted by others" (p.7). The writings of the Reformers were diffused (works of Luther, Melenchthon, Zwingli, Bucer, Calvin) together with the Bible in Latin, French and Italian. In 1537 the works of Italian reformers began to appear (Vergerio, Valdes, Vermigli, Ochino, Paleario and many others), amount them the *Sommario della Sacra Scrittura* and the *Trattato utilissimo del Beneficio di Cristo crocifisso* (p.13).

On September 7, 1523, Martin Luther himself wrote to Carlo III, Duke of Savoy, a lengthy letter in which he carefully presents his doctrine of justification by faith. I have read the letter in its Italian translation (Jalla 1914:15-19). Luther hoped to win the Duke for the Protestant cause. In this he failed. The Waldenses and others still in the Catholic Church had already protested against indulgences and other abuses. But all was in vain. The Inquisition was directed against the Lutherans and the Waldenses.

We are told of some 100,000 Waldense faithful scattered throughout Italy and other places. At a 1526 synod 140 *Barbi* are reported to have begun to initiate relations with German reforms (p.25).

The Pope encouraged and commended Carlo III in taking severe action against the "heresies". Many were accused, turned over to the Secular Arm, condemned, and burned at the stake. Nevertheless Reformed doctrines spread, taking root especially in Turin.

In 1536 the French occupied the territories of Carlo III, beginning a period of disaster for Piedmont. "The victims of the Catholic repression...saw that both the regimes were fatal to religious liberty. Nevertheless under the French there was some let up in the rigors of the Inquisition..." (Jalla 1914:47). In 1542 Rome itself became alarmed and began to exterminate "heresy" - directed against B. Ochino, Peter Martyr, and others.

Upon the death of Franceso I, 31 March 1547, his son, Henry II, ascended the throne. His intentions for a renewed, fiery persecution against "heretics" were frustrated by Giovanni Caraccioli, prince of Melfi.

Henry II on June 27, 1551, to please the clergy, signed a new edict: "it was prohibited to bring any book from Geneva or other heretical places, to keep books not approved by the Sorbonne, to print or sell...translations of the Bible or of doctors of the Church..." (Jalla 1914:67). Many other prohibitions were applied.

Carlo III died on August 17, 1553, in Vercelli. His son, Emanuele Filiberto, was far away in the service of the Emperor (Jalla 1914:70). Protestants were persecuted with renewed zeal. Nevertheless the Reform cause moved ahead. A letter to Switzerland contained the following glowing points: "...Several valleys and many thousands of men who profess Christ openly...The Supper has been celebrated openly in Angrogna, with a concourse of at least 6,000 persons...Not a one is to be found, not a woman, not a child that would not have responded to be ready to suffer everything rather than abandon Christ, their Savior" (Jalla 1914:85). The greater the threats, the more the progress.

The Pope in 1557 extended the inquisition to France and in all the States subject to Enrico II. Case after case is cited of Believers becoming martyrs for the truth of Christ. In 1557, a certain Bartolomeo, seller of books, was arrested on the street, in possession of sacred books. Taken before the Senate, "he confessed his faith with much spirit and force". In the face of the Archbishop and the Senators, and to the wonderment of all, he refuted "the errors of the Antichrist".

He was tried in many ways, and finally, after being examined by the Archbishop of Turin, was condemned to the flames by the Senate. "He faced death victoriously for Christ and His Word" (Jalla 1914:99). This is one illustration among many cited in a letter directed to the chief German Protestants by the churches and ministers of Piemonte in 1559. It was read in the Italian translation of the Latin text (Jalla 1914:97-104). The letter requests to be circulated among the rulers and churches of Germany that all might know their sentiments and religion. It shows both the degree of Reformation inroad and severity and the Catholic counteraction.

Emanuele Filiberto in 1559 returned to Piemonte. Shortly Enrico II died and was succeeded at the French court by his young son, Francesco II. As a result of actions against them, Italians of Reform persuasian under Filbert scattered not only to Geneva, but to Lucerne, and we hear of illustrious individuals who found a place of safety and usefulness as far away as Russia.

War was made against the Waldenses in 1560-1561. As a result, privileges that had been denied were restored. In a limited sense freedom to preach and meet as congregations was to be permitted in some of the valleys. One source indicates that the number of Lutherans at the Court in Piemonte was very great, sufficient to counterbalance the Catholics. A member of the House of Savoy, Claudio, married a Protestant. This aroused the disdain not only of Emanuele Filiberto but of the fanatically Catholic faction. The years 1562-1567 were to see wars of religion unleashed in the Alps. The Inquisition proved insufficient to maintain its orders, and in 1563 Catholics were prohibited from conversing or having any kind of relation with the "heretics". Where the Waldenses were the majority this had little effect, but it was disastrous for them in other areas (Jalla 1914:219). Nevertheless the Reform moved ahead. A number of attempts against it failed. In April, 1566, the Discipline or Constitution of the Waldensian Churches was voted by the synod in convocation in Lucerne Valley. Calvin wrote one of his final letters, on behalf of the Waldenses to the French, shortly before his death. It is a time of confusion, of correspondence between French, Spanish, the Vatican, Emanuele Filberto and Geneva concerning the Waldensian "problem". A policy was enacted which had as its object the destruction of churches outside the Valleys. The Count required all non-Catholics in one area to register within six days as such under threat of total confiscation (of body and property), not wanting to tolerate two kinds of religion in his territory. He had the approval and encouragement of the hierarchy for using even violence against the Reform, "for the glory of God" (Jalla

1914:235). Many were imprisoned probably for the purpose of determining the number who could bear arms.

This was an era of religious bloodshed throughout Europe. Sentiments favoring liquidation of Protestants were increased with the election in 1566 of the Cardinal of Alessandria and grand Inquisitor as Pope Pius V. His successor in the north aimed at "purging Piedmont of heresy" (Jalla 1914:248). Persecution instead appeared to fan the fervour of the persecuted. There were martyrs, but the reformists continued numerously.

The Jesuits were to have a role in the persecution. The St. Bartholomew massacre was to have an effect even in Piedmont. The years 1570-1574 saw a series of crusades against the Protestants. News of the massacre was celebrated joyfully by the fanatical in Piedmont. The Waldenses secured their families in mountain hideaways as they did in times of greatest danger (Jalla 1914:310). The Duke was coerced by extremists to prohibit sheltering of French refugees who were described as "pests, filth, poisonous snakes, whose tongue bites like a cancer, and the heart emits poison" (Jalla 1914:311). But the Waldenses opened both heart and home to their Hugenot brethren fleeing from the slaughter.

Refugees, French and Italian, swelled the population of Geneva to 2300 simultaneously. Duke Emanuele Filiberto tried to starve the city. But the Duchess, friend of the Reform, secretly sent 4,000 florins to Theodore of Beza for the refugees. This she repeated annually until her death (Jalla 1914:314). The Italian Church in Geneva grew large.

In the days immediately following St. Bartholomews, forces proceeded against the Waldenses in several actions. A state of war existed in August of 1573. Following the signing of the peace, the Waldenses insisted upon following their ancient beliefs passed on from their ancestors. A state of civil war continued. Jalla devotes an entire chapter to the St. Partholomew period of 1570-1574 (1914:299-331).

The Duchess of Savoy, Margaret of France, was instrumental in securing for the Waldenses "a century of legal religious liberty, although continuously disturbed by the illegal decrees of the son and the grandsons of this generous mediatrix" (Jalla 1914:339). She intervened directly on behalf of many individuals. Protestants of Italy and France mourned her death on Nov. 5, 1570. Ten years later Emmanuel Filbert, Duke of Savoy, followed her in death, being in his fifties. The throne passed to his only son, Carlo Emmanuele. Filbert; though free from many vices, had been a bigot. He published and executed the decrees of Trent in Piedmont. "In spite of good principle and generous resolutions he too frequently used violence against...the dissidents" (Jalla 1914:369). In spite of his rigors, at the death of the Duke the Reform was well rooted and organized in the valleys of Piedmont. Repression did prevent Protestantism from "flowering" there as it did north of the Alps.

Jalla includes in his book (1914:373-382) a list of Piedmontese enrolled in the Register of "Inhabitants of Geneva" from 1549 to 1574, another of those who became residents of Geneva after the Reform, and a list of students from Piedmont at the Geneva Academy.

Bad as was the sixteenth century for the Italian Waldensians, worse was yet to come. The sixteenth century had seen gains despite the difficulties. In the next century the Waldenses would be all but totally wiped out.

DEATH

The seventeenth century was the height of sorrow. The pestilence of 1630 was followed by the Capuchins. In 1650 the Council of the Propaganda of the Faith was established in Turin, having as its object the complete destruction of the Vaudois. The massacre which took place Easter, 1655, was accompanied by unbelievable tortures "which the rage of even a Nero shrank from inflicting" (Wylie n.d.:144). The Waldenses were practically exterminated in 1655. All that remained of the fighting men were 500 (Wylie n.d.:159). In the midst of tragedy the Waldensian hero was Giosue' Gianavello. When ordered to the mass within 24 hours or die, Gianavello replied, Mille volte meglio la morte piuttosto che la messa!" (A thousand times better death than the mass). When Gianavello was wounded and his successor Jahier killed, the situation seemed hopeless. Fortunately the Duke, pressured by the Swiss and English as well as the King of France, decided it was time for peace. The history of this period was recorded by an eyewitness, Giovanni Leger, moderator of the Waldensian Church.

The end was not yet. On Easter, 1685, another massacre was unleashed. Those not killed were imprisoned. Duke Victor Amedeo II purged the Valleys for the Pope. The area was left desolate. In January, 1687, the prisons were opened. The three thousand surviving the horrors of imprisonment were exiled to Geneva (Comba 1930:232). Two years later, let by their pastor and colonel, Enrico Arnaud, they returned to reposses their Valleys. The Duke in 1690 proclaimed an edict permitting their free return. Peace had come. Not all difficulties were over. There would be lapses. But the Waldenses were about to enter the new century with a greater degree of freedom. In spite of troubles there was hope.

RELIEF

The relief of the eighteenth century was not accompanied by spiritual advance. The French Revolution brought an evil influence to the Waldenses who once more passed under the dominion of France. The skepticism of Voltaire "threatened to inflict more deadly injury on the Church of the Alps than all the persecutions of the previous centuries" (Wylie n.d.:205). Pastors and churches lost their first love under the spell of rationalism. When revival came early in the nineteenth century, it divided the Church.

> Rather than a true revival of conscience, the movement of 1825 was mainly doctrinal: it was a lay protest against certain ecclesiastical deficiencies of the time, it was the reaction of the spirit of faith against rationalism and paralyzing formalism (Comba 1930:309).

The dissention healed, and new life was breathed into the ancient Church. Again there was an interest in missions, in the distribution of Scripture, and in door-to-door evangelism in every village (Comba 1930:310).

Help came from the outside during this era in the person of an Anglican pastor, William S. Gilly. Another benefactor was General Carl Beckwith. These men and others were instrumental in providing church structures and institutions among the Waldenses as well as provoking controversy. From this time on Italian Churches were to show a reliance on foreign sources in such things as finance.

Much more significant than funds or buildings was the Emancipation of 1848 signed by Duke Carl Albert. Political and civil emancipation were explicit - in short, everything except religious freedom (Comba 1930:348). Still, great progress had been made. The following year an evangelistic effort was made in Florence and Pisa. This was followed by thrusts in Piedmont itself and in Liguria. A Faculty of Theology was founded in 1855 in Torre Pellice and shortly thereafter the Claudiana Publishing Society was opened in Turin.

The Revolution which brought greater freedom to the Waldenses, also apparently stirred them to new evangelistic endeavors. Pioneer evangelists entered Milan, Bergama, Como, Pavia, Brescia as Lombardy became part of "Free" Italy. Then it was Tuscany: Leghorn, Florence, Elba, Lucca and Pisa. As the Red Shirts of Garibaldi added Sicily and Naples to the Kingdom of Victor Emmanuel, these were entered by Waldensian evangelists (Comba 1930:369). From various centers the Gospel spread to other cities and towns throughout Italy. In 1870 with the fall of the Papal States, Rome was penetrated by soldiers and by a Waldensian colporteur.

The century ended much better than it had begun. In 1848 when civil rights were granted, the Waldensian Church had determined a bold program: "Although its constituency numbered only about twenty thousand it adopted as its aim the evangelization of Italy" (Latourette 1959:219). By the close of the century many new congregations had come into being. There was "a modest growth" (Latourette 1941:140). The theological seminary was relocated in Rome. A royal decree had recognized the Waldenses as the "Italian Evangelical Church" (Latourette 1959:219).

THE WALDENSIAN CHURCH TODAY

The nineteenth century closed with a proliferation of Waldensian institutions - school, orphanages - and publications. In the first decade of the twentieth century the Waldenses reported nearly 3,000 pupils in 56 day schools and nearly 4,000 in 54 Sunday Schools. The Waldensian Valleys, Pinerolo and Turin, were divided into 17 parishes. There were 44 settled congregations and 65 mission stations in all parts of Italy. The mission field for the Waldenses was the peninsula. They also organized seven churches among the emigrants to South and North America and one in Germany. Foreign funds helped maintain the program of the Church in Italy (Clark and Clark 1909:50).

Italy around the turn of the century was nominally Roman Catholic (97.12 per cent). Protestants numbered some 65,000 of whom half were said to be foreigners. Of the Italian half 22,500 were Waldenses (Villari 1926:17-18).

From the Report of the Moderator, 1920, a degree of progress is visible: 60 churches, 150 mission stations, 68 ministers, 10 evangelists, 6 colporteurs, one seminary with three professors, two high schools and one nomal school having 21 professors, 13 elementary schools with 40 teachers, an evangelistic weekly paper and a theological review (Rose 1922:48).

Fascism introduced a difficult period for Protestants. The Waldensian Church did not apparently suffer the oppression felt by some other non-Catholic groups during the Mussolini era. The regulations prescribed by the Concordat between the Vatican and the Fascist State were interpreted as reaffirming the principle of liberty of conscience (Comba 1930:401).

Ernesto Comba sumarizes the ideals of Waldensianism:

> To restore the simplicity and purity of primitive Christianity;
> To separate religion from the political elements which cause it to degenerate into clericalism;
> To demonstrate that every legitimate progress of civil life is not only compatible but indissolubly connected with true and genuine Christianity;
> To offer hospitality to souls who, emancipated from sacerdotal tyranny, are seeking brotherly communion with other believers in Christ;
> To unite these believers in a vigorous sheaf to fight every manifestation and to extirpate every root of evil and misbelief, causing the leaven of the eternal Gospel to penetrate into the Italian soul (Comba 1930:403-404).

Commendable as these ideals are, they betray a tragic loss of mission. There is no strong evangelistic goal.

Post-World War Waldenses have shown chiefly social and ecumenical concerns. Improtant as they are, it seems unfortunate that they preclude an evangelistic emphasis. The ancient Church whose *barba* and missionaries went everywhere teaching the Gospel appears to have largely stopped evangelizing. Jemelo blames the Italian State:

> ...The authorities reveal an inflexible determination not to allow the ancient Waldensian sect to extend its influence beyond the boundaries of its two small Alpine communes and not to permit any Protestant propaganda (Jemelo 1960:315).

Waldenses of other centuries evangelized despite restrictions and persecution. The judgment of Jemelo, which may have applied to the years immediately following the War, no longer is valid. Other Protestants have evangelized openly, aggressively, and successfully.

At present there are around 35,000 Waldensians in Italy according to Santini (1969:63). However the figure of 25,000 seems more likely. The number of churches was reported as 150 in the *World Christian Handbook* whose figures are not always reliable (Coxill and Grubbs 1968:199). A recent list totals only 126 (Santini 1969). The 1967 Directory lists 77 communities and 92 groups *in diaspora*, or a total of around 170 places of public or private worship (Consiglio 1967). About 50 institutions are maintained.

Robert Evans reported that in a typical post-war year the Waldenses were instructing 581 catechists for church membership (1963c:287). This low rate may still be typical. It seems to indicate biological increase rather than additions from without by conversion. The Waldenses once constituted the majority of Protestants in Italy. This is no longer true since the post-war growth of the Pentecostals. (See figure 8)

Figures 9, 10, and 11 portray Waldensian growth. It is evident that the Church never recovered from the decimation of the seventeenth century. The blood of martyrs is not always the seed of the Church.

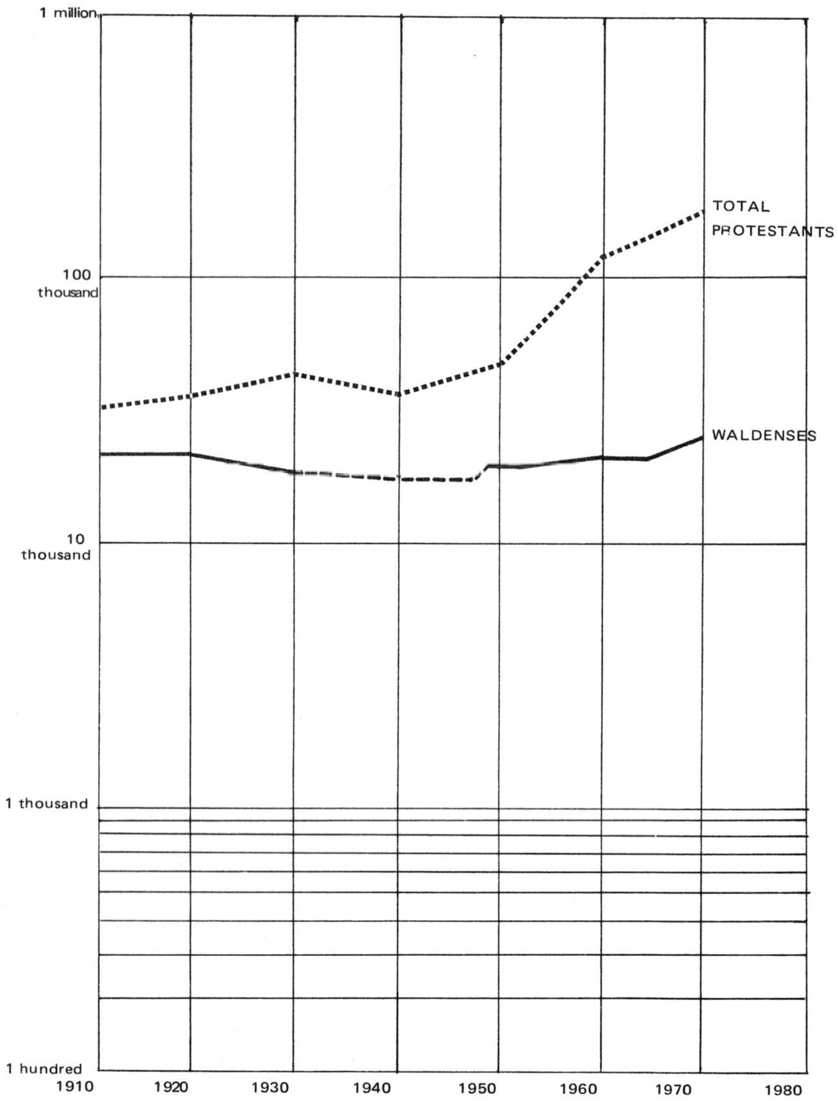

WALDENSIAN MEMBERSHIP GROWTH COMPARED TO TOTAL PROTESTANT MEMBERSHIP GROWTH

FIGURE 8

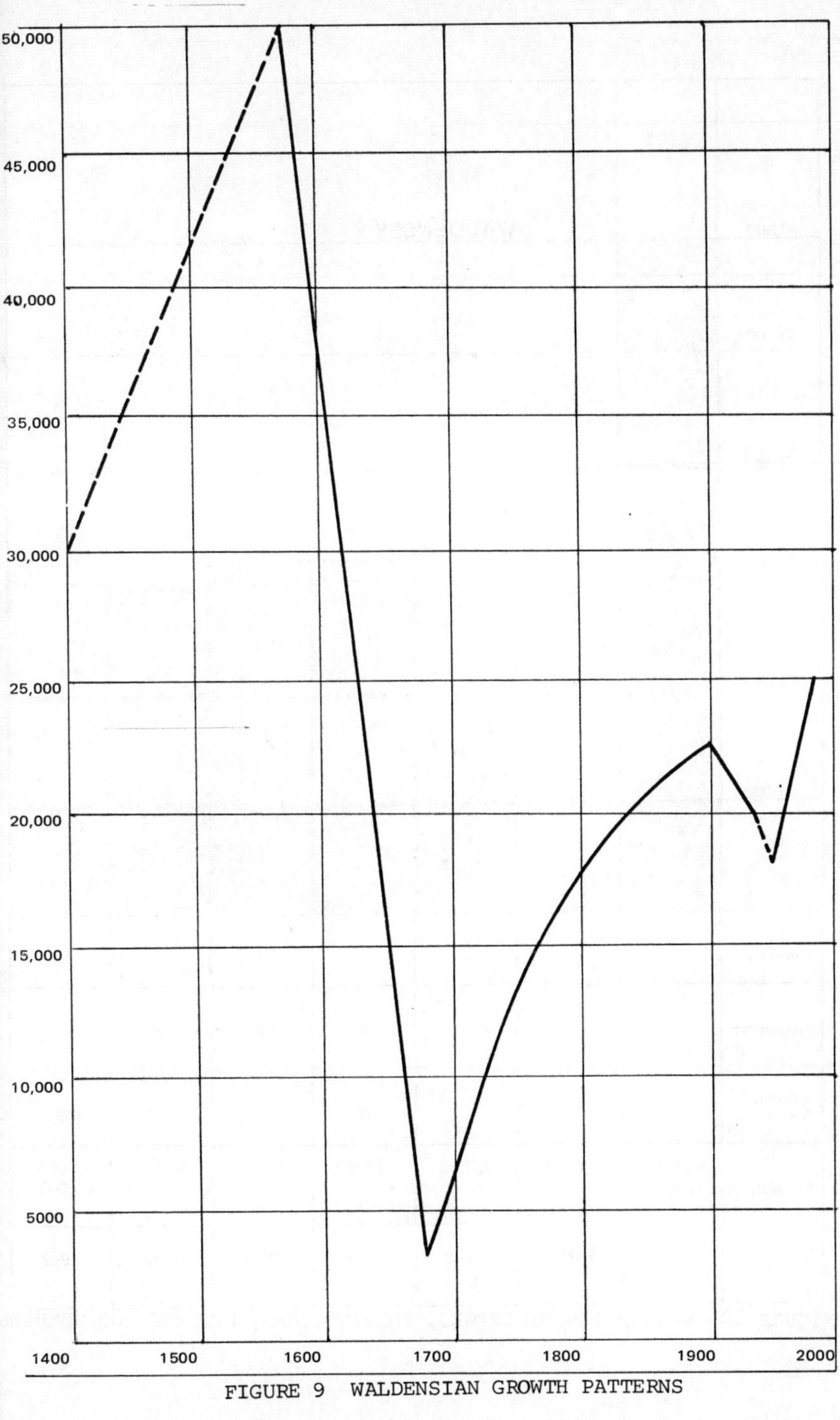

FIGURE 9 WALDENSIAN GROWTH PATTERNS

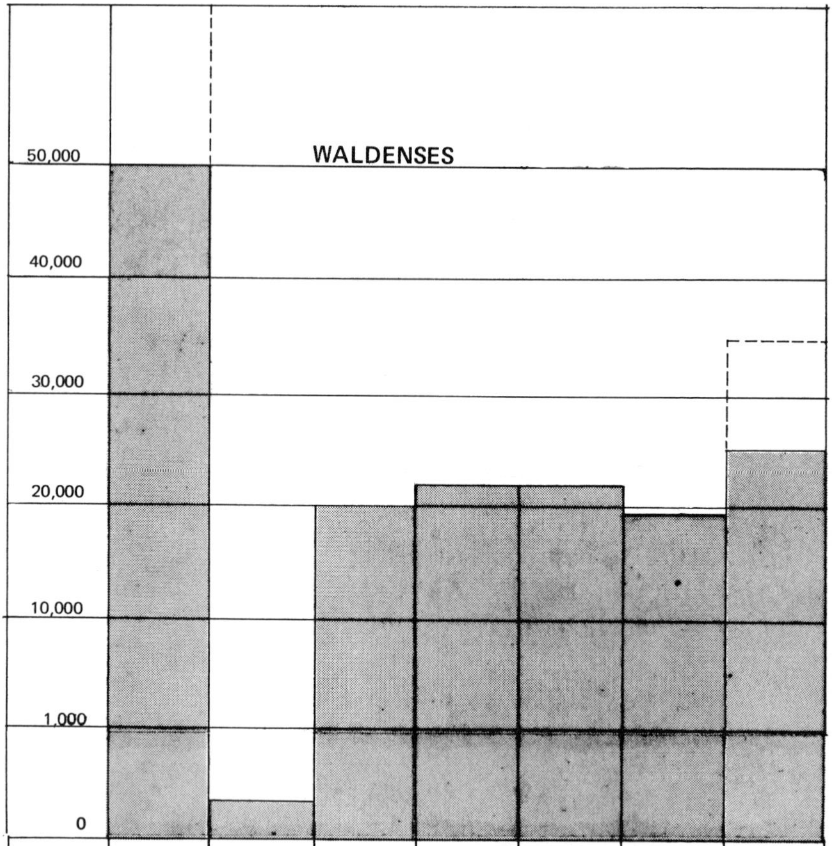

Ministers					78	64	85
Institutions				58	20+		50
Churches & Stations				109	210	244	169
Members	50,000 (100,000)	3,000	20,000	22,500?	22,500?	19,691	25,000 (35,000)
Year	1500's	1687	1848	1900?	1920	1932	1969

FIGURE 10 WALDENSIAN MINISTERS, INSTITUTIONS, CHURCHES AND MEMBERS

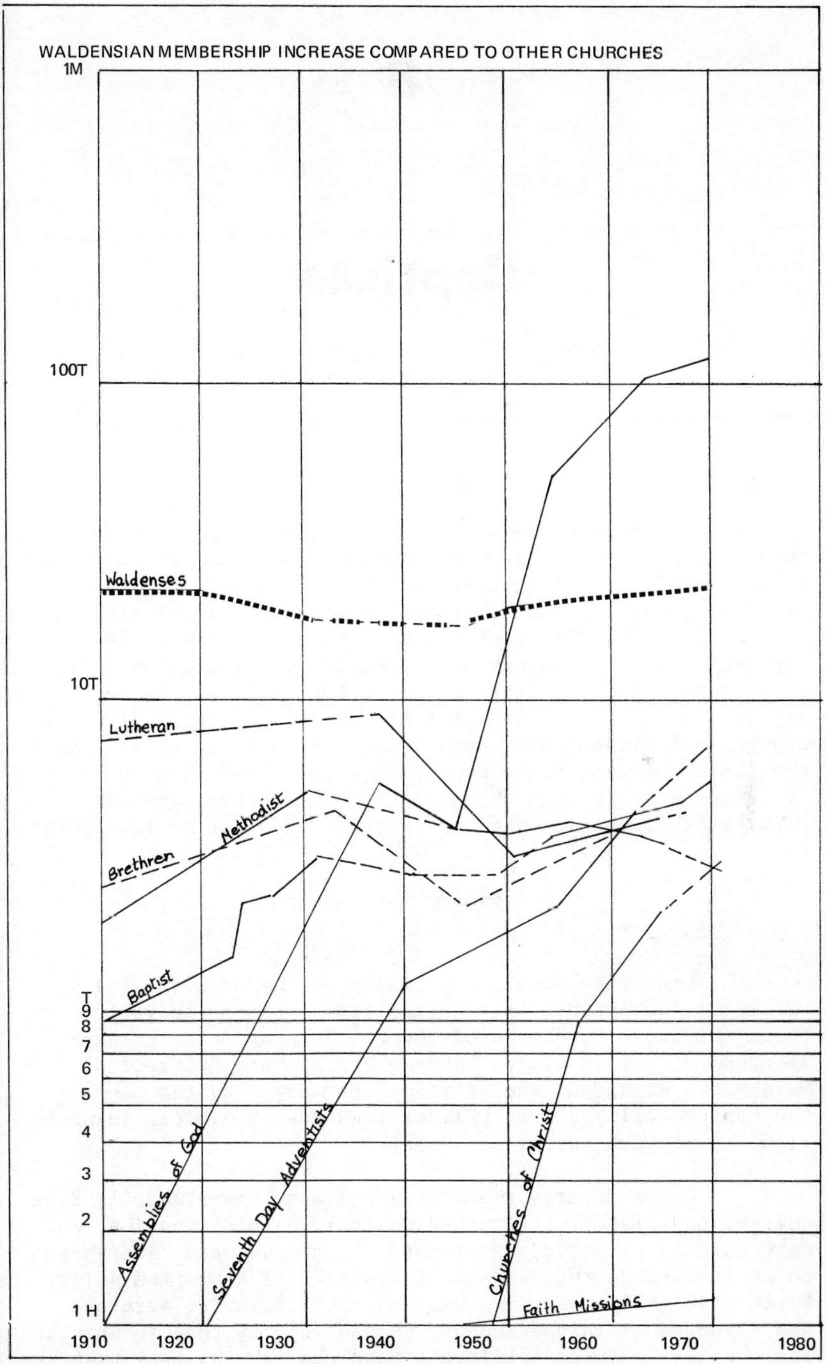
WALDENSIAN MEMBERSHIP INCREASE COMPARED TO OTHER CHURCHES
1M
100T
10T
T
9
8
7
6
5
4
3
2
1 H
1910
1920
1930
1940
1950
1960
1970
1980
Waldenses
Lutheran
Methodist
Brethren
Baptist
Assemblies of God
Seventh Day Adventists
Churches of Christ
Faith Missions

FIGURE 11

8

Baptists

The Baptist denomination of Italy began in the nineteenth century. Baptist missionaries, Wall and Clarke, came from England in 1863. It was the time of the Risorgimento. Garibaldi, Cavour, and Mazzini were busy unifying Italy. In 1870 Southern Baptist sent Dr. Cote to Italy, their first European Field. Cote may have been the first missionary to enter Rome (Southern Baptist Convention 1970:2). If so, it is probably of his preaching that Calvin Guy remarks: "the first evangelical preaching in Rome after Victor Emmanuel II came to the Italian throne found spectacular response" (1965:203). It is unfortunate that the resulting church was organized on anticlerical reaction and had to be reorganized in four years.

HISTORIC PRECEDENCE

Centuries before the coming of the missionaries a colony of Anabaptists from Switzerland had come to Venice. These spiritual forebears of the Baptists are said to have emerged in over 70 places between Ferrara and Switzerland before the middle of the sixteenth century. By the end of the century all had been obliterated under Dominican inquisition. Some were martyred. Some fled.

Moore reports that two survivors, Francis della Sega and Anthony Rissetto, returned to Italy as missionaries, but were quickly arrested, imprisoned, condemned, and "sentenced to be drowned in the lagoons of Venice." A converted priest while conducting a service was, in 1542, likewise arrested and disposed of in the lagoon. Moore reports that in Northern Italy still today are believers "who cherish the fact that they are descendents of the Baptists who dared to die for their convictions" (1951:47-48).

ENGLISH BAPTISTS

The Baptist Missionary Society of Great Britain was responsible for beginning Baptist work in Italy. One of the original missionaries, Edward Clarke, in 1866 formed the "La Spezia Mission" - an independent Baptist mission which endured until 1969.

By 1911 the English Baptists had planted 32 churches having a membership of 815. Five churches were located in Rome, one with a membership of 168 (Crivelli 1938:174). These figures do not agree with Luzzi's report from the same period which states that there were 56 churches and mission stations with 663 communicants. Luzzi also speaks of the La Spezia Mission as "flourishing" (1913:225). Actually a report from around 1933 lists 7 churches for La Spezia (Crivelli 1936).

After a good beginning the Baptist Missionary Society in 1920 turned their entire operation over to the Americans. At that time the *Opera Cristiana Evangelica Battista* ofItaly was born.

Five churches from La Spezia (now known as A.M.E.I. - *Associazione Missionaria Evangelica Italiana*) joined the Baptist Union in 1967. The remaining 4 A.M.E.I. churches of Naples became, for all practical purposes, independent churches at the final dissolution of the La Spezia Mission in 1969, but cooperate with the Conservative Baptists.

BAPTISTS FROM AMERICA

Southern Baptists, working in Rome, cooperated with the English missionary in that city. The year after Cote's arrival the first church was formed in Rome. In 1872 churches with 271 members were reported in 6 cities. By 1907 membership had risen to 825 in 32 churches and 65 out-stations. Although scattered, the Southern Baptists in the 19th century worked most in Rome and Italy south of Rome (Laturette 1941: 140).

It is not clear in some reports whether all Baptists are included or whether a certain branch is intended. At any rate, for the year 1908 one source shows twice as many Baptist in the South as in the North. The 14 churches of the South had 403 members in such cities as Bari, Boscotrecase, Gravina, and Naples. Sicily had 3 churches in Messina, Noto, and Palermo with 76 members. On the island of Sardinia there were 43 Baptists in the 2 churches in Caglieri and Iglesias. The mission also extended to Tunis, North Africa, when it cared for one church (Clark and Clark 1909:58-59).

The North, in conrast, had 248 members, 12 churches, and 26 mission stations. There were 14 Italian helpers.

The transfer of the English assets took place in January, 1923. "The total number of Baptist churches in Italy at that time was reported to be 51. The membership of 2240 represented an increase of more than six hundred over the preceding year" (Southern Baptist Convention 1970:33).

Ten years later the pressures of Fascism combined with financial stress caused a decline. In 1933 six churches and ten out-stations were closed. Persecution was intense in 1936. The following year 8 churches and 5 out-stations closed (Southern Baptist Convention 1970:35). Curiously a report lists 88 Baptist churches during this period (Crivelli 1936), slightly more than at present.

After the War, in 1956, the Italian Baptist Union was formed. The Italian Church was constituted an autonomous body.

Evans states in 1963 that there were 57 congregations and 41 out-stations, half with church buildings. Fifty-one pastors cared for about 4000 baptized believers. The total community was estimated at 12,000 (1963e:281).

In 1967 when the 5 La Spezia churches joines the Union, membership reached 5,001. Churches totalled 85 (Southern Baptist Convention 1970:39). The directory published that year, however, lists 116 Baptist Union churches and groups (Consiglio Federale 1967).

The report for 1968 indicates that 13 churches were self-supporting and that an equal number of mission points were operating. The previous year had seen 117 baptisms. The Baptist denomination was served by 53 national pastors and 29 missionaries (Southern Baptist Convention 1968).

At the beginning of 1970 a Baptist pastor, active in evangelism and denominational work, gave as a reasonable estimate 6,000 baptized believers in the churches of the Union (Jones 1970).

Baptist growth is portrayed in figure 12. Figure 13 compares Baptist growth with that of other churches.

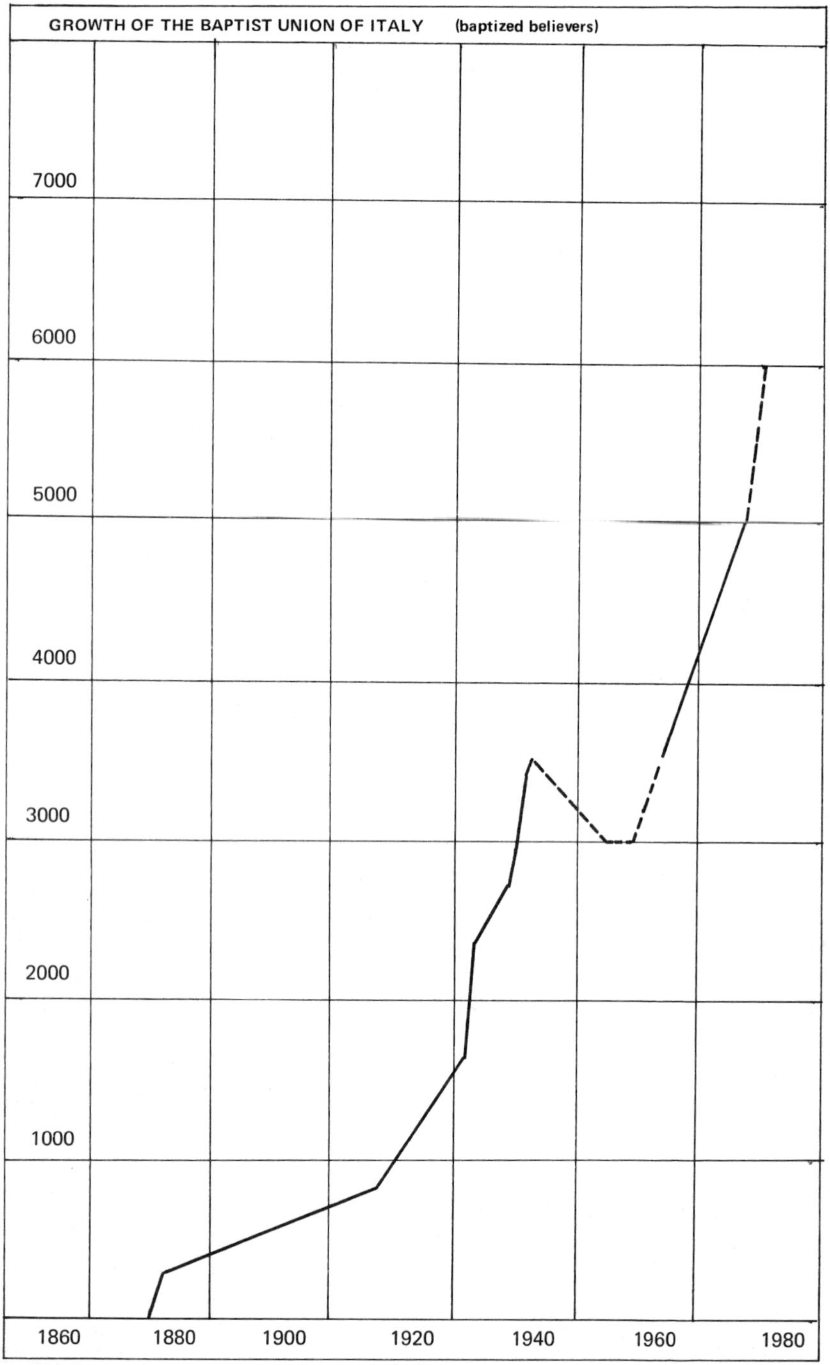
GROWTH OF THE BAPTIST UNION OF ITALY (baptized believers)
7000
6000
5000
4000
3000
2000
1000
1860
1880
1900
1920
1940
1960
1980

FIGURE 12

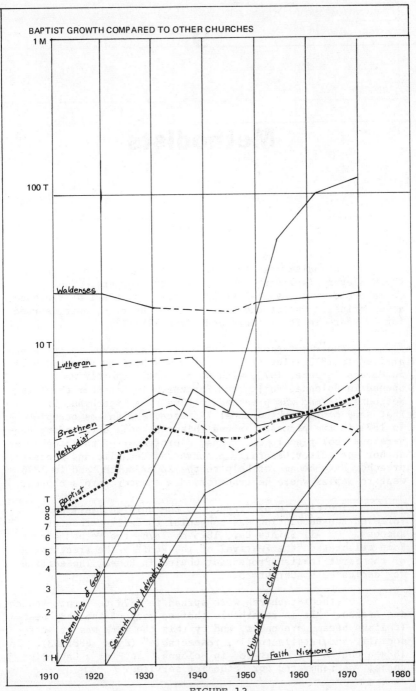

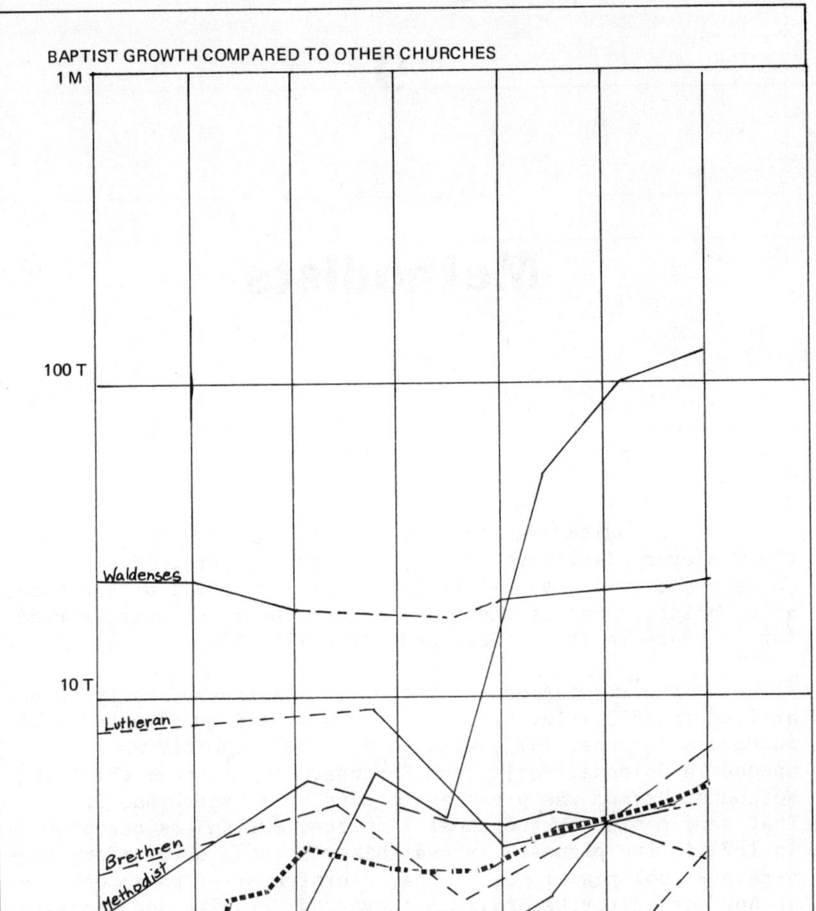
BAPTIST GROWTH COMPARED TO OTHER CHURCHES
1 M
100 T
10 T
T
9
8
7
6
5
4
3
2
1 H
1910
1920
1930
1940
1950
1960
1970
1980
Waldenses
Lutheran
Brethren
Methodist
Baptist
Assemblies of God
Seventh Day Adventists
Churches of Christ
Faith Missions

FIGURE 13

9

Methodists

FOUNDATIONS

Methodism came to Italy first from England. In 1861 the Wesleyan Missionary Society sent two workers. They collaborated with Evangelist Bartolomeo Gualtieri of Florence, an ex-priest. One of the missionaries, Henry Piggott, served for 40 years in Italy (Holt and Clark 1956:125).

The first American Methodist missionary, Leroy Vernon, arrived in 1873. The first service was held in a rented hall in Modena in June, 1873, with 60 present. Shortly work was opened in Bologna, Forli, and Ravenna. In Decmeber the first Methodist sermon was preached in Rome by a Frenchman, Dr. Gay. That same month work began at Florence. Milan was occupied in 1874 in two places. Around this time some outstanding conversions took place: Dr. Lanna, a professor of philosophy; an author and editor,Caporali; a converted Catholic and Protestant preacher Rave became of help to the Rome church, and in 1876 went to Naples where he transformed a theater into a church.

The climate of freedom in the unified Italy which followed the Revolution was congenial to early Methodist success. On All Saints Day, 1875 or 1876, the Methodists of Rome celebrated "the Festival of the Roof" - the erection of the first Italian Protestant church in Rome. The edifice was dedicated at Christmas.

Methodist church work spread in 1876 to Terni, Venice, and Arezzo. "It is remarkable that so many of the very best Italians became preachers, and by this the work was at once, socially and intellectually, respectable" (Hyde 1888:303). In 1884 a church was dedicated in Bologna. In Pisa a Catholic chapel was renovated for Methodist services.

Hyde says that in 1888 Italian Methodists numbered 1200 "in society, with 25 preachers" (1888:303). The strongest society, at Florence, consisted of about 200.

American Methodism from the start was involved in social service. The famed Casa Materna Orphanage near Naples was opened at an early date.

INSTITUTIONS

Methodism quickly assumed a pattern which seems characteristic of the work of this Church in many parts of the world. Benevolent Christian institutions to demonstrate the love of God were chosen as a tool of evangelism.

At first there was a direct evangelistic ministry. However in 1888 an orphanage and a home were opened. The latter developed into a school for girls. A famous student and later head of the school was Miss Garibaldi, granddaughter of the heroic unifier of Italy. Around the turn of the century some three or four hundred girls were fast on their way to becoming an institutional mission. A report of the Methodist Episcopals tells of three couples and five single women in Rome. The Wesleyans also had personnel there. Churches were established. But one hears of not only orphanage and girls' school, but also of a boys' college, a theological school, a publishing house and a womens' work all in Rome, and an industrial institute in Venice. Besides churches and Sunday Schools, Italian Methodist partors have the care of "day schools...in Genoa, Milan, Naples, Pisa, Turin, Bologna, Florence, Pistoia, Venice, and many other cities" under the direction of an American bishop (Clark and Clark 1909:56).

A case has sometimes been made for constructing beautiful church buildings for Protestant worship in Italy. Luzzi felt that evangelism among Italians would be enhanced by such chapels. The Methodists apparently did just that. A report told of the "prestige" provided by the headquarters building in the capital, "holding its own in proportion and elegance with the architectural triumphs all about it - a building fo which every Protestant who sees it is justly proud" (Clark and Clark 1909:57). But was a more effective evangelism the result of building? The Methodist Church has not made great progress in growth in Italy in spite of the 1909 report of mission stations in 40 cities and towns, 46 Italian pastors, 70 teachers, 46 Sunday Schools "and a large church membership" (Clark and Clark 1909:57).

One is grateful for Methodist evangelistic concern which sent them into the cities to establish churches. The Wesleyans carried this concern to the Italian military. One wonders how much greater could have been the impact had their energies not been expended inso many projects, some of which were in competition with the Catholics: "All about this institution are the rival schools of the nuns, offering better accommodations at lower prices...But all to no purpose; the college has gained in every way, and never were its prospects brighter" (Clark and Clark 1909:57).

Where is that school today? What did it contribute to the evangelization of Italy? What imprint has it left on the country, or on the Evangelical Church? I do not know. However I do have some acquaintance with one institution of the Methodist Church which continues to serve today. It is respected; it performs a much needed function; it demonstrates the love of Jesus Christ. However I must also comment that I doubt that it contributes to the evangelization of Italy. Its graduates are fine people, but they are not necessarily converts to the Evangelical church.

THE DENOMINATION

Around the beginning of the century the Italian Free Church had evangelized and trained numerous converts. Conceived of originally as an Italian Church superceding all denominations, its churches merged into other denominations. The Methodists were the chief recipients (Clark and Clark 1909:51).

The two Methodist branches (British and American) worked in cooperation for many years. They were fully merged in 1946 (Latourette 1961:372). A connection was maintained to the Methodist Missionary Committee of London.

The Evangelical Methodist Church of Italy was proclaimed autonomous in 1962: A "Pact of Cooperation" was signed with the British Methodist Church. The Church is a member of the World Methodist Council and the Council of Churches (Consiglio Federale 1967:53).

CHURCHES

Institutionalism seems to have mitigated against the expansion of Methodist Churches. In the decade 1901-1911 evangelicals in Italy had doubled. Yet a few years thereafter a Methodist superintendent was quoted as saying, "Our Italian Protestant missions are still in the seed-sowing period; the harvest is not yet" (Rose 1922:52).

The 1967 *Annual* of Evangelical Churches (Consiglio Federale) lists 85 Methodist churches and places of worship, including private homes. If *World Christian Handbook* figures mean anything at all they would indicate that Methodist membership in recent years had declined while the number of churches has increased. Figure 16 tabulates graphically a number of these facts.

Of the ten Methodist circuits, four are in the North having 40 of the churches. The two Central circuits have only 11 churches between them although they include Florence and Rome. The remaining 35 churches are in the four Southern circuits. Methodism seems to have done best in the northern regions and worst in the Central area and the islands (the tenth circuit consists of the 3 churches of Sicily; there are none on Sardegna).

Methodism today seems to lack an evangelistic thrust. There apparently is no effort to begin new churches. Social and ecumenical concerns seem uppermost.

The growth and decline of Methodists is shown by graph in figure 14. A comparison with other Evangelicals may be seen in figure 15. Figure 16 attempts to show the size of the Methodist Church at various times in terms of number of ministers, churches, believers, and total community. The War years are not shown, but normally all Protestants declined in Italy at that time. The number of institutions supported is not shown, but it should be remembered that they are numerous at most times. According to one estimate there are only 2,000 Methodist communicants in 1970. That seems too low. If true, however, the rate of decline would be shocking.

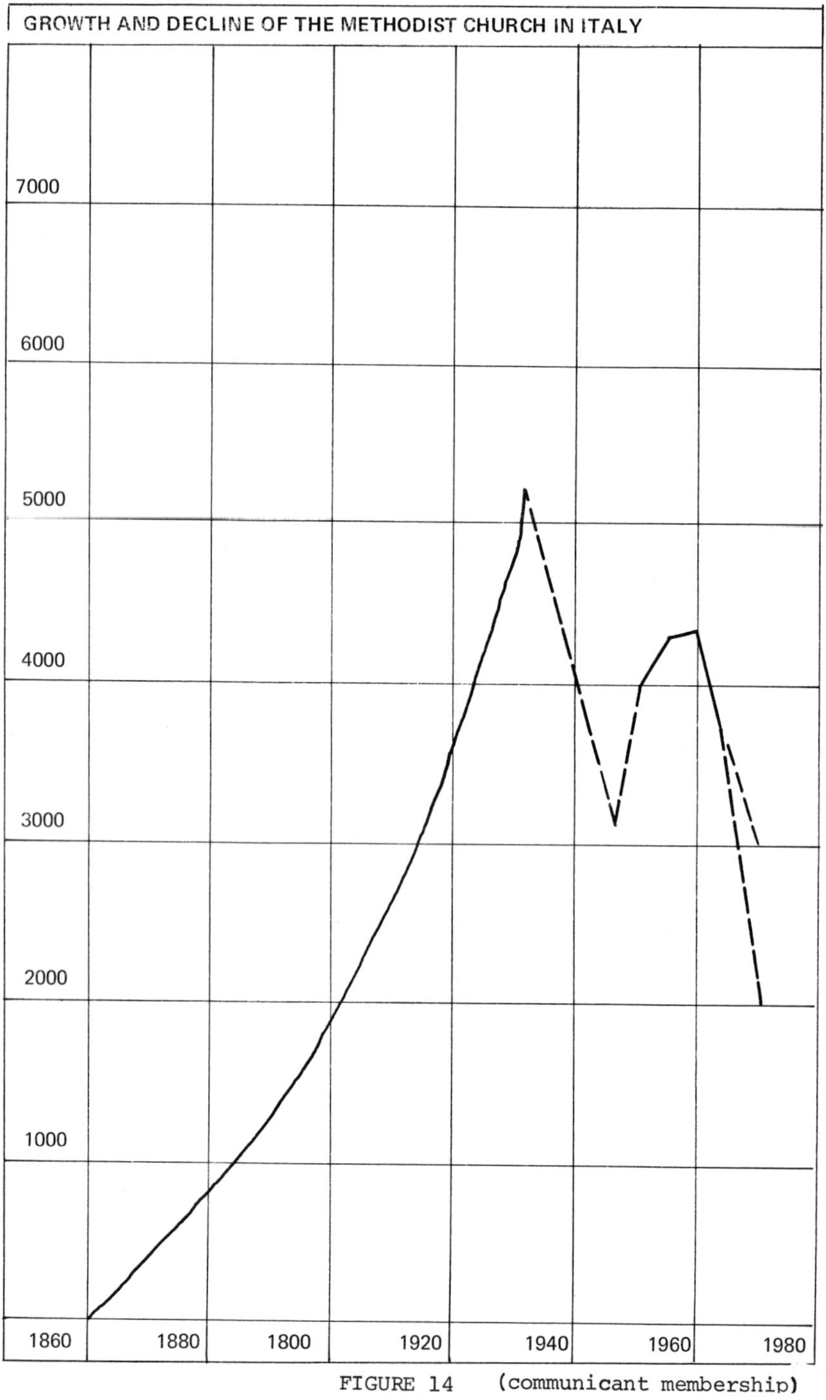

FIGURE 14 (communicant membership)

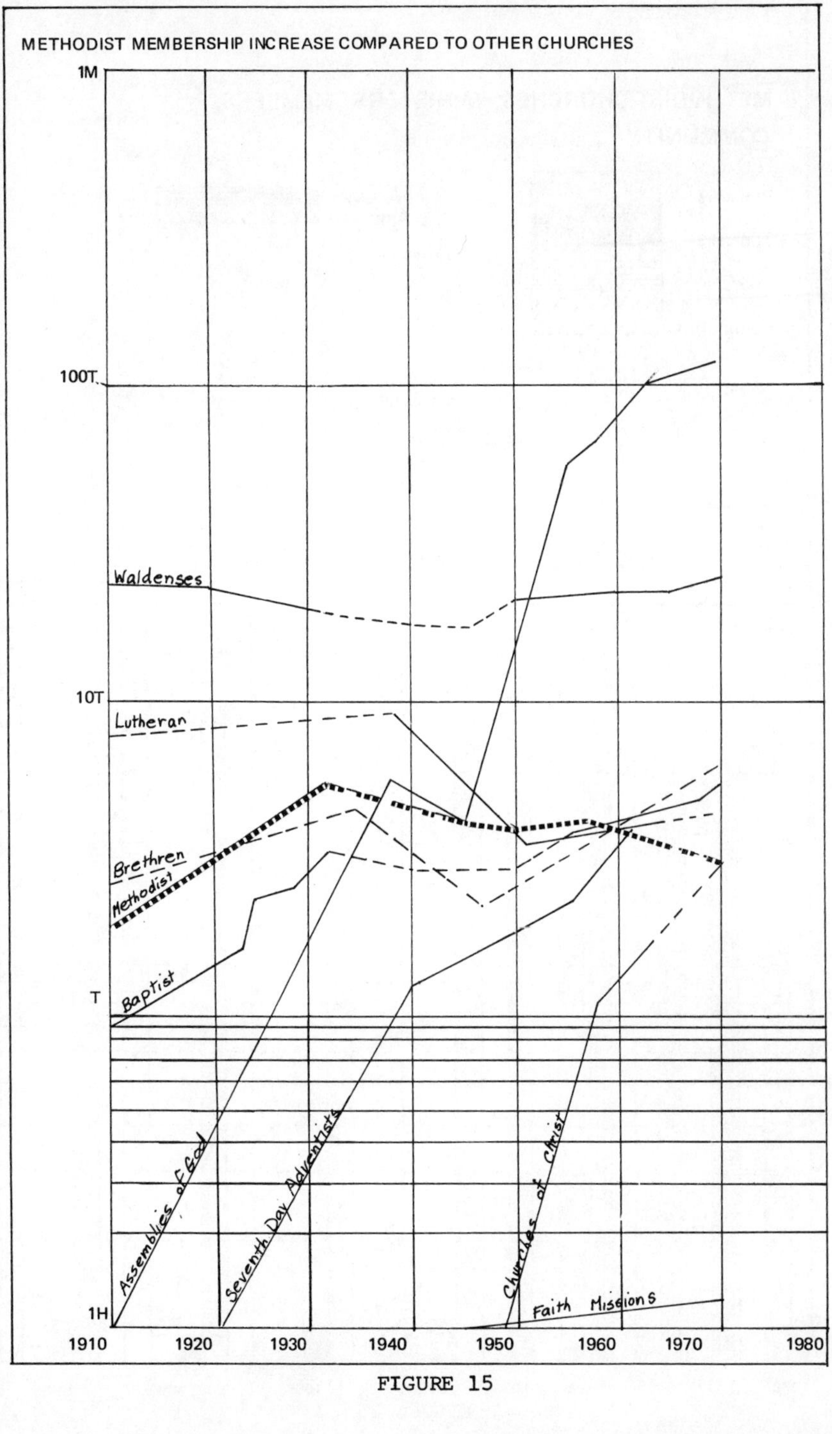
METHODIST MEMBERSHIP INCREASE COMPARED TO OTHER CHURCHES
1M
100T
10T
T
1H
1910
1920
1930
1940
1950
1960
1970
1980
Waldenses
Lutheran
Brethren
Methodist
Baptist
Assemblies of God
Seventh Day Adventists
Churches of Christ
Faith Missions

FIGURE 15

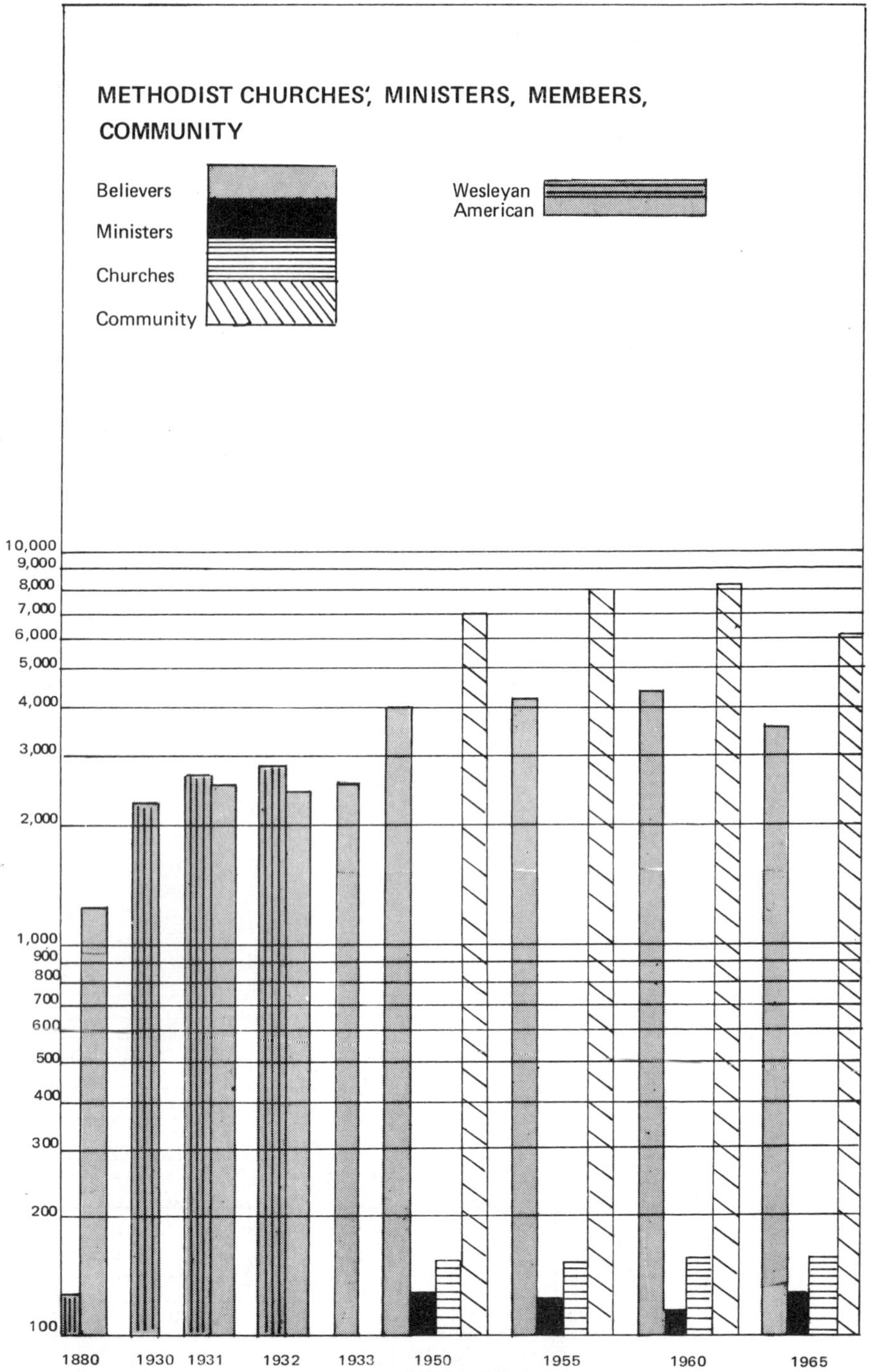
METHODIST CHURCHES', MINISTERS, MEMBERS, COMMUNITY
Believers
Ministers
Churches
Community
Wesleyan
American
10,000
9,000
8,000
7,000
6,000
5,000
4,000
3,000
2,000
1,000
900
800
700
600
500
400
300
200
100
1880
1930
1931
1932
1933
1950
1955
1960
1965

FIGURE 16

10

Seventh Day Adventists

EARLY HISTORY

Italy was the first country in Europe in which Adventist doctrine was preached. The messenger was a Polish ex-Catholic priest who had been baptized in Findlay, Ohio (Nuefeld 1966:620). M. B. Czechowski arrived in Torre Pellice (the heart of Waldensianism) in 1864 under the auspices of another Adventist denomination and there opened a hall. His converts became Seventh Day Adventists. Among the first converts were Catherine Revel and J. D. Geymet. The latter became the first Seventh Day Adventist Colporteur in Europe. Mrs. Revel's grandson was later sent by the Torre Pellice church into France.

The first Seventh Day Adventist missionary to Europe was J. N. Andrews. In 1877 he came from Switzerland to Naples and baptized H. P. Ribton, M.D. with his wife and daughter in the Bay of Naples near possuoli. Ribton held meetings and soon made 5 converts. By 1878 the number had increased to 22. In 1884 the tract, "Il Georno del Signore" (the Day of the Lord), was published in Naples. That year also a church of 10 members was orgainzed in Naples upon the visit of D. T. Bourdean who the following year went on to Torre Pellice. Ellen G. White also visited Italy (Torre Pellice) in 1885. The first Seventh Day Adventist periodical was *L'Ultimo Messaggio* (the Last Message).

Workers were sent from California in 1902 and took up residence in Rome. Already a few persons in that city were observing the Sabbath. The first convert, Lattoni, carried on the first Seventh Day Adventist public evangelism in the city in 1904. A convert from Waldensian aristocracy, Miss L. Chiellini, translated White's *Steps to God* into Italian.

"At the time of the 1909 General Conference there were

44 members in Italy, 26 of them in Torre Pellice (Neufeld 1966:621).

Florence was entered in 1910 and Pisa in 1912. A church is spoken of in Gravina.

FOLLOWING WORLD WAR I

The Adventists were few in number around the time of the War. But they were growing. "By Decmember, 1918, there were 7 churches and 110 members in Italy. In 1920 members are mentioned in Torre Pellice, Bolzano, Montaldo, Bormida, Genoa, Pisa, Bari, Gravina, and Firmo (Neufeld 1966:621).

A publishing house (Casa Editrice "L'Araldo della Verita") was established in Florence in 1926.

The Italian Union Mission was organized in 1928 with 19 churches and 410 members. A year later there were 482 members, and the churches had increased to 22.

Sicily had been entered in 1916. Six were baptized in 1920, and the first church was organized the following year. An evangelist established a church in Palermo in 1928 and "companies" (groups meeting in homes, etc., but not organized as churches) in Catania, Piazza Armerina, and San Michele di Ganzaria. By 1966 Sicilian churches numbered 17 with 788 members (Neufeld 1966:622).

Adventist growth was never phenomenal, but it was consistent even in the Fascist era as a Catholic critic recognizes (Crivelli 1938:222-223). By 1932, for instance, membership has gone up to 534 and the churches to 25. These were rather evenly distributed. In Central Italy 7 churches with 157 members were bo be found in Florence, Genoa, Rome, Gaeta, and Pisa. In the north 9 churches and 197 members were located in Acqui-Cassini, Bolzano, Merano, Milan, Montaldo-Bormida, Turin, Torre Pellice, and Trieste. The 9 churches and 180 members in the South were in Bari, Messina, Gravina, Naples and Palermo. Figure 17 illustrates the growth of the 30's.

It was necessary in 1940 to establish a training school for young people. The "Instituto Adventista di Cultura Biblica" (Adventist Institute of Biblical Culture) is located in Florence. In 1957 the faculty consisted of personnel in art, Bible, commerce, English and French, Geography, History, Italian, Latin, Math and Physics, Music, and Science. Industries included Farm, Food Director, Poultry and Garden (Seventh Day Adventist 1957:222).

ITALIANS IN THE UNITED STATES

While work was being started and growing in Italy, Italian immigrants in America were also being evangelized.

The first Italian Seventh Day Adventist Church was formed in New York in 1907. The following year a second was organized in the same city. In 1912 a work was begun in Chicago which has since grown to some 200 members. A monthly paper, *La Verita* (The Truth) is published. A number of churches were founded in the 1920's on the Pacific Coast. Italian Seventh Day Adventists in the United States now number about 1,000 (Spaulding 1962:317).

WORLD WAR II

The War created confusion and difficulties for all Churches throughout Europe. In the Axis countries Adventism experienced persecution, suppression, confiscation (Spaulding 1949:649).

Despite oppression the Adventist cause progressed. In Italy it is remarkable that during the War years, the Adventist Church "increased its membership 50 per cent" (Spaulding 1949: 650), the only denomination to grow during this period.

Is it possible that circumstances which were unfavorable worked to the advantage of the Adventists? Spaulding gives the account of a Seventh Day Adventist recruit in the Italian Army. The young man requested to have the Sabbath free. His officer roughly refused. When the soldier failed to report on Saturday, he was abused and then sentenced to prison. After a year a change in officers freed him. The new commander took him into his home, then paid the boy's way home to visit his mother. Apparently the officer was impressed by the high moral quality of this convert.

> Shortly after this, orders were sent out from general headquarters to all Italian military officers, to grant Seventh-day Adventists in the service freedom to worship on their Sabbath. Thus because of one young man's faithfulness, unheard of liberty was granted to his fellow members (Spaulding 1949).

POST WAR

The denomination emerged form the War years with an increase in each of the areas of the country. All other Churches had declined during the War.

The North Italian Mission was working among a population of 18,500,000 in the regions of Piemonte, Lombardia, Liguria and Venezia as well as the cities of Genoa, Reggio Parma and Piacenza. 433 members were gathered in 12 churches.

The territory of the South Italian Mission included Lazio, Campania, Abruzzo Molise, Puglie, Lucania, Calabria and Sicily. There were 19 churches with 574 members out of a population of 16,000,000.

The Central Italian Mission, organized in 1946, had 8 churches and 323 members out of a population of 11,500,000. Territory included Emilia, Tuscany, Marche, Umbria, Sardegna, and Lazio (Rome, Viterbo and Rieti) (Seventh Day Adventist 1948:203-204).

Missionaries, ministers and evangelists formed a total of 108 workers in 1950.

In 1955 the work was reorganized into two missions. The Sardinia Mission reported 40 members in one church. The Italian Mission incorporated the rest of Italy plus San Marino. That year there were a total of 51 churches in Italy with 2,194 members. During the year there were 169 baptisms plus 14 additions by professions of faith. The total tithe was $52,279. (Seventh Day Adventist 1957:189-190).

An amazing feat has been the growth of the Publishing House since the war. Volume and employees quadrupled between 1950 and 1968 (see figure 17). Periodical sales have surpassed book sales for a number of years.

A Bible Correspondence Course, organized in 1947, by 1962 had served 37,274 registered students. Of these 2,058 had finished the course, and 477 had been baptized.

Radio programs were aired over local radio Bologna from 1947 to 1950, over Montecarlo for 1950 to 1957, and over radio Cogliari from 1947 to 1952. The Adventists, like other groups in Italy, have been unable to broadcast on the national network (Neufeld 1966:622).

Robert Evans in 1963 estimated there were around 50

Advent places of worship in Italy and that the denomination had perhaps 10,000 followers (1963e:281). Actually the membership is still less than that although the number of churches in 1963 was 58. "On June 30, 1963, the union mission had 58 churches with a total membership of 3,019; the denomination owned 24 church properties and used 31 rented halls" (Neufeld 1966:622).

Seventh Day Adventist growth, which is not spectacular, continues steadily. In 1968, 189 baptisms took place. With 52 apostacies and missing members the membership at the close of that year was 3,278 - an increase of 56 over the previous year - in 61 churches. Though modest, these gains are solid and ahead of those of the traditional denominations in Italy.

The tithe for 1968 totaled $238,602.30 - an almost unbelievable sum for Italy.

Figure 17 indicates the degree of growth in recent years.

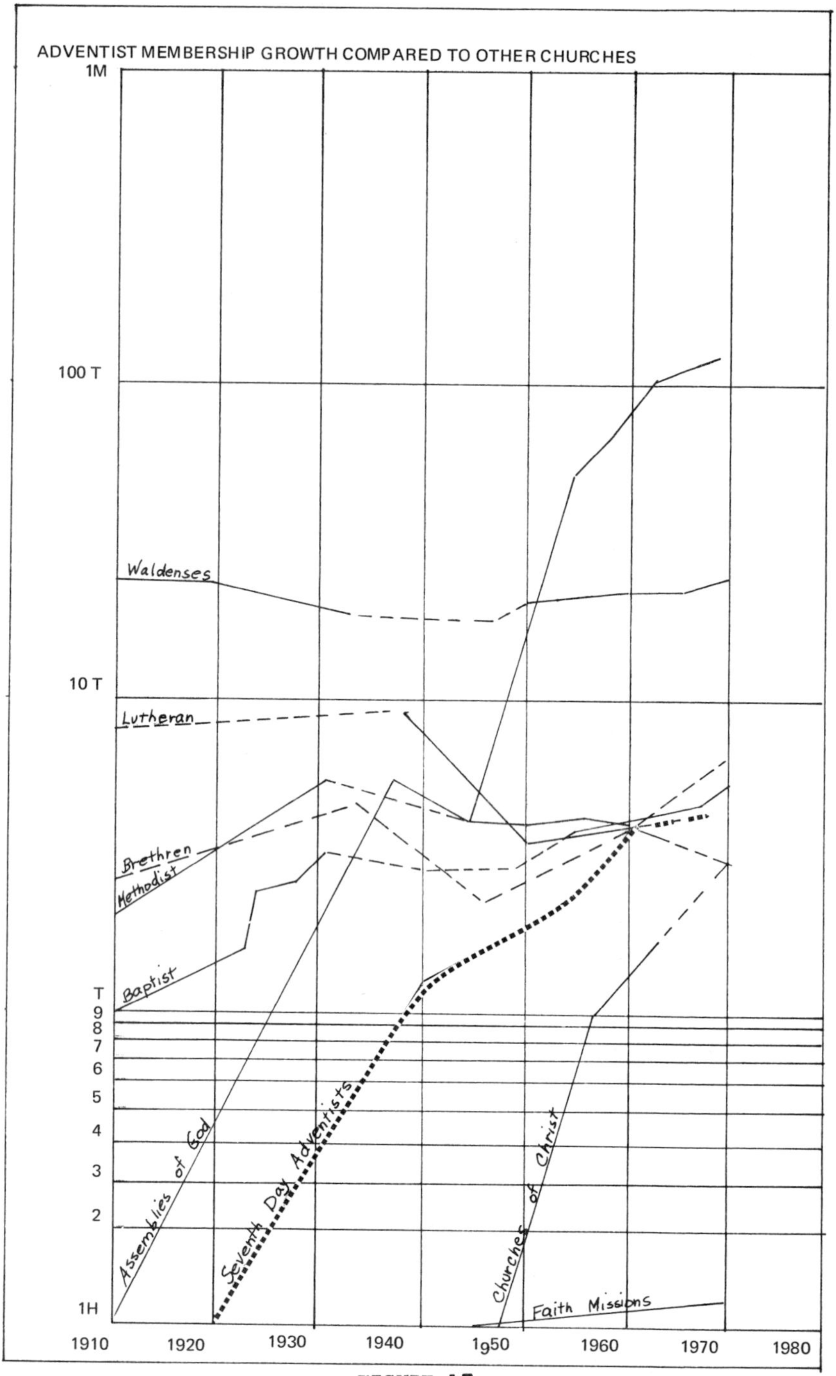
ADVENTIST MEMBERSHIP GROWTH COMPARED TO OTHER CHURCHES
1M
100 T
10 T
T
9
8
7
6
5
4
3
2
1H
1910
1920
1930
1940
1950
1960
1970
1980
Waldenses
Lutheran
Brethren
Methodist
Baptist
Assemblies of God
Seventh Day Adventists
Churches of Christ
Faith Missions

FIGURE 17

11

Churches of Christ

BEGINNINGS

A most interesting story is that of the coming and early experience fo missionaries of the American Churches of Christ. This venture began because an American soldier during World War II was touched by the "pitiable conditions of the people of Italy. He returned to America with a burning desire to return there as a soldier of Christ" (Gibbs 1958:4). He did return with others whom he had inspired to help evangelize Italy. I have read the account of the first nine years of activity (Gibbs 1958).

In 1947 a team of two came to survey the country in preparation for the venture. They visited Genoa, Milan, Rome, Naples and other major cities. The original intent had been to make Milan their center, but as a result of the survey they chose Rome instead. Favorable reasons included its central location, the presence of numerous Protestant groups there as well as the American Embassy. Gibbs mentions also the appeal of this "center of Apostacy" and the appeal of "again establishing a church in the city to which Paul addressed a letter and where he labored during the last years of his life" (Gibbs 1958:13). The survey completed, the two returned home for final preparation and to raise support. Mission accomplished, the workers with their families then came to initiate the evangelism of Italy.

A beachhead was made at Frascati, near Rome, with the establishing of the Frascati Orphans' Home. The purpose was "not only to care for homeless youngsters but ultimately to develop gospel preachers in a Christian environment" (Gibbs 1958:22). In those post-war years of hardship the work of the missionaries consisted also in the distribution of packages of clothing. The emphasis was "spiritual", however, rather than social. Eventually both package distribution and the orphanage work were abandoned, but not before years of conflict had passed.

The first Bible studies were in January, 1949. In March two converts were baptized in the sea. The beginning Church had 17 members in April, and by mid-May there were 30. By the first week of June there were 56 members (Gibbs 1958: 27,29). Contacts were made outside and efforts spread beyond the town. It was a beginning year of amazing growth. The list of places where there were classes, Christians, members, contacts, and people attending includes Monte Compatri (which grew from 10 to 20 Christians), Rocca Priori (where 70 were attending a class), San Cesario, Zagarolo, Villa Speranza (100 attending), Pantano Secco (30 attending with 9 baptisms), Squarciarelli, Rome, Marino, Rocca di Papa, and Boiana.

PERSECUTION

All sorts of legal difficulties were encountered in relation to the orphanage. The Churches of Christ did not have legal status as a moral and spiritual entity in Italy. Difficulty led to opposition toward the missionaries themselves. Open persecution flaired. Priests managed to label the Americans "communist". In their struggle the missionaries received no support from the American government. United States active support of the Christian Democratic Party after the War, as a bulwark against communism, may explain some of the hostility encountered at the hads of the Truman Administration (Fried 1963:237). Catholic leaders, by making the charge of "Communism" were cleverly able to channel hostility against these Christian workers.

Gibbs quotes a letter from Missionary Harold Paden in 1949 which reveals the bitterness of the persecution.

> When we left, while trying to push through the angry mob of people, their shouts became louder. "Get out of town", they cried. "We don't want Protestants...stirring up our people...we don't want your teachings...get out and don't come back." They would shake their clubs and fists in our faces and shout these things. Some of them blasphemed and spit on us; we were covered with their spittle. Some one threw a bucket of cold water on us. Some of our supporters were beaten after we left. We did not take their advice about not returning. We returned for our next scheduled class meeting. At that time we had more than one hundred present...and

there was no trouble (Gibbs 1958:38).

GAINS

The evangelists persisted despite persecution, and their efforts were rewarded. During 1950 calls for preachers came from Turin, Milan (where there were 6 baptisms in June and 16 members by September), Florence, Genoa, Rome, and Centicelli. In September, 1950 there were 500 active members.

The following year was much the same. New centers of evangelism were opened throughout the North. Milano is mentioned as growing and reaching out to new cities through American and Italian evangelists (Gibbs 1958:86). A new building for Borghetto is built for $2,000. At Catanzaro in the South a denominational church is made available, and here there are 24 members by July. The work is expanded in other places in the South around this time. At least 8 are mentioned. In one case an abandoned Pentecostal congregation became a Church of Christ, and in another it was an abandoned Waldensian congregation. A building is purchased in Rome at this time.

During 1952 and 1953 persecution continued as did the growth. Three new churches are spoken of for 1953. The following year there are four, and Florence is reported to have 18 members. Naples is a new work in 1955. That year there were 25 established congregations from which came reports of 263 baptisms, as compared to 142 in 1954. "As 1956 began there wer 1,142 enrolled in the Bible correspondence course" (Gibbs 1958:154). Several new works were inaugerated that year, including a second congregation in Rome. At Pistoia a Baptist church was rebaptized.

The list of established congregations at the end of 1956 include 32 meeting in public rooms and 6 meeting in private homes. During the year there were 231 baptisms, and membership totalled 904. That was the year it was decided to begin closing the orphanage. Gibbs for 1957 provides a list of 24 Italian preachers (Gibbs 1958:167-168).

The six largest congregations in 1956 were as follows: Milan - 68, Rome - 50, Palermo - 50, Padova - 50, Catania - 45, Allesandria - 41 (Gibbs 1958:169).

During 1957, 230 persons were baptized. Membership reached 1,134. At the time Gibbs wrote his thesis he could safely assume that membership was over 1,200, excluding some 400 others who had been baptized but had not remained faithful

(Gibbs 1958:182). Robert Evans is therefore mistaken in saying the "Texas" Churches of Christ numbered around 22 with 500 members. Evans does correctly add that there were representatives of another Church of Christ branch also in Italy. I do not know how accurate he is in stating that these "Midwest" Churches of Christ numbered about seven congregations (Evans 1963e:281). In 1958 seven American evangelists and their families were in Italy, and two more were anticipated within a year (Gibbs 1958:1).

In 1969 a list of 42 workers appeared in an Austin, Texas, publication (Churches of Christ 1969:8). It was also reported that hundreds of Italians were meeting in over 40 cities, actively engaged in spreading New Testament Christianity in Italy. No indication is given as to membership. Nor is the present number of churches told. A 1964 document is quoted in the Yearbook of Churches as reporting over 2,000 members (Consiglio Federale 1967:111). The membership in 1970 may be assumed to be considerably more.

METHODS

The amazing growth of the Churches of Christ is portrayed in figure 18. In 15 years they achieved 2,000 members, beginning from zero. This is even more astounding when we consider that other groups coming in the same post-war period have made little impact. If we were to lump all the faith missions and independent missionaries coming since the War into one, the total number of countable converts (i.e. church members) would probably equal about 200. The Churches of Christ can claim 10 times that number. They alone of the newcomers have achieved success. If the rate of growth since 1964 has remained fairly constant, membership should now approach that of the Methodists and Adventists.

What possible explanation can be found?

Part of the answer may be in the attitude of the missionaries. The Church of Christ evangelists came for the sole purpose of planting churches. True they engaged in orphan and relief work, but these were kept subservient to the goal of winning the lost. When the orphanage proved a poor approach, it was abandoned. Thus the work was never burdened with the baggage of institutionalism.

These men were determined to plant New Testament Christianity, as they saw it, in Italy. All energies were directed to that end, and from it they could not be deterred

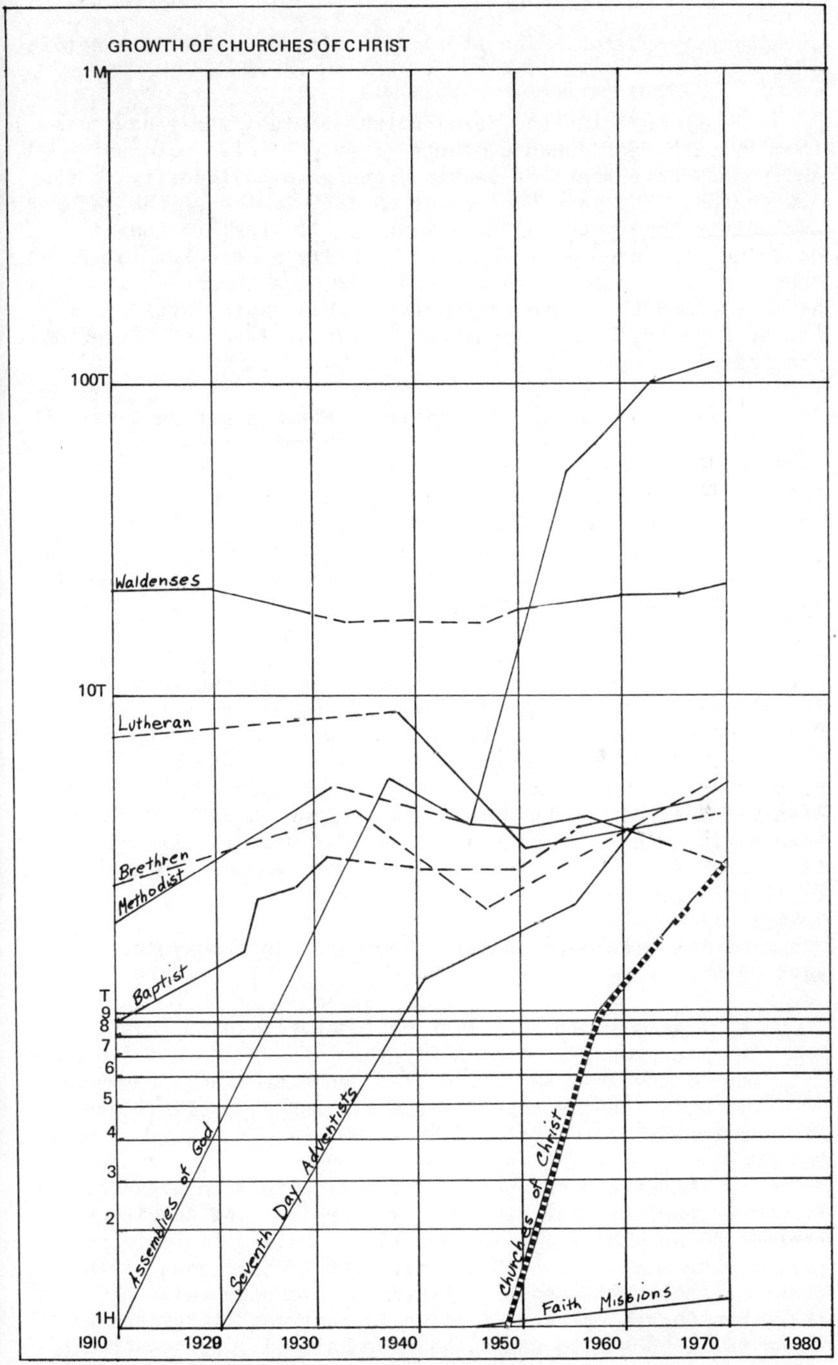
GROWTH OF CHURCHES OF CHRIST
1M
100T
10T
T
9
8
7
6
5
4
3
2
1H
1910
1920
1930
1940
1950
1960
1970
1980
Waldenses
Lutheran
Brethren
Methodist
Baptist
Assemblies of God
Seventh Day Adventists
Churches of Christ
Faith Missions

FIGURE 18

even by persecution. The story of their struggles is a heroic one.

If anything the persecution eventually may have won them sympathy and enhanced their cause. It also no doubt sharpened their sense of destiny, and gave an identity to the new Church. The name "Church of Christ" indicates the rather exclusivist character of this Church. Its restorationist doctrine also creates a sense of identity as the People of God. Other Churches are something less. To be a Christian is to be baptized into the Church of Christ. This "hard" attitude may not be popular, but it apparently works in favor of the group that has it.

A strong sense of identity creates a strong sense of Mission. The Churches of Christ must evangelize Italy. The only was to do so is to plant churches. A theology which is Church dominated is accompanied by an evangelism that is Church centered. Evangelism, in Church of Christ thinking, must include baptism and incorporation into local bodies of believers. Conversion is therefore very specific. Evangelizing must consist in church extension.

To this philosophy the workers coupled hard work and every available resource. American financial aid was welcomed. In fact for continued growth such aid was declared to be "imperative" (Gibbs 1958:186). Funds were used to pay for printing and advertising costs, for legal expenses, and to provide larger buildings. In no way does this seem to have been a detriment to the work. The Italian churches did not become dependent upon this aid. Applied wisely, and for one-time expenses, foreign funds probably served to accelerate early growth.

The missionaries were themselves in a teaching ministry.

> The logical role that American evangelists can play in this program is primarily that of a guide and instructor to the less experienced and younger Italian evangelists, while the more capable Italian evangelists are preaching the Gospel (Gibbs 1958:186).

That the missionaries fit well this role seem apparent from the results. Teaching was by example. The Americans shared in the ministry of evangelism. Italian converts took part in the ministry which was not kept in the hands of the missionaries. This sense of brotherhood coupled with the fact that this Church makes no distinction between clergy and laity tends to cause all to share the responsibility for evangelism.

12

Others

SALVATION ARMY

The first Salvation Army Corps was opened in Rome in 1886 by Captain Vint. Although the Rome work was forced to close the work expanded in other areas, especially Piedmont. In 1892 the Salvation Army was granted legal recognition. Revival services were conducted "in all the villages of the Waldensian Valleys". Salvationist Corps had come into being in 4 Piedmont towns in 1891. Within two years corps were opened in Florence, Leghorn, Milan, Venice, Bologna, Pisa, La Spezia, and other towns of the North.

Salvation Army witness was begun in the South by emigrants who returned "with the joyous message of salvation by faith and of loving service" (Santini, Artissi, Capezzani 1969:106).

Fascist persecution was fierce. Works closed during the war were later reopened. At present there are said to be "35 centers of activity, 8 social institutions, and 2 youth centers" (Consiglio Federale 1967:69).

Fifteen corps and 25 outposts are centers of worship and evangelism. Sixty five officers (52 active and 13 retired) plus 33 employees serve the Army (Salvation Army 1968).

MENNONITES

The Mennonites commenced work in Italy in 1958. Bodies of believers have come into being in Florence, Scerni, (Abruzzo), and Palermo. Radio, music, and publication ministries are carried on.

Mennonites enjoy the leadership of one of Italy's outstanding evangelicals, Elio Milazzo. Italian Mennonites through the Virginia Conference (Brunk 1969).

CHURCH OF THE NAZARENE

Nazarenes came to Italy in 1948. Churches have been opened in 10 centers scattered from Turin to Sicily. The ten churches are cared for by Italian pastors. The church in Torre Annunziata has opened brance ministries in Naples, Ottoviana, Scarfate, and Torre del Greco.

Nineteen persons were baptized and received membership in 1969 (Fuller 1969). Total membership figures were not available to me. In 1963 Evans wrote of a few hundred adherents in 5 congregations (1963e:281). One missionary couple served under the Church of the Nazarene in 1969 at Rome.

Direction of Nazarene work from Kansas City seems an obstacle to future growth. Pastors' salaries are apparently subsidized and buildings have been constructed with American funds. While this practice is not necessarily harmful, it tends to reduce incentive. The degree of control would seem to mold this Church in an American rather than Italian pattern.

LUTHERANS

The Lutheran Church in Italy is unique, an ethnic church representing the German minority of the north. As such its presence dates from the 18th century.

Since World War II an Italian ministry has been carried on. The Church since 1948 has been known as the Evangelical Lutheran Church in Italy (Chiesa Evangelica Lutherana in Italia). Of the 4 Italian communities, 3 are in Naples province. Sixteen additional congregations are German.

How many Lutherans are there in Italy? Crivilli in his 1938 book suggested 10,000. That is exactly half as many as claimed by the *Lutheran World Almanac*. Criville is a Catholic and a sharp critic (1938:65). The *Lutheran Encyclopedia* of 1965 reports only 6,000 Lutherans for Italy (Bodensieck 1965). Figure 19 reveals that the Lutheran Church is similar to the Baptists, Methodists, Brethren and Adventists in size.

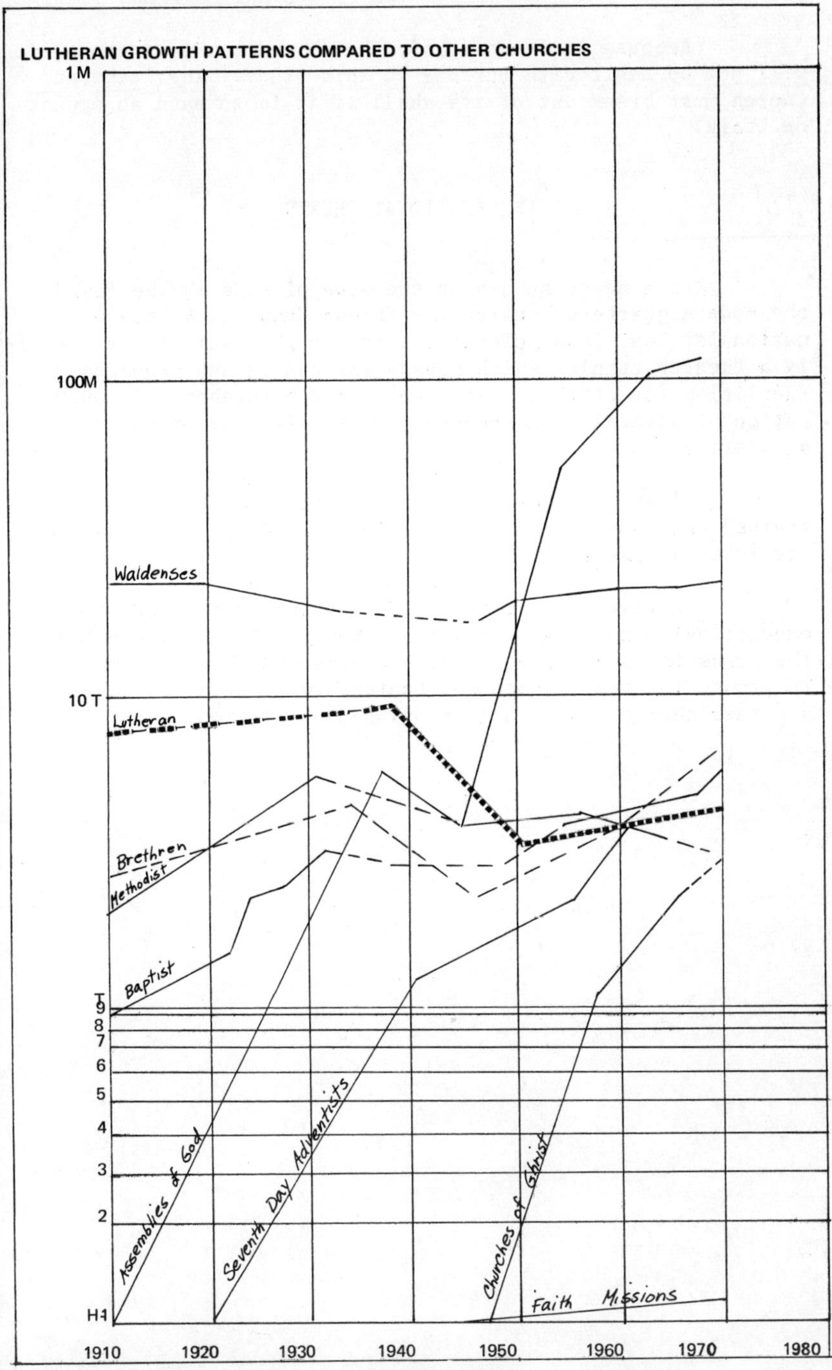

LUTHERAN GROWTH PATTERNS COMPARED TO OTHER CHURCHES
1 M
100M
10 T
T
9
8
7
6
5
4
3
2
H1
1910
1920
1930
1940
1950
1960
1970
1980
Waldenses
Lutheran
Brethren
Methodist
Baptist
Assemblies of God
Seventh Day Adventists
Churches of Christ
Faith Missions

FIGURE 19

Because it is an ethnic Church and rather ingrown, it will not be dealt with further in this study. The Lutheran Church must break out of its shell if it is to have an impact on Italy.

INTERNATIONAL CHURCH

In a newer suburb on the edge of Rome may be found the modern quarters housing the Chiesa Evangelica Internazionale, Rev. John McTernan, pastor. The facility is actually a theater complex which houses the church and provides facilities for offices, classrooms, and printshop. A congregation of several hundred does not yet fill the thousand seat auditorium.

Classrooms serve students in the Bible School who are trained and sent out to minister in small Pentecostal churches scattered across Italy.

An Italian assistant aids the pastor in youth and educational ministries. Plans are being made for expansion. The press is used effectively, and other media give promise to growth in this independent Pentecostal church - both as a mother church and as a developing denomination.

PART THREE

Two Case Studies

TWO CASE STUDIES

Two significant movements were selected for special attention at the beginning of this study. It was my hope to accumulate a mass of data for each, and then to abstract the dynamics which have made each an important segment of Italian Evangelicalism. Unfortunately pertinent information has been difficult to obtain. Therefore the treatment of both groups is much abbreviated.

The Assemblies of God Field Representative for Italy, the Rev. Alfred J. Perna, Sr., has been most gracious in supplying recent information on that Church as well as correcting statistics gathered from several sources. Similar assistance was not available from the Brethren, so that I am unable to give as recent a picture of that Church.

13

The Brethren Church

ORIGINS

The Brethren movement in Italy has its earliest roots in groups of converts meeting in Florence in the year 1833 (Consiglio 1967:100). Among them was Count Piero Guicciardini, member of one of Florence's most ancient families and descendent of the famed historian, Francesco Guicciardini.

An evangelical revival of small scale accompanied the *Risorgimento* in 1848. Open evangelical meetings were begun in 1849. When the revolution was squelched the following year, the evangelicals became the objects of suspicion and were repressed (Coad 1968:189).

Count Guicciardini had begun years before to read the Bible in private, "at first with his caretaker, and later with other secret evangelicals, many of them of the working classes" (Coad 1968:189). In May, 1851, Guicciardini and six others were surprised and arrested. Because of his nobility, the Count could have been exempted, but chose rather six-months' imprisonment.

"Numerous arrests of evangelicals followed in Florence, in some cases acquitted by the courts being followed by re-arrest and by banishment or imprisonment by police edict" (Coad 1968:190).

In 1852-1853 occurred the notorious case of Francesco and Rosa Madai. Arrested in August of 1851, they were imprisoned without trial until June, 1852. Francesco was then sentenced to four years and eight months solitary confinement and hard labor, and Rosa to three years, nine months of the same. Their crime was that of professing the Evangelical faith and "holding private Bible readings in their home" (Coad 1968:190).

Eventually their release was secured, but only after great protest involving a deputation from England and a letter from the Evangelical Alliance of Geneva. They were also exiled. Francesco is said to have never recovered from the effects of his confinement. This episode is treated in detail in Italian sources dealing with this period.

Guicciardini himself was forced to flee from Italy, and came eventually to England where he came in touch with leaders of the Plymouth Brethren. There he also met with Teodoro Pietrocola Rossetti who had come as a political exile from Naple in 1851. An uncle, Gabriele Rossetti, provided Guicciardini's contact with T. P. Rossetti whom he later converted to the Evangelical faith. All three names are familiar in Brethren circles in Italy today. Guicciardini was to become the "guiding light" to early Italian Brethrenism. T. P. Rossetti was to be its hymn writer.

The two men were able to return to Italy in a few years when the Grand Duke was forced out of Tuscany. Florence and Alessandria became the centers for a series fo congregations established in Northern Italy. Alessandria was situated near traditional Waldensian territory in the more liberal Piedmont. There were churches established in Liguria and Lombardy as well as Piedmont and Tuscany (Coad 1968:191).

Rossetti and Guicciardini were not alone in their mission. Other preachers associated themselves with them, in the first years totaling about 15 (Vinay 1965:187). These came from the lowest walks of life. Among them are mentioned one who sold sweets in the piazza, an *excaffettiere*, a *brigadiere di finanza*, an *incisore*, and

> ...Several colporteurs...who distributed everywhere the Holy Scriptures furnished by the Bible Societies. All of them maintained themselves with their own work and received only some subsidy for their travels and when the necessities of evangelism constrained them to neglect their usual occupation. <u>They had a minimal culture, but</u> were well acquainted with the Bible (Vinay 1965:187).

The enthusiastic preaching of these humble men was effective for the diffusion of the Gospel in town and country (Vinay 1965:288). As evangelizers however they experienced every difficulty: pressure from religious authorities, disregard of religious liberty, persecution from those who attempted to deny their "right to propagate their faith" (Vinay 1965:291).

DISTINCTIONS

It is not the intention here to engage in a capitualtion of Brethren beliefs, but to indicate certain features that seem germain to the Italian Protestant movement (movement may be taken to imply growth and non-growth).

Indigeneity. The Brethren movement has been described as a "completely indegenous development" under the leadership of Guicciardini and his associates (Coad 1968:189). The Bible-reading Evangelical group at Florence was entirely Italian and did not owe its birth to any outside impetus. True, the movement introduced by Rossetti and Guicciardini was "Brethren", and received that stamp in England. Certain earmarks identify the movement: the Sunday "Breaking of Bread" service, the absence of ordained clergy, the particular function of elders. Evidently these marks did not set the movement off as "foreign"; it was rather felt to be "indigenous" i.e. "Italian", from the start.

Laity. The Brethren differ from most other evangelicals in their view of the Church. The absence of clergy is a noteworthy feature. It may be one secret of Brethren success.

However, "success" is itself difficult to measure. In terms of numbers - that is, individuals won into the fellowship of the Church - it is especially hard to calculate since the Brethren do not have a membership roll as such. It is my impression, however, that the Brethren have been successful in terms of evangelizing. Exactly how successful is difficult to determine.

Since there is technically no clergy, the Brethren Church might be called a "lay" Church. This is not to obscure the fact that elders function both in local congregations and in the national Church much like professional, ordained ministers. But there is no ordination ceremony. Elders are recognized as such on the basis of spiritual gifts which they possess. The absence of ordination means there is no distinction between the leaders and the "people". All who are believers are considered "Brethren". The wall of separation which tends to create two classes in the Church is broken down. Therefore the Church tends to function as a unit. It is the Church - Christians - rather than a few representatives of the Church that carries on the work of the Church.

The Brethren pattern from the start has been this. Ironside tells us that the Brethren movement was from the very first an evangelistic endeavor, and that the evangelists were laymen. In Great Britain noblemen, ex-clergymen, and uneducated men from the humblest occupations preached the Gospel in all sorts of public places (Ironside 1942:27). In Italy likewise the evangelists have been and are lay-preachers.

The system has many advantages. The Church that is a layman's Church more naturally has more involvement. The people - all the people - are responsible for the spread of the Gospel. The absence of clergy sets this Church apart. It is obviously not Roman Catholic. But neither is it typically Protestant. In a country which is anti-clerical, this feature undoubtedly works in favor of the Brethren much as it apparently does for the Church of Christ and for the Jehovah's Witnesses. Criticisms aimed at the priests cannot be applied here. Communist attacks on the "leaches" of society may be directed as much against Protestant ministers as at Catholic priests, but there is no object of the attack in the Brethren Church.

Unity. I once heard a Brethren missionary describe the Brethren as an ecumenical movement. The movement has always opposed denominations, its members preferring to be called "Christians" and "Brethren". Many observers would disagree with the epitaph "ecumenical", however. The kind of unity expressed seems to be one of exclusion rather than inclusion. Opposed to denominationalism, the movement tends to extract people from other groups or to exclude them entirely. In so doing the Brethren tend to form a tight-knit body of their own, in other words another denomination. This is true in Italy where the movement is recognized as a legal entity known as the Brethren Church.

The relationship the Brethren have had with other groups bears out their separatistic quality. The earliest leaders at first associated with the only Protestant body in Italy, the Waldenses. The relationship apparently was strained from the start, and division was inevitable. The year 1854 became the year of schism. Various efforts were put forth to reunite the Evangelical Church in Italy, but to no avail. The Waldenses understandably considered the Brethren schismatic. The Brethren felt the Waldenses to be apostate. Unity of the Body was the desire of the Waldensian Church. The Brethren felt that union would be dangerous.

Finally to combat the efforts of the Evangelical Alliance and others to reunite the two groups, T. P. Rossetti in 1863 (with the agreement of Guicciardini, according to Vinay) published anonimously a tract entitled *Principii della Chiesa Romana, della Chiesa Protestante e della Chiesa Christiana*

("Principles of the Roman Church, of the Protestant Church and of the Christian Church"). The tract was an attempt to prove the apostacy of the various denominations and to show that the life of the true Church was to be found only in the communities of the Brethren (Vinay 1965:331). Rossetti's criticism was severe: "Without being able to speak correctly our language, they set about to preach not the Church of Christ, but the Waldensian Church, not the Gospel, but their Constitution" (quoted by Vinay 1965:334-335).

A cultural basis for the rift is apparent. The Waldenses from the North spoke either French or a dialect of of Italian which contained a mixture of French, not the "pure" Italian of Tuscany as did the Brethren from Florence. The Waldenses were also regional, having their own Waldensian sub-culture in the valleys of Piedmont, the product of a ghetto-like existence resulting from centuries of persecution. The Brethren were new believers, coming from other parts of Italy and various levels of society. Brethren beginnings coincide roughly, with the Risorgeinento. It was the time of the birth of a new Italy. It was perhaps natural for the Brethren to feel themselves part of this new beginning. Psychologically the Waldenses seemed to represent the "old". So it is not so surprising that the Brethren felt themselves to be the true Italian Evangelicals. This tendency was reinforced by the Darbyite doctrine of the Church.

Around the time of the unification of Italy, Baptists and Methodists began missionary endeavor in the country. Baptists particularly thought the Brethren practice of believers baptism by immersion indicated the two could work as one. Belief in a regenerated Church which admitted only believers to the Lord's table also appeared common ground. The attempted cooperation, however, failed.

In similar fashion the Wesleyan Methodists from England sought and failed to work in union with the Brethren. The warm evangelistic messafe of the Methodist missionaries no doubt explains the rapport which was at first established. The cordiality did not endure. Vinay judges that the Brethren simply did not want the Methodists in Italy, even as they did not want any other Protestant denomination (Vinay 1965:331).

Identity. Spurning other Evangelical groups, the Brethren are a people set apart. In the classic Plymouth Brethren tradition, their communities are assemblies of converts meeting for edification and observing the Lord's Supper as they await the Second Coming of Christ.

Vinay admits that Brethren Assemblies today are

numerous but dismisses them as "closed in themselves", and "without any influence on the life of the Italian people" (Vinày 1965:350). In terms of social service Vinay may be correct. But if influence may be measured in terms of lives changed (as I have indicated elsewhere I believe this can be a valid measurement of social influence), then the judgement is too severe.

In this connection it is interesting to read the description of Brethren believers in an area of the South, Puglie, where they have become fairly numerous. The writer, who observed them at worship and in daily life, is non-Christian (Jewish) and seems the most unbiased observer available.

> In general these Christian Brethren are excellent people. I was told on all sides of the harmony reigning in their families, the absence of discord between husband and wife, sufficiently remarkable in a country where conjugal relations are often stormy, these folk, all *brucctanti*, day-laborers, are humble working men (their pastor is a hairdresser by trade), live honest frugal lives; they are poor, but their children are clean, well cared for and very likeable" (Cassin 1959:156).

Transformed lives seem to negate somewhat the criticism by Vinay who represents Waldensian "backlash". Brethrenism was a complete reaction to the Waldensian pattern which contained much from Catholicism - liturgy, creed, a gowned clergy, etc. The Brethren feeling that the Waldenses (and others) were apostate, drove them to themselves and to a feeling that they were <u>the Church</u>. Exclusiveness has created an identity. Although the Italian Brethren Church is of the "open" variety (it admits most Christians to the Lord's table) the psychology of exclusiveness prevails, and it apparently works in their favor. Evangelism consists of discipling people to Christ within the framework of the fellowship of His true People.

PROGRESS

Evangelists in the mid-nineteenth century preached faith in various localities of Piedmont and Liguria as well as in Florence. In 1856 there were workers in Genoa and Alexandria (Vinay 1965:289).

Statistics are notoriously hard to collect from Brethren, so that it is difficult to measure actual progress in this way. In his lectures delivered in the United States during 1912-1913, Luzzi gave what he believed to be "as complete and exact an idea of the missionary work carried on in Italy as it is possible to give" (1913:225). In his report it is stated that the Plymouth Brethren group "in Italy has churches in about 20 towns, and in about 68 smaller places" (Luzzi 1913:222). It appears that there were at least 88 churches in 1910 assuming Luzzi's figures three years old at the date of publication.

Luzzi gave no membership estimate. However in a treatment of all Protestants in Italy published by a Jesuit opponent, Camillo Crivelli, a Brethren missionary by the name of W. Hoste is quoted as having written in 1911 that there were around 25 assemblies in the North, seven or eight in the Central area, and five in the South for a total of 40 (Crivelli 1938:147). From a 1918 source Crivelli learns there were then 62 churches or meeting halls. Both figures fall short of Luzzi's 88 which he published in 1913. The discrepency is probably accounted for by different ways of counting. Luzzi is reporting 88 places where there were Brethren groups. The 1911 report was of 40 Assemblies, and probably does not include outstations. In 1918 the number of buildings (churches or halls) was 62. Crivelli does considerable research and is able to provide a list of cities and villages where there are Brethren "proselytes" as of 1932. These total 122. But he is able to go further, and on the basis of his knowledge calculate the number of Brethren throughout Italy as approximately 5,000. Since Crivelli displays a very critical attitude toward Protestant statistics, it is safe to assume his estimate to be very conservative.

Using the above figures as a base, the average-size church in 1932 had 41 communicants. Projecting backward to 1910, we may estimate 3,520 Brethren if we use Luzzi's claim of 88 churches. If we choose the more pessimistic report of 40 for 1911, however, we arrive at only 1,600. In the one case "membership" more than doubled in 21 years. In the other it increased by 60 per cent in 22 years.

During the War years all denominations declined (with one exception, the Adventists), and it is fairly safe to assume that in this the Brethren Church was typical. The picture is not clear. Robert Evans mentions the report of a Brethren missionary that 168 had been baptized in one post-war year, and that these came from about that many different assemblies (1963:287). At the time of writing, Evans claims, "there have been reported to be more than 170 assemblies, counting 10,000 followers, concentrated especially...around Turin" (1963:280). He mentions the existence of "recent" groups in Sicily, Emilia, and Liguria.

Every evidence, including my own impressions while on the field, indicate that the Brethren are growing. But how much is difficult to surmise. A 1967 publication says that missionary and national labors have pushed the numbers of assemblies to over 200 (Goddard 1967:150). The *Yearbook of Churches*, also published in 1967, gives a list of Brethren churches which totals only 142. Since the yearbook is nearer to the Italian situation I assume it to be the more correct.

A report for 1969, given in Italy, states that there were 171 assemblies with three opened that year for a total of 173 at the beginning of 1970. That is an increase of 31 churches since 1967, if the *Yearbook* is correct.

How many members are there? Most estimates of 4,000 or 5,000 seem low. The *World Christian Handbook* reports 7,000 communicants, but says there are only 40 places of worship (Coxill and Grubb 1968:199). It seems safe to say this is a very conservative estimate, and that there are probably more. But using this as a base and recognizing the age of the figures when published, it is safe to assume that the average church in 1965 had 49 members, and that by 1970 there were 8,500 Brethren communicants.

The vagueness of the numbers of churches reported may simply be due to Brethren exclusiveness: previous reporters simply had to guess! Consistent low membership estimates also indicate that no one has been aware of recent Brethren growth.

Figure 20 plots Brethren progress in terms of communicant "members". The total community would probably be about twice as much.

PRESENT STATUS

The Italian "Church of the Brethren" is obviously not in the stagnant state that is typical of most denominations today. Its present growth rate appears to be much greater than that of the general population. If this rate can be maintained the future is promising.

The strength of the movement has been and continues to be in Piedmont. However it is now expanding in the South where it has success especially in Puglie, where there are now probably some 30 churches.

While there are some dangers, the movement seems to be mature. Aid is sometimes received from foreign sources,

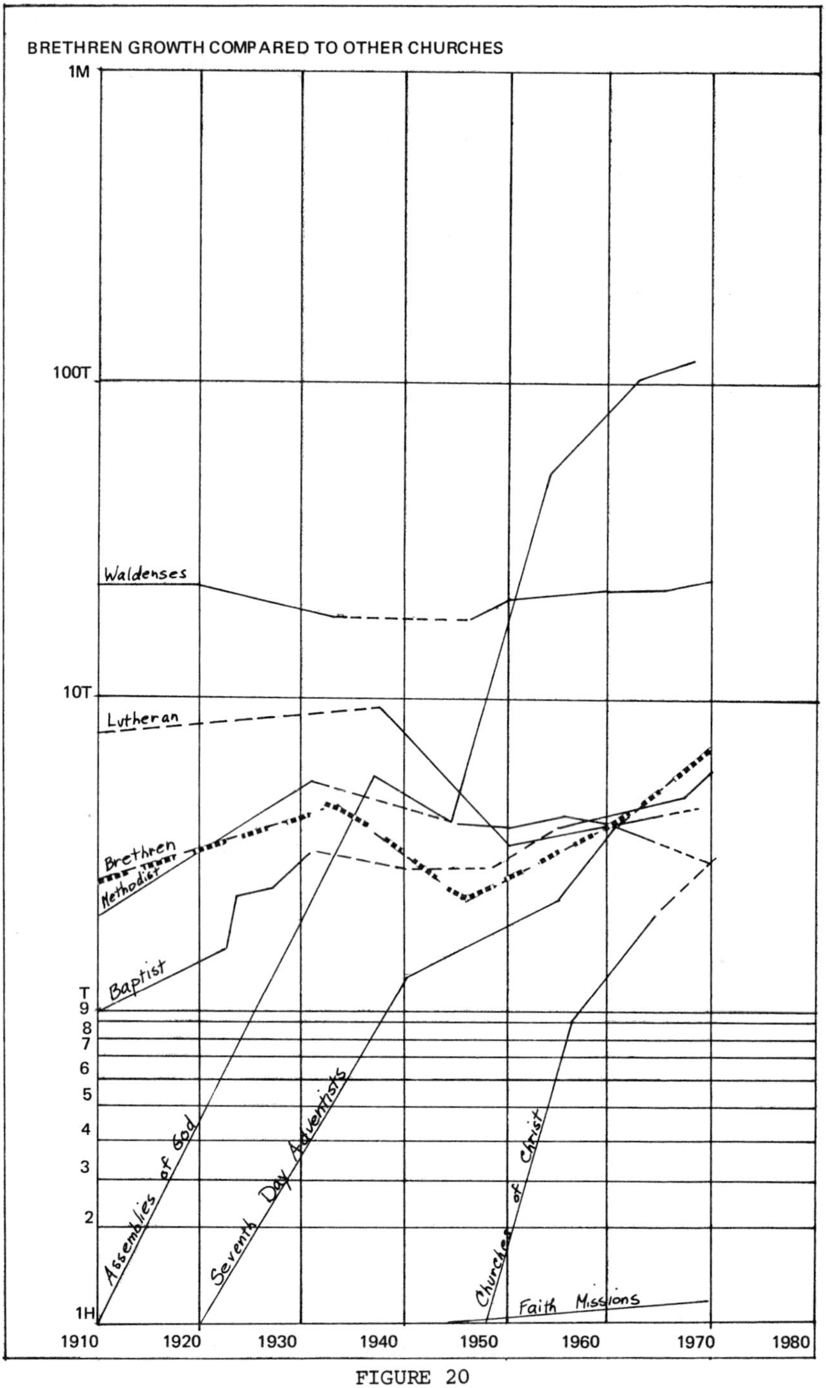

BRETHREN GROWTH COMPARED TO OTHER CHURCHES
1M
100T
10T
T
9
8
7
6
5
4
3
2
1H
1910
1920
1930
1940
1950
1960
1970
1980
Waldenses
Lutheran
Brethren
Methodist
Baptist
Assemblies of God
Seventh Day Adventists
Churches of Christ
Faith Missions

FIGURE 20

but there does not seem to be a great deal of unhealthy dependency on foreign subsidy. Relations between missionaries and Italian leaders have sometimes been strained, but generally the situation seems healthy. No foreign mission apparatus is imposed by these missionaries from England, America, Switzerland, New Zealand, on the Italian Brethren. Foreign workers participate as members of the local assemblies.

Tent campaigns are used to establish new Assemblies. An increase in this kind of evangelism should multiply Brethren churches throughout Italy.

14

Assemblies of God

A Roman Catholic priest, writing about Pentecostals says that they are considered unconventional and even amazing by Catholics and other Protestants (O'Hanlon 1963:634). In this day of ecumenical diologue it is not likely that Pentecostals will be included at the tables. There are formidable social and cultural as well as theological barriers according to Father O'Hanlon (1963:635).

This points up the fact that Pentecostals have had great success among the humbler peoples of the world. The poor, the oppressed, the migrant, the forgotten - these are attracted to Pentecostals because they feel themselves loved and understood. This fact, says Father O'Hanlon, constitutes "the first reason for the growth of Pentecostal churches" (1963:634). Warmth attracts; people feel at home among them. Pentecostals are providing "many of these elements of true Christianity which Catholics and other Protestants frequently neglect" (O'Hanlon 1963:634).

Other reasons for their growth may also be found. They are not encumbered with ecumenical concerns, and are free to preach the Gospel. While they may be criticized for a lack of social involvement, they have given evangelism its rightful first place. Nor has Pentecostalism been terribly concerned over great theological issues. But again its simplicity is an appealing feature. The doctrinal essentials they practice are few - such as repentance of sins, the gift of the Holy Spirit, a life of holiness and dedication, and the Hope of the imminent Second Coming of Christ (O'Hanlon 1963:635).

Traditional Protestant Churches, on the other hand, are much involved in an ecumenism which is an "intense movement toward unity in keeping with the hopes of the World Council of Churches and the Second Vatican Council" (Evans 1965:19). Pentecostalism is different, as the story of the Assemblies of God in Italy should demonstate.

ORIGINS

Pentacostalism began in Italy of 1908 with the return of an American immigrant from Chicago. Giacomo Lombardi had received the baptism of the Holy Spirit in 1906 when the Azusa Street Revival jumped from Los Angeles to Chicago. He returned "home" to preach the message of Pentecost. Assemblies established in Calabria, Abruzzi, and Rome became the centers for diffusing the message throughout the country. In this ministry Lombardi was joined by numerous other returned Italian emigrants who bore witness to their people of the experience that had transformed their lives on the other side of the ocean. In this way the work spread across the South and into Sicily until 1934 when the Fascist persecution began (Winehouse 1959:112).

PERSECUTION

During its beginning years of fantastic success, the Assembly of God movement was not without opposition. Evans cites one Pope who, apparently with some sense of alarm, overstated the case in speaking of Pentecostals as "that movement (which) has invaded every parish of our blessed country" (Evans 1963c:280). Surely such a statement could never have been caused by any regular body of Protestants!

With the signing of the Lateran Pacts the Vatican was able to appeal to the State to take measures against Protestants. The totalitarian regime was most rigorous toward Pentecostals who were prohibited from having services.

Fascist persecution began in earnest in 1934. Pastors were sent to prison or to concentration camps. Secret meetings were held "in caves, cellars, or in private homes behind barred doors" (Winehouse 1959:112).

Pentecostal believers have described to me those difficult days when, near Naples, some met out in open fields when the grain was high and in other unusual places.

The most unusual account was furnished by a missionary.

It is the story of the "Pentecostal" dog. While the believers met secretly a watchdog was posted to stand guard. No one was able to get past the dog except by giving the password, "Pace" (peace). Since this Pentecostal form of greeting was known only to believers, the police and other outsiders were unable to surprise the secret worshipers.

Mussolini's reign of terror ended in 1944. With the liberation armies came freedom (Winehouse 1959:112). Pentecostals worshiped freely under the Allied occupation.

Then, from 1948 to 1958, a period of persecution was endured once more (Consiglio 1967:72). It was this which caused Jemelo to protest "the most savage persecution is reserved for the Pentecostals, of whom there are many among poorer classes in the south of Italy (1960:315).

Finally the persecution ended with the legal recognition of the Assemblies of God in 1959, following a long battle and through the intervention of the Federal Council of Churches as a moral entity for worship.

GROWTH

From its origins in 1908 the Movement spread so that in his 1938 volume Crivelli is able to list 144 stations throughout Italy. Fifty-two are in Sicily. Crivelli admits that his list is not complete, but tends to look down on the Pentecostals as insignificant because many of their groups are tiny, and calculates that there can be few more than 5,000 full members in all of Italy (1938:239). Nichol, who researched various Pentecostal source materials, asserts that the work of Lombardi, Ottolini, and Arena had resulted in 149 Pentecostal Assemblies by 1929 (1966:205). Therefore Crivelli's estimate seems low; we may assume there were over 5,000 Pentecostals at the beginning of Fascist repression. Clearly Pentecostals in two decades had attained a similar size to other denominations in Italy (except the Waldenses).

Understandably membership fell off during the persecution. All churches remained closed until 1944 when 120 were reopened. Approximately 29 churches had been lost. But in the next decade places of worship increased to 300 (O'Hanlon 1963:634). In 1955 the Assemblies reported 399 groups, "of which 365 were in Southern Italy" (Latourette 1961:372). A writer from this period reports that the 60,000 members of the "350 Pentecostal Assemblies" make it the largest evangelical community in Italy (Steiner 1957:51).

The map (figure 21 shows the distribution of the Pentecostal movement in 1969. This may be compared with the distribution of non-Pentecostal Evangelicals (figure 22).

Several sources seem to indicate that in 1954 there were 300 churches. There is evidence that these churches had 50,000 members. This is interesting, because Nichol's work indicates that in 1961 there were 600 churches with 100,000 members (Nichol 1966:206). Membership doubled when the number of churches doubled.

By 1970 there were 700 churches (Perna 1970). Without exact membership records, it is difficult to estimate the membership. However Perna who is as close to the situation as anyone, feels that "we are very safe in saying that the total membership of the Italian Assemblies of God is well over 100,000" (1970).

The problem is deciding just how much "well over" actually is. On the basis of 100,000 members in 600 churches, however, we may conservatively estimate that there would be 120,000 in 700 churches (if an average congregation has over 166 members.

The Pentecostals now are more than twice the size of all other Protestants combined. Figure 23 plots the growth of the Assemblies of God as against that of other denominations. Figure 24 compares Pentecostal size with that of the combined denominations. The Pentecostals tower above the other 7 chief denominations, as shown in Figure 25.

PROBLEMS

Pentecostal success is noteworthy. Still I venture to suggest certain problems.

First, it is alarming from the standpoint of church growth that in spite of continued growth a tabling off seems to be happening. The post-War growth was sharp, but the last ten years was scarcely more than the population rate of increase.

Why has the growth slowed? Has Italian receptivity changed? Many possible explanations need to be explored. One possible reason relates to another problem. That is the lack of training of leaders and a failure to teach new converts. The Assemblies do not seem to have solved this problem yet.

PENTECOSTAL CHURCHES

FIGURE 21

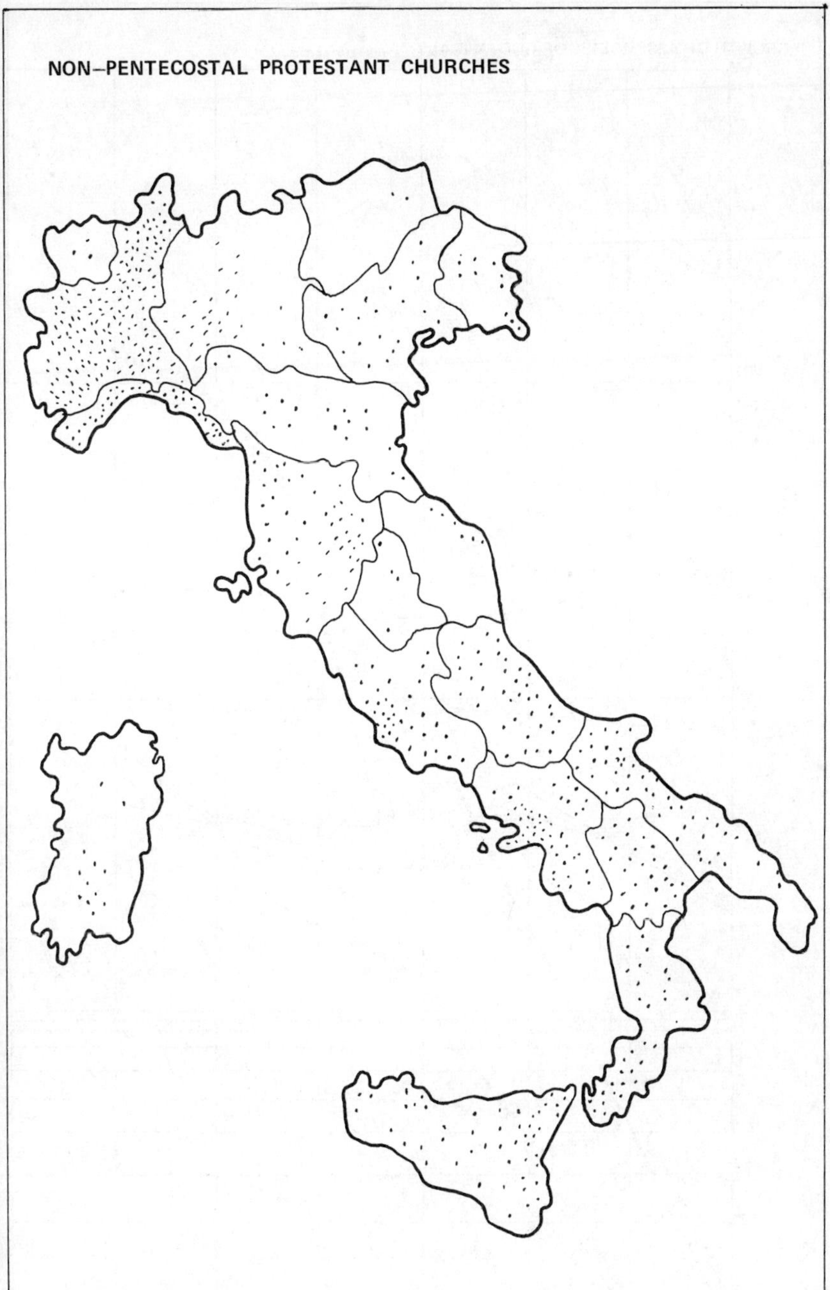
NON-PENTECOSTAL PROTESTANT CHURCHES

FIGURE 22

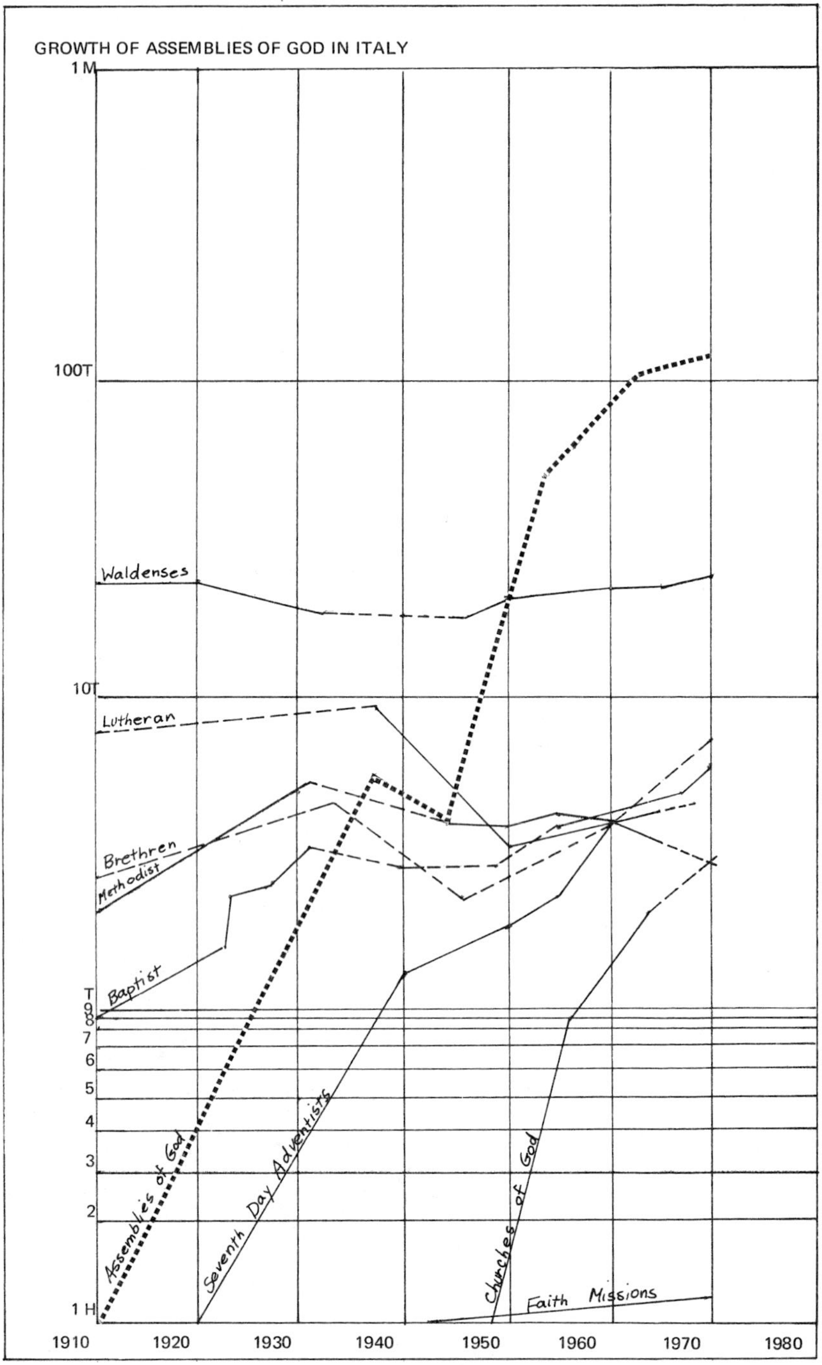
GROWTH OF ASSEMBLIES OF GOD IN ITALY
1 M
100T
10T
T
9
8
7
6
5
4
3
2
1 H
1910
1920
1930
1940
1950
1960
1970
1980
Waldenses
Lutheran
Brethren
Methodist
Baptist
Assemblies of God
Seventh Day Adventists
Churches of God
Faith Missions

FIGURE 23

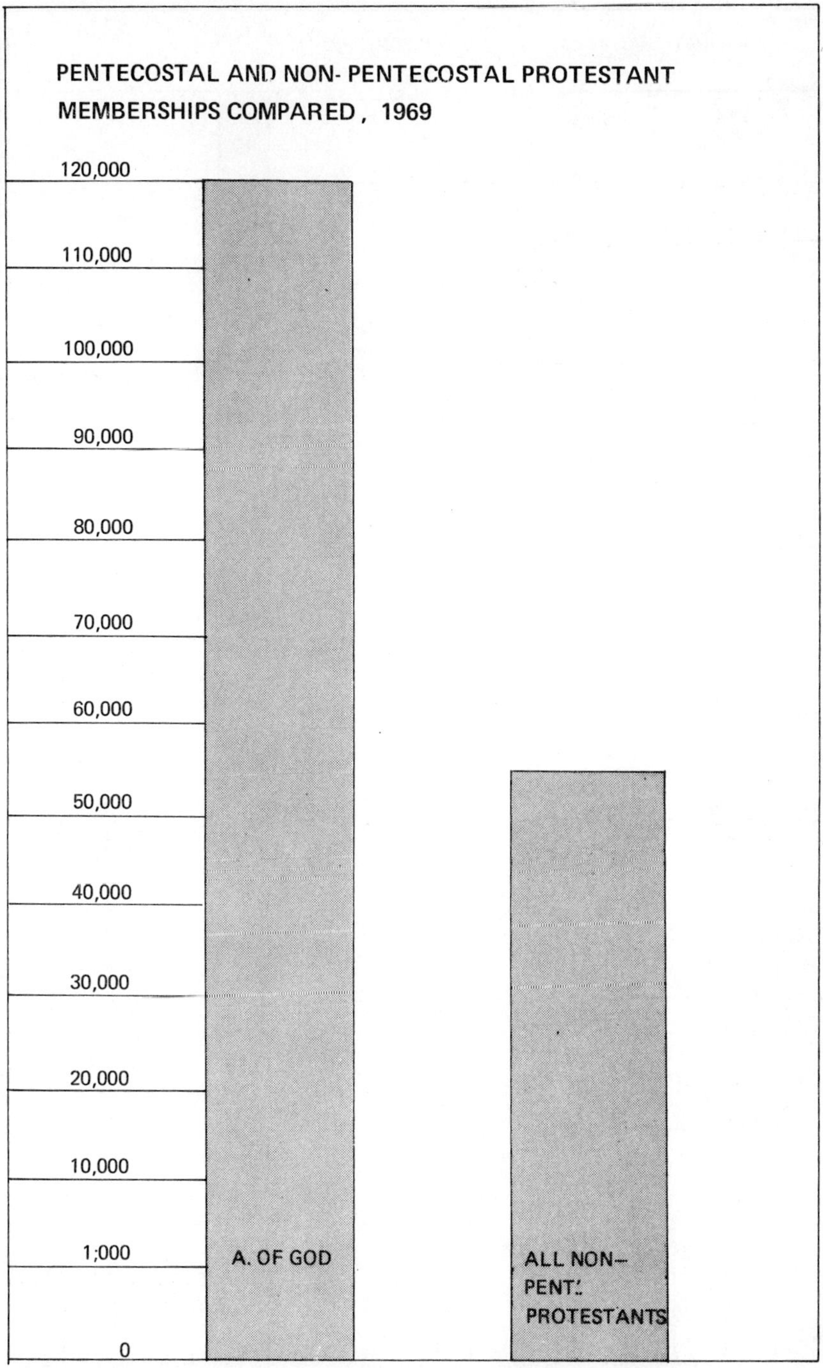
PENTECOSTAL AND NON- PENTECOSTAL PROTESTANT
MEMBERSHIPS COMPARED, 1969
120,000
110,000
100,000
90,000
80,000
70,000
60,000
50,000
40,000
30,000
20,000
10,000
1;000
0
A. OF GOD
ALL NON-
PENT.
PROTESTANTS

FIGURE 24

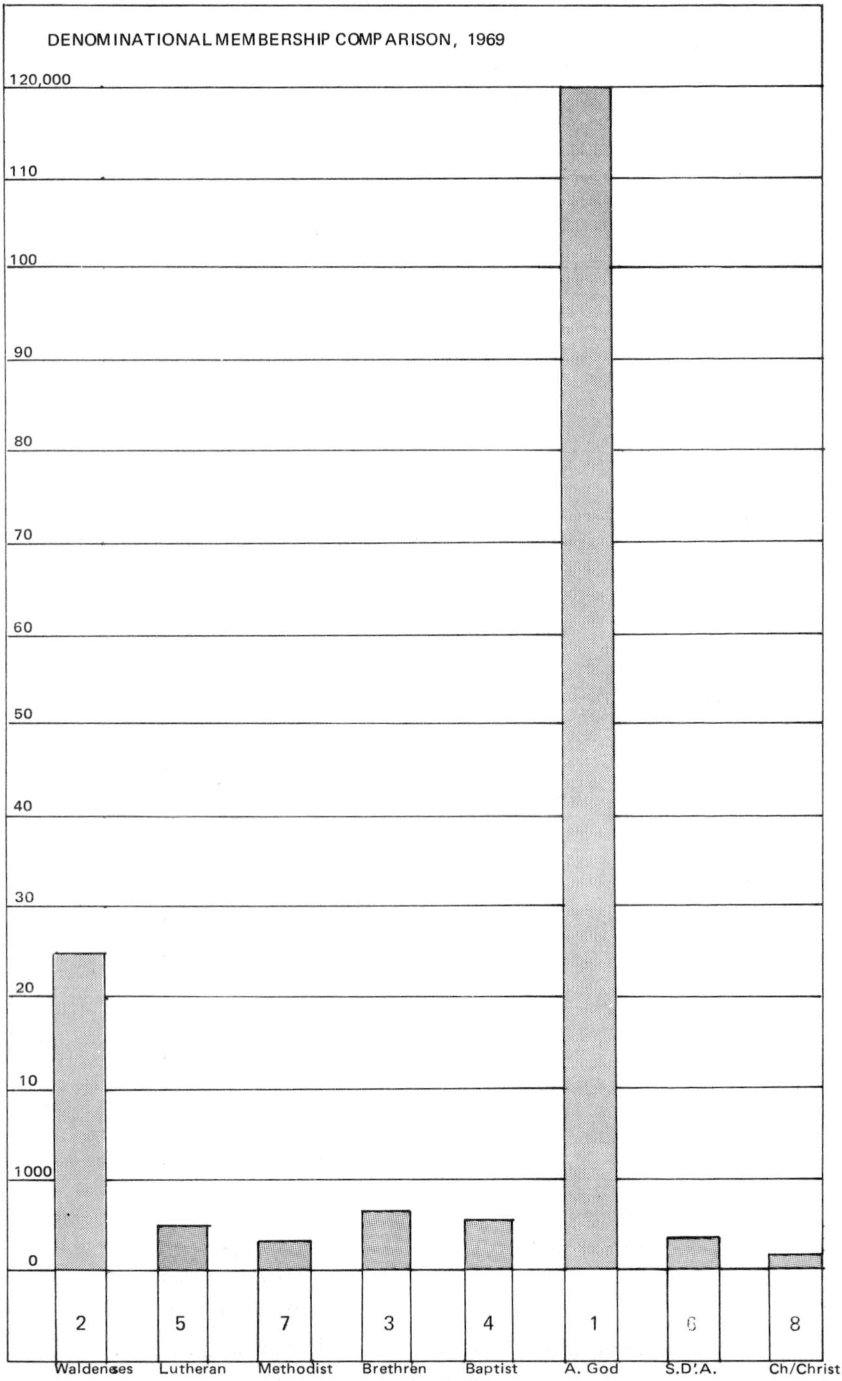
DENOMINATIONAL MEMBERSHIP COMPARISON, 1969
120,000
110
100
90
80
70
60
50
40
30
20
10
1000
0
2
5
7
3
4
1
6
8
Waldenses
Lutheran
Methodist
Brethren
Baptist
A. God
S.D.A.
Ch/Christ

FIGURE 25

A step toward solution is being taken by the preparation of a *Regolamento* to govern the internal affairs of the Church (Perna 1970). The Bible School at Rome serves to give advanced training to those who minister in the churches.

One of the strong points of the movement is also a weakness. Lay leaders serve as the ministers of the churches. Perna states, "our pastors are recruited from among the lay people and only after they have given proof of their calling and ministry are they encouraged to attend our Bible School and get advanced training to better minister to the churches" (1970). This arrangement is marvelous for evangelism and spontaneous expansion. I believe it is one of the keys to the rapid growth that has occurred. As a plan it seem Scriptural, logical, and practical. But the problem comes if these leaders are not trained. Perna reports 23 in the student body of the School at present. This would indicate that very few are actually taking the training. The result is a ministry that is poorly equipped. If follows that the instruction of converts is mediocre.

My own impression is that this is tragically true in a number of cases. In one province where there are a number of Pentecostal churches more than one pastor was described to me as "illiterate". Individual Christians had abandoned the Pentecostal churches because of the poor quality leadership. One complaint was, "He preached the same sermon every Sunday." Understandably that particular church was declining. Present decline in growth may in part be accounted for by numbers who are leaving the churches for this reason. I do not actually know how widespread this problem may be. If a rapid growth rate is to be recovered, however, it seems clear that corrective action must be taken. Leadership must be trained. Since lay pastors are self-supporting they can hardly be expected to go to the Bible School in Rome. Another plan must be found.

One suggestion would be for initiating an extension training program modeled after the extension seminary which is proving successful in Latin America today. Since the pastors cannot go to Rome, Rome should come to them with the help needed. Missionaries and leaders of the Italian Assemblies of God might profitably explore the possibility of extension training in light of the experience of others (Winter 1969). If personnel is lacking to begin such a program, the denomination might consider calling in the aid of other mission organizations who could work into the situation harmoniously.

In addition something could perhaps be done administratively. Qualified pastors and missionaries might be deployed in strategic areas where they would have a full-time ministry of weekly instruction of all lay leaders. In this way not only would natural and gifted leaders rise to the top, but they would be trained to more effectively use their gifts and talents for the ministry of the Church. This would seem a better alternative than the trend which Perna mentions, of "swinging over to encouraging young people to come to the Bible School, and no doubt in the not too distant future we will have reverted to a preministerial preparation as it is done elsewhere" (Perna 1970).

At the moment it seems as if some sort of "crash" training program is needed for the lay pastors of the 700 churches. Greater growth must be recovered. Perhaps the denomination could pour all of its energies into a one-year stint of training every untrained leader <u>for</u> growth. It is not my prerogative to suggest the curriculum of such an intensified course as I am not close enough to the problem. But the goal should be to equip the Church for growth - to win new people and to hold the converts, in large numbers. Therefore something of the dynamics of church growth should be included in the training.

A third type of problem is a tendency toward extremism. Warmhearted evangelicals of other persuasions have sometimes found themselves rejected by their Pentecostal brethren. This is unfortunate in Italy where the unity of true believers needs to be displayed before the Roman Catholic majority. Pentecostals could possibly gain from association with others of like faith. Other evangelicals need the fellowship of Pentecostal brethren.

I do not wish to criticize the Pentecostal style of worship. It is free and spontaneous, recognizing the priesthood of all believers. This is important in a Roman Catholic environment. Pentecostals have provided a corrective that might well be followed by other Evangelicals. In certain cases, however, extreme emotionalism has occurred to the detriment of church expansion.

Lurking in the minds of some are incidents of proselytism or of attempted proselytism. The vastness of the movement and the zeal of its members make it inevitable that there be such charges. No doubt a like charge could be made against Baptists, but since Baptists are much smaller (and less zealous) it is not likely and would certainly not be frequent! A feeling of exclusiveness and of suspicion toward this kind of extremism.

POTENTIAL

Pentecostals are the bright spot in Italy in terms of evangelism and growth. In a half century they have come from nothing to twice the size of all other Protestants. Some reasons for this astounding geat have been indicated above. Certainly the employment of lay leaders is a key. Growth is not limited to availability of professionally trained men or money. Where phenomenal Pentecostal growht has occurred elsewhere in the world, the situation seems similar. Coupled with the active lay ministry is an authoritarian form of church government. Kessler feels that this combination, vitalized by spiritual experience, explains their success in contrast to other Churches in Chile (1968:301).

A common assumption on the part of North Americans is that Pentecostalism attracts because it is emotional. This is an oversimplification. The Italian is admittedly emotional, but this does not account for his attraction toward Pentecostalism, although this temperament may have some bearing. Nor is it proper to equate Pentecostalism with emotionalism.

Therefore we must look beyond the emotional factor to find the dynamics of Pentecostal growth in Italy. To outsiders the emotional style of the Pentecostals may appear more significant than is actually true. At the same time a degree of emotion is important in the drab lives of the people who comprise many of the Assemblies. Where emotionalism seems excessive this may be understood in the light of lay leaders whose intellectual training has been limited.

The Pentecostal practice of concert prayer in public worship is a splendid funtional substitute for the liturgy of the Catholic mass. Protestant worship often fails to provide for full participation in spite of the doctrine of the Priesthood of believers. Catholics are accustomed to reciting prayers in unison during the mass. Therefore everyone praying aloud together as is done in Pentecostal worship does not strike the Catholic as strange, but it does fill much the same function of participation.

Pentecostals also go to the proper audience, to the masses where 75 per cent of the people of Italy are. But so have some others who have failed to grow. The Salvation Army, for instance, which traditionally appeals to the masses, has not known phenomenal growth in Italy.

What is the difference in the appeal? Kessler, who analyzes from the setting in Chile and Peru, feels it has to do with the message.

> We are convinced that several of the Protestant churches... owe their slow rate of progress to the way in which they have presented the message of salvation. When they stated that Christ had already done everything for us and that all the sinner had to do was to receive this finished work, converts tended to become introverted and even selfish. When, on the contrary, the Pentecostals declared in effect that salvation was only complete with the baptism of the Spirit, which could only be experienced in the complete consecration of oneself to God, they were too prone to become supremely satisfied with their own salvation (Kessler 1968:301).

Radical conversion, encounter, is part of Pentecostal teaching and practice. The importance of the dynamics of what Dr. Tippett calls "verdict theology" has been discussed in relation to spiritism. The defeat of Satan through a crisis experience is an important ingredient in an Italian adaptation of the Gospel.

The element of consecration involves obedience. Pentecostal proclamation is not only the responsibility of leaders. Every convert is expected to witness. The salvation of Christ not only acts upon the individual. The individual becomes a participant. Participation involves activity. Therefore expansion is spontaneous, for every one engages in witness, and little groups of believers emerge here and there. We see the results in stark contrast to that of others; the indictment of Pck made four years ago, still stands:

> Apart from Pentecostal achievement (which is principally a national movement and not missionary inspired), 18 years of postwar missionary effort have produced little that is tangible. Neither missionary nor Italian has much success to report (Peck 1966:20).

The Assemblies of God is an Italian Church, run by Italians in an Italian way. Organized under that name in 1944 and later officially recognized as such (Winehouse 1959:113), it is "national" and not "missionary" in orientation. Its American missionaries work under the Italian Church - an arrangement sometimes difficult for the missionary, but apparently beneficial to the Church. One possible reason for the failure of the Missions is that their missionaries preach the Gospel in foreign dress.

Pentecostals have pecularities. Their form of greeting sets them apart, for instance, from the world, and distinguishes them from other Christians. Their legalistic insistence upon certain externals (the veil, divided seating) sometimes chafes the outsider. Actually these practices probably work in favor of the movement. Psychologically it strengthens their identity. Also there is historic precedence in the distinguishing uniforms, language style, forms of greeting, rites and the Roman salute of the Fascists. Even the Italian language was changed or adapted by the Fascists (i.e. "voi" instead of "lei"). Jemelo likewise points out (1969:191) that the anti-Fascist was noticeable for his refusal to follow Fascist forms! Thus the Pentecostal use of "Pace" in greeting is not so "peculiar" in Italy. This as well as other distinguishing marks are an effective means of identification in the Italian culture.

In a disintergrating society identification with a vital community offers hope. Pentecostalism has grown during days of stress. Barnett in his study of innovation as the basis for cultural change, states, "the collapse of controls during periods of social and political upheaval opens the way for innovation" (1953:71). Pentecostalism is a meaningful option to the people of disrupted Italy. Not a mere novelty, it brings meaning to their lives.

LESSONS FOR OTHERS

A Catholic observer of Pentecostalism in Latin America gives this sense of belonging high priority; "the first reason for the growth of Pentecostal churches is that when a forgotten human being comes to one of them, he feels himself loved and understood" (O'Hanlon 1963:634). He goes on to cite the example of a convert who summed up his experience as "I felt at home." O'Hanlon then concedes that Pentecostals proved many elements of true Christianity which are forgotten by Catholics and other Protestants.

Simplicity of belief is identified by Father O'Hanlon as another appealing feature. A few essentials are concentrated upon in song and sermon (1963:635). One need not be a theologian to be a Pentecostal. But then one need not be a theologian to be a Christian either.

Melvin Hodges is probably the outstanding Assemblies of God missiologist. In *A Pentecostal's View of Mission Strategy* he gives several significant points (1968:306).

(1) The role of the Church. A local church is defined as wherever two or three are gathered in the name of

Christ. Its function is to become a living cell of the Body of Christ, the Agent of God for bringing the message of redemption to its community. The supreme task therefore is church-planting and church growth which is cell multiplication (Hodges 1968:305).

(2) Mission strategy. "The Holy Spirit is the Chief Strategist of the Church in evangelism and mission." The Church is responsible to adopt the particular strategy which the Spirit has given for a given age and place. "Human planning is valid only as it reflects the Divine Mind" (Hodges 1968:305).

(3) The human part. While the role of the Spirit is prominent, the role of man is not passive. He must engage the best mental, physical, material and spiritual powers that he possesses "in the planning and execution fo God's work" (Hodges 1968:305).

(4) The role of the individual. "Pentecostal methodology for church growth emphasizes the importance of the individual's response to the Holy Spirit. Every Christian is called to be a witness and upon receiving the gift of the Spirit, is empowered for this service" (Hodges 1968:306).

(5) The role of the laity. Ministry is in the hand of the laity. Laymen are active in their local churches, then develop into pastors or evangelists. They may begin their "pastoral" ministry by opening an out-station. As the station becomes a church, the layman may become the pastor. Many such lay leaders attend Bible School for training in Christian doctrine and church administration. "They have the advantage of being close to their people and identified with the local culture" (Hodges 1968:306).

PART FOUR

An Overview of Mission Agencies

PRELUDE

One way to survey mission organizations at work in Italy is to arbitrarily divide them into two categories: those which plant churches and those that do not. Such a scheme is simplistic. For one thing most mission organizations are involved in several activities, one of which may be church planting. Some persons and organizations obviously involved in programs specifically not dedicated to church planting would protest that their particular ministry does contribute to the establishment and growth of churches. Radio and literature are examples of such ministries.

In another sense missions whose avowed purpose is to plant churches sometimes find themselves involved in additional activities, so that it is difficult to know in which category to place them. To be very critical, the question might be asked, "Are so called church-planters really planting any churches?" If there are no visible results, should this particular mission be classed as "church-planting"?

Any procedure seems likely to stir protest. Nevertheless I am attempting to make such an arbitrary division. It is admittedly subjective. The classification is made on the basis of what appears to be the major emphasis of the organization in question. That is, if 50 per cent or more of the effort appears to be placed on church-planting, the mission will be classed as a church-planting mission. If less, it is to be considered a non-church-planting mission. I regret that detailed information was not available to me on many of the groups. It is possible that significant ommissions occur.

Much of this information is familiar to workers in Italy. It is included not only for the benefit of other readers, but to offer a type of self-evaluation. Royal Peck has declared that "18 years of postwar missionary effort have produced little that is tangible" (1968:20). Italian brethren have been critical of much missionary activity. Could it be because of a wrong emphasis? Much activity with few results?

A directory (Missionary Research Library 1968) lists 31 agencies with 139 missionaries doing mission work in Italy. This list does not include a number of independent missionaries. Some agencies may have been omitted. I make no attempt to discuss all. I lack information for many.

15

Agencies Primarily Devoted to Church Planting

BAPTISTS

Baptist missions in Italy have emphasized church planting. This was true of early English and Southern Baptist work. The story of those two groups is told in a preceding chapter. Southern Baptists today have the largest group of missionaries in Italy. Since their ministry is tied to the Baptist Union it need not be discussed at this point. The Baptist Union is not actively planting new churches at present to my knowledge.

Baptist Mid-Missions has in recent years maintained two missionary couples in Italy. Because of ill health these have either withdrawn or are in the process of withdrawal. An effort in Verona did not result in a church, but the work of this small staff has produced two churches in the South at Salerno and in a suburb of Naples, Soccavo.

Literature has been a major concern of the Conservative Baptist Foreign Missionary Society. Naples has been the center of operation since arrival in 1950. The following year a Bible Center was opened. The first church planting was begun by Robert Lillard in 1959 at Caserta. At present over half of the missionaries under appointment are related to planting churches. In 1968 eleven small groups had come into being with a total membership of 70. The Caseta church had 30 members and its own pastor. Twenty baptisms took place during the year. Groups of believers met regularly in Avellino, Aversa, Gragnano and San Giorgio. Acerra, Castelvolturno, Castellammare, Scanzano, San Tommaso, and central Naples were preaching points.

An English speaking Baptist Church was organized in Naples during 1969 with 36 charter members. A Christian

Servicemen's Center also is part of the responsibility of CBFMS.

BIBLE CHRISTIAN UNION

This mission has formed small churches in Ravenna and Viareggio. Since the churches are on opposite sea coasts, isolation and lack of fellowship seem major problems.

Some missionaries are in radio and literature work.

EUROPEAN CHRISTIAN MISSION

The church planting of this British-based organization is carried on by three couples in the Northeast. A start has been made in the cities of Trent, Bolzano and Verona. In or adjoining the German part of Italy, this is the area of the country which is more intensely Catholic than any other.

Most members of this mission are engaged in church planting. It is also commendable that they have gone to minister in what is probably the most neglected section of Italy. The German speaking area has, however, been resistent to the Evangelical message. Therefore it would seem wise for this mission, while continuing to maintain a witness in the Trento-Bolzano district, to consider expending future energies among more responsive people.

WORLDWIDE EVANGELIZATION CRUSADE

W.E.C. has been maintaining a number of workers on the island of Sardegna at Nuoro and Oristano. It is my impression that all these missionaries (five or six) are engaged in new church work and in re-opening closed Baptist churches. A degree of contact seems to have been maintained with the Naples pastors of the former Spezia Mission for Italy. The 1967 Yearbook lists 5 churchs and stations on the Island.

INDEPENDENT MISSIONARIES

A number of missionaries in Italy have no organizational sponsorship. Several of these are engaged in church planting. The 24 Brethren missionaries could be so classed since they have no apparent connection. However they are considered part of the Brethren Assemblies, in the work of which has been elaborated upon in the previous chapter.

At Sassare, Sardegna, Seviss missionaries are engaged in evangelism, Apparently a church has been begun, and the work is expanding to another town.

An independent Brethren worker from Australia meets with a church in Castellammare di Stabia. A converted priest pastors a church in Rovigo.

Other independent missionaries are engaged in various other ministries.

16

Agencies Primarily Engaged in Other Activities

BIBLE SOCIETIES

The British and Foreign Bible Society in 1951 sold 119,554 copies of the Scriptures in Italy. The following year the figure rose to 121,513. At the same time a "Million Testament Campaign" destributed theirs free of charge. The Bible Society had no salaried colporteurs, but the work was carried on by 104 volunteers in that post-War time of spiritual hunger (Chochrane 1953:334).

Bible distribution is a necessary corollary to church planting. The work of the Bible Society is strengthened by the various literature efforts. *Action Biblique*, a Swiss mission working in Rome, makes effective use of literature and has channeled converts into a church. *Centro Biblico* of Conservative Baptists at Naples is a leading distributer as is also the Christian Literature Crusade at Florence and more recently in Milan.

BIBLE CLUB MOVEMENT

One couple serves in Italy under this organization. Their ministry among children and youth serves to strengthen the local church. This ministry has been closely related to the Brethren Assemblies.

CHILD EVANGELISM FELLOWSHIP

This work is very similar to that of the Bible Club Movement. Up to the present however, there has been little direct working with the churches. This seems to be due to the policy of the organization rather than to the workers who seem very willing to cooperate. Conservation of results would be more likely if the workers were permitted to function as part of some Church.

GOSPEL MISSIONARY UNION

Voce della Bibbia (Voice of the Bible) radio broadcast is the chief ministry of the Weins who serve under this Board. An extensive literature ministry is conducted in relation to the broadcasts. Weins is conscientious about follow-up. Names of contacts are passed on to other missionaries and pastors, and Weins visits personally many who write in.

GREATER EUROPE MISSION

This mission sponsors the Evangelical Bible Institute at Rome. Recently church planting has been initiated in a suburb of Rome. Students are involved in mass evangelism campaigns as part of their training.

Of the 18 missionaries on the field, two are engaged in church planting. Additional couples have been appointed for this ministry. During 1969 staff and students were reported to have won approximately 15 persons to Christ. At the beginning of 1970, 13 students were enrolled in the School (Peck 1969).

INDEPENDENT FAITH MISSIONS

The approach of this Mission is 3-pronged; Publications (2 periodicals), Bible Correspondence School (14 courses), and church-planting and direct evangelism centered about the Mission Center in Rome where a local church is being organized. Several missionaries cooperate in this project. A former Waldensian church is being reopened in the Monte Rotonda area. Home Bible studies, childrens clubs and other activities form part of the evangelistic program in Rome.

A missionary observer from another group remarked that he was impressed by the church-planting being done by this mission. Although a "part-time" activity, he felt these missionaries were doing a more effective piece of work than many who were in it full-time.

I know of seven missionaries serving with this Board in Italy.

INTERNATIONAL FELLOWSHIP OF EVANGELICAL STUDENTS

Two single ladies publish the Inter-Varsity magazine and books, and engage in student evangelism.

L'ABRI FELLOWSHIP

A self-sustaining church (the only Italian Presbyterian Church in the country), and extensive student work form the nucleus of the ministry of Hurvey Woodson who cooperates with Frances Schaeffer of Switzerland.

MISSIONE DI BEATENBERG

Eleven individuals serve at Isola del Gran Sasso under this Swiss mission. Among the varied activities are openair evangelism, Bible studies, literature distribution, camping and Bible conferences in German and Italian. Regular services are held at the Mission hall.

OPERATION MOBILIZATION

Evangelism is the sole purpose of this organization which brings international teams of young people into the country. Massive literature distribution takes place during the summer. The participants also make an impact through tent campaigns and general visitation and witnessing. This Mission effectively collaborates with local churches and is a direct aid to church growth.

Many young people serve for short terms under O.M. In one recent year there were 20. O.M. has been the inspiration that causes many to return for "full-time" service. Probably 4 or 5 workers are permanent with O.M.

WORLDWIDE EUROPEAN FELLOWSHIP

Radio, church planting, and literature are the activities of the 12 missionaries of this Society. In the Florence studio - programs are prepared for release over Monte Carlo. Workers in Trieste minister through literature. A church planting effort is being made in a German-Italian bilingual city.

OTHERS

Here and there across the country may be found individuals engaged in various activities which serve to strengthen the Church. Two single ladies, Miss Albina Tedesco and Miss Margaret Scipione, have contributed greatly in the field of Christian education.

POSTLUDE

The Directory of the Missionary Research Library, published in 1968, includes the names of 8 organizations concerning which I have no information whatsoever. I do not doubt that they work in Italy; I merely do not know about them personally. These are Church of the Brethren (Brethren Service Commission), Garr Memorial Church, International Pentecostal Assemblies (Missions Department), North American Baptist Association (Missionary Committee), Southern European Mission Inc., and World-Wide Missions. Church of God World Missions is also listed. This is probably the Cleveland, Tennessee, Pentecostal group which has churches in Southern Italy and Sicily. According to the *World Christian Handbook* (1968) there were 1449 members in 24 churches.

A number of other organizations also have missionaries in Italy. At present I have little or no information about the Barbican Mission to the Jews (2 workers), Christian Churches of North America (Italian Pentecostals - 2 workers), Crusaders for Christ (probably 2 workers), European Evangelistic Crusade (1 worker), European Missionary Fellowship (6 persons), Hebrew Christian Testimony to Israel (from England 1 person working with Jews in Rome), Missionary and Soul-Winning Fellowship 3 workers (from Long Beach, California, church planting in Rome), Missione Svizzera per Dischi (Swiss organization, 4 representatives distribution Gospel records), Servizio d'auito Amichevole (also Swiss) Slavic Gospel Association (from Chicago, one couple in Rome), Scripture Union

(Unione Biblica Italiana devotional books), and Unione Biblica Ospedaliera (Nurses Christian Union, one worker in Rome). The Pocket Testament League is also in Italy engaged in the distribution of free Gospels. Recently Campus Crusade for Christ has nominated a representative for Italy.

These 14 organizations should be appended to any future directory of mission work in Italy. A corrected listing should of course include also Action Biblique (8 workers), the Brethren Assemblies, L'Abri Fellowship, the Beatenberg Mission and Operation Mobilization. The *World Christian Handbook* (1968) tells us that a United Church Board for World Ministries is also working in Italy.

To this list should be added the names of the forgotten "church planting" missions listed earlier. Previous directories have omitted the European Christian Mission (12 workers) and WEC (Worldwide Evangelization Crusade, 5-6 missionaries). Therefore instead of 31, a complete list of mission organizations would be more like 53.

Some 237 missionaries serve under all these groups. I know of an additonal 16 independents, which brings the total to 253.

Each of these workers is engaged, no doubt, in very important activities. Most missionaries have arrived since World War II. The fruitfulness of their labors is probably variegated. But in terms of extending the Church they seem to have had little effect. In some cases results are hidden. Brethren and Assemblies of God missionaries work within their respective Churches where growth has been taking place.

But by and large few churches have been planted by these missionaries. The majority of the missions work independently of the existing denominations, and their work is not hidden as part of the activity of some Church. Therefore at least their church planting results should be visible; that is, we should be able to see the churches they have begun and count, in some fashion, the number of members. From the absense of this kind of visible evidence I am forced to conclude that most missionaries are apparently engaged in something other than church planting. Even those officially involved in direct church planting have not had phenomenal success. The 253 missionaries in Italy of all groups have not since the war planted 200 churches, nor 100, or even 50. In fact my investigation leads me to ponder whether the total number of converts in churches started by these foreign missionaries since the war would be much over 200 (excluding the accomplishments of the Brethren, the Pentecostals, and the

Churches of Christ). For purposes of comparison it seems generous to allow even 200 as the number of new or additional members in congregations not part of any Italian denomination and started by missionaries. The "Faith Missions" designation in Figure 18 (page 111) refers to these churches and converts, and includes such diverse groups as Conservative Baptists and the European Christian Mission all lumped together (put separately they would not show up on the graph). The lack of progress is especially disturbing when compared to that of the Churches of Christ who also began operations in Italy after World War II.

PART FIVE

Some Conclusions

17

Some Challenges

"CULTS"

Jehovah's Witnesses. The "cult" problem in Italy may be expressed in two words: Jehovah's Witnesses. The *Testimoni di Geova* seem everywhere present. People who have never met a true evangelical have had contact with these cultists who also appropriate the label "evangelical". Towns without an evangelical church may be found to have a group of Jehovah's Witnesses. The cultists are zealous in propagandizing. They are of all groups most fanatical.

The strong anticlericalism expressed is attractive to Italians already having that bent. The message is negative.

Christians have been impressed with the familiarity with the Bible which Jehovah's Witnesses seem to possess. The Old Testament is frequently used. Italian evangelicals are much better versed in the Gospels, and the Old Testament sometimes remains incomprehensible to them. Evangelicals often feel incapable of confronting the Jehovah's Witness. However a number of pieces of literature have been prepared in Italian expressly for the purpose of helping the believer at this point. Most significant is a translation of *Jehovah of the Watchtower*, by Martin and Klan. The tract, "Questions for Jehovah's Witnesses" is especially useful.

The cultists are aggressive in door-to-door visitation. Where an entrance is found they will return again and again. A favorite technique is to leave books for the interested person to look at; then the Witness returns for the book, and begins a "Bible" study in the home. A number of times in my own calling I have encountered persons who said, "Oh, I already have the Bible." What they thought to be the Bible turned out to be actually a Watchtower Society book.

I have encountered a number of these Witnesses in Italy. All of them were Italians. None I met were foreign missionaries.

Yet in spite of the bitter attitude and non-Christian teachings of this cult, I have known persons who became interested in the Gospel because of initial contact with the Witnesses. Some evangelicals actually see no difference between themselves and the *Testimoni di Geova*. Others who have become non-Catholic but who are still nominal Christians fail to see any difference between this cult and the evangelicals.

Two points should be made. (1) Persons once contacted by the Witnesses are not necessarily lost to the Gospel. (2) Religious interest stirred by the cultist may be channeled into real Bible teaching and conversion to Christ.

The proselyting activities of the cult make it important that believers be properly taught. The sect's aggressiveness requires evangelicals to stir themselves to the task of personal evangelism. We must rise to the competition. Christian workers tend to become so enamoured with administration that evangelism in its various phases is neglected. The Witnesses are then given a golden opportunity. I once called on a family that had completed an evangelical correspondence course only to find that a Jehovah's Witness had already contacted them and begun a study in the home. They were a lost opportunity. Follow-up, as an essential part of evangelism, must not be neglected or we will be feeding the cultists' ranks.

Today the Witnesses operate freely in Italy. It was not always so. Under Fascism they were severely persecuted. Earlier activities, following entrance into Italy in 1903, apparently neeted results, for the religious and political persecution caused around 300 of them to be arrested. Of these, 100 wer imprisoned and 26 were deferred to the Special Court of Rome which in turn condemned them to various sentences of four to eleven years of confinement. In 1943 they were released, and the cult was reorganized (Santini, Artissi, Capezzani 1969:239-240). The war period must have decimated the religious group. For in 1946 there were apparently only 95 members.

Since the War growth has been phenomenal. From 1950 to 1965 the membership increased from 1,000 to 9,586, which is an average annual growth rate of 16% per year. The little table found in Santini, Artissi, and Capezzani (1969:240) is here reproduced (Figure 26). Its significance is not so much in the record of growth shown as in the corresponding

PROGRESS OF JEHOVAH'S WITNESSES IN ITALY

year	ministers	hours dedicated to preaching		visits to interested persons		studied with families		books, magazines, tracts distributed	
		per capita	total	per capita	total	per capita	total	per capita	total
1946	95	83	7,921	37	3,443	.85	82	450	42,653
1950	1,005	157	157,107	60	60,309	.66	665	102	102,864
1955	2,829	140	403,217	67	188,912	.57	1,600	118	333,176
1960	5,413	127	688,125	55	299,826	.66	3,570	142	766,494
1966	10,313	155	1,593,250	68	699,667	.89	9,244	216	2,232,406

FIGURE 26

activities whose figures give the reasons for the growth. Growth corresponds roughly with the number of hours given to preaching, with visits made, with studies conducted and with pieces of literature distributed. This relationship is shown in Figure 27.

It is meaningful that figures given are for "ministers". Each Witness is a "minister". This is no empty title. Each one carries on an active ministry: hence the four activities. Faithfulness is the execution of responsibilities accounts for the astronomical figures in the activities columns.

The table does not tell all the story. What is shown are the specific (proselyting) hours. In addition members attend five different hours of instruction weekly and locally. Note too that visitation hours are reported only of visits to interested persons. It does <u>not</u> indicate the additional multiplied hours given to door-to-door, "cold-turkey" calling for the purpose of propagandizing every home in every locality and thus finding interested persons.

The relationship between membership growth and number of studies is roughly even. However the number of hours dedicated to preaching in 1966 averaged 154 1/2 per person! The average person made over 67 visits to interested persons that year and distributed 216 books, tracts, and magazines.

The Witnesses are cause for concern because of their aggressiveness and rapid expansion. Awareness of their tactics and teachings is essential. More than this, Evangelicals, in power of the Spirit, need to equal the Witnesses' zeal. Methods employed are largely copied from the New Testament. From this we might take a lesson. To my knowledge <u>no</u> church anywhere has achieved the growth rate maintained by Italy's Jehovah's Witnesses.

<u>Mormons</u>. In the fall of 1969 I talked with a Mormon missionary in Los Angeles who told me that the Mormons had recently baptized "thousands" in Italy, chiefly in the traditionaly Protestant districts of Piedmont. I have not been able to either disprove or verify his statement. Mormon missionaries are not entirely strange to Italy, however, and I am inclined to question the report.

The Church of Jesus Christ of Latter Day Saints has extablished branches in some of the large cities of Italy. But to date I doubt that much of an impact has been made. An instance is known to me where Protestants entertained two Mormon missionaries for dinner. The hostess in telling about it admitted laughing at their strange beliefs. The Mormons'

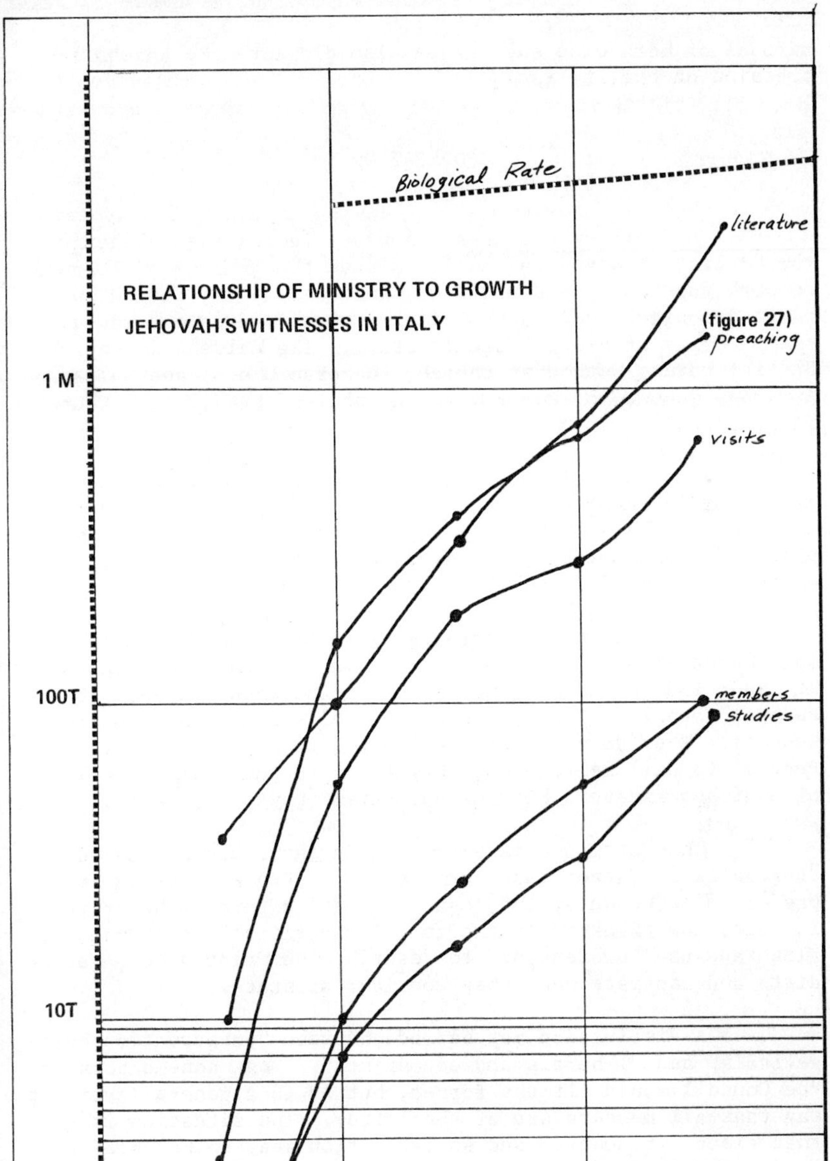

RELATIONSHIP OF MINISTRY TO GROWTH
JEHOVAH'S WITNESSES IN ITALY
(figure 27)
Biological Rate
literature
preaching
visits
members
studies
1 M
100T
10T
1000
10T
1T
1940
1950
1960
1970

FIGURE 27

refusal of both wine and coffee also did not make a good impression on the Italians.

COOPERATION

Council of Churches. Besides facing the challenge of the "cults", Italy's Evangelicals have the problem of learning to work together. A Council of Churches exists, having been first organized in 1945, but its membership does not include the majority of Protestants in Italy. The Waldensian Church, Baptist Union, Methodist Church, Lutheran Church and Salvation Army are members of the Federal Council of Evangelical Churches in Italy.

The Assemblies of God, Adventists, Brethren, and Apostolic Churches as well as the various smaller Bodies are not members, though they may adhere to the Council for purposes of rapport with the government and the defense of religious liberty (Consiglio Federale 1967:17).

The Council of Churches therefore actually represents only about 38,000 Christians who belong to its member Churches. At least 133,000 Christians belong to Churches not part of the Federal Council. Many non-members feel strongly against the Council. They do not want the Council to represent them. The Federal Council is related, they feel, to the World Council of Churches and to a kind of ecumenism they do not want.

This attitude is expressed in their use of the word "evangelical" rather than "protestant". Protestants in Italy prefer to be known by the less connotative term. The Brethren, in fact, sometimes apply the term "evangelical" to themselves alone and use "protestant" to describe the Waldensians, Methodists and Baptists whom they consider apostate.

A distinction may be made between "conservative evangelicals" and "liberals and ecumenists". Most non-members of the Council would fit the former, but it is a generalization to say that all members are of the latter. The situation is not that clear. Ecumenism and social action seem to be chief concerns of Council members however, while the conservatives' main emphasis is that of evangelism. Therefore perhaps the distinction made by the Brethren and others between Protestant and Evangelical may, in fact, by useful.

Pentecostals go a step further, appropriating the nickname "Evangelista". So widespread and helpful is this usage that other evangelicals working in Pentacostal areas have found it helpful to borrow it.

Exclusivist tendencies in the evangelistic groups make it understandable that they want no part of a Council of Churches. Practically all of the Missions are distinctly conservative too. Missionaries with such missions do not have much interest in the Council. Evangelism is a prior concern, as is commendable. The results speak for themselves. Progress in evangelism is a fact, not so much of Council Churches (Methodists are in decline), but of non-Council Churches (Pentecostals, Churches of Christ, Brethren).

The result is fragmentation. Little cooperation has taken place between Evangelical bodies. Evangelism may be more successful carried on separately. But sometimes small groups struggle on by themselves with little awareness of other Christians. Fellowship, even friendship, is lacking. Christians, who are truly Evangelical, are often suspicious of one another.

Missionaries of various persuasions meet in an annual conference. It is mainly a fellowship meeting, open to all evangelical workers. In the last two years this conference has been at least partially opened to Italian workers. But it is a missionary oriented affair.

Proposed Union and Fellowship. On September 21-22, 1969, meetings were held to consider formation of a Union of Free Churches and a Fellowship of Free Churches in Italy. The meeting was called by the four AMEI related churches of Naples. The AMEI (Association of Italian Evangelical Missionaries) had recently been dissolved, leaving these churches totally independent. Pastor Maselli (also a professor of history at the University of Florence) has for some time had a vision of such a Body encompassing evangelical churches of various backgrounds.

> Both missionary and national groups were in attendance from considerable distances. Statements of Purpose and Doctrine were presented to the group by Pastor Maselli for the consideration of prospective members. The Unione di Chiese Libere (Union of Free Churches) would give the Italian pastor recognition before the government as ministers which they now stand to lose as a result of their dissolved relationship with AMEI (as of 31 December 1969). The Communione (Fellowship) of Free Churches would have a mission organization and would be open to all who would subscribe to the Doctrinal Statement. An additional meeting is proposed for February 11, 1970, for further consideration to these organizations. A committee com-

> posed of six persons was selected to prepare for the coming meeting...(CBFMS 1969).

The six-man committee was representative regionally: two each from North, Central and South of which one was an Italian, the other a missionary. In this way several independent groups were represented by missionaries and some of the churches by the Italians. Formation of such an organization may give the churches founded by independent missionaries a strategy for the future and thus bring a number of individual churches closer together. It may be that entire groups, such as the Conservative Baptists' Italian churches, may become members.

In the minds of the founders this Union or Fellowship is not intended to become a denomination. Member churches may keep their identity as Baptist, Brethren, Pentecostal. It is my impression that neither is it envisioned as a competitive Council of Churches or Association of Evangelicals. The Assemblies of God or the Church of the Brethren could, conceivably, become members in their entirety, but I do not know that that is the intention. My impression is that the plan is more to attract local churches on an individual basis.

One hundred years ago (circa) a Christian Free Church was in existence in Italy. Over the years the name was changed several times. Early in this century many of its member congregations became Methodist churches. Other divisions occurred and the association eventually disappeared.

The present plan for a new fellowship is promising. Evangelicals may find opportunity to express their unity of faith without compromise or forced union.

Ecumenism. Meanwhile ecumenism continues as a major theme both for Catholics and Protestants. Protestant evangelists welcome the friendly climate which is following Vatican II. Ecumenical concerns, however, sometimes mean a shift in emphasis from evangelism to "our need for a common witness before atheistic materialism."

Thus, writing on "Ecumenical Experiments in Italy", Maria Vingiani states:

> Catholics and Christians of every denomination are urgently aware of the need to give a common evangelical reply and witness to the problems of peace, justice, liberty, revolution, education, the renewal of structures, hunger, the third world, and so on, but on account of their different mentality, they find that they argue and

> disagree in their judgments -- hence the need to insist on the fundamental problem of the "reform of mentality", so that a path toward ecumenism can be cleared (1969: 165-166).

Vingiani admits that the path of ecumenism is a difficult one. She describes the Protestant attitude as a critical one toward the Catholic Church and toward Italian religious life in general. "Proselytism" is scorned. Waldensian experiences of the past are recognized as an obstacle. On the Catholic side, she refer to "a deep-seated triumphalistic mentality, the use of dialectics without dialogue, intolerance, and, above all, mutual ignorance" (Vingiani 1969:163).

The Catholic seminaries Vingiani sees as a negative influence, but cites as positive the activities and writings of Waldensians Janni and Miegge, the Protestant ecumenical village of Agape, and the YWCA. She praises the work of Catholic associations, reviews, and religious groups such as Unitas, Foyer Unitas, Lega di Preghiera, Oriente Cristiano, and Russia Cristiano. The Foccolari movement is particularly singled out for praise, as are several cultural and spiritual reviews and centers, mixed meetings of Catholic and Protestant clergy, study and research centers in Rome and Florence, and ecumenical centers for prayer and encounter. Several publishing houses are mentioned as specializing on ecumenical subjects, and she reports an unofficial attempt to translate the Bible with the help of every denomination (Vingiani 1969:164).

Joint Bible translations have been received with mixed emotions in some countries. A Plymouth Brethren missionary who was a consultant for such a translation project in the Philippines expressed himself in favor. "Surely we who base our stand so decidedly on the Scriptures should contribute our share toward faithful translations when given the opportunity to do so" (Brooks 1969:174). The project with which he worked included a priest as a committee member.

In Italy perhaps the case is slightly different. I am not personally acquainted with the translation project. Several Catholic versions of the Bible are now available, and there are two Protestant editions. Perhaps a new rendition would be useful. Protestants sometimes use Catholic editions in evangelism. A joint translation could help break down the barrier of suspicion.

But ecumenism has two phases: that of Catholic-Protestant relations, already mentioned, and that of the relationship of Protestants to Protestants. This second phase was discussed under previous topics and is very closely related to the first. It is because of the dialogue with Catholics on the part of the Council Churches that problems arise. Evangelicals fear church union. A Federation of Churches is seen as an attempt toward union. Evangelicals such as the Seventh Day Adventists, Assemblies of God, Church of Christ, and the Brethren "will not countenance even a cautious rapprochement with the Roman Catholic Church" (Mollar 1968:119), which they consider to be apostate.

Related to this fear is another, that evangelistic activities could be compormised. Membership in the Council of Churches could lead to comity (Mollar 1968:119). Comity could mean the foreclosure of evangelistic activities amoung our "Roman Catholic brethren".

Dialogue. Ecumenicity involves dialogue. The question is, should the Evangelical engage in dialogue? To this the ecumenical Protestant gives a resounding "Yes". Some who have known Catholic repression and whose present concern is evangelizing Catholics would answer "no". In between are the others.

R. Pierce Beaver is an articulate advocate of dialogue as the rewarding path toward "new knowledge, an enlarged understanding of one's own religion, and a chance to witness relevantly to Christ and the Gospel" (Beaver 1968:119). This sounds impressive. Every Christian desires to bear witness. Some may wonder as to the subject of witness. Is it a witness to brotherhood, to unity, to ecumenism? Beaver's answer is: the role in dialogue is "to be a witness to the Gospel, to introduce Christ, to be himself the manifestation of Christ's love." The Evangelical cannot object to that. Beaver clearly intends that the Christian engaged in dialogue be the agent of the Holy Spirit. "When there is acutal confrontation with Christ a man cannot be indifferent to Him: he either accepts or reject- Him" (Beaver 1968:125). This far the evangelist can only say "Amen". But there is another element. Despite his stated concern that dialogue be the arena for the Holy Spirit's working, and that it is "a form of apostolic witness demanded by the times...more consistent with the spirit of Christ than many methods of the past", Beaver excludes conversion. Dialogue is not a form of evangelism. No man is able to convert another, nor should he attempt to do so. Every man has in some measure been enlightened by God. Dialogue recognizes and respects this illunination (Beaver 1968:124,125, 118). "Dialogue presupposes that the participants do not strive for conversion and restrain themselves from any form of coercion and pressure to achieve conversion" (Beaver 1968: 124).

The people representing the "No" side of the dialogue question are quick to reply that dialogue is then a waste of time for the Evangelical deeply concerned for evangelism. Conversion to Christ and His Church is the meaning of evangelism, they point out. From the standpoint of aggressive evangelism, the- would seem to be right. From the church-growth viewpoint dialogue might be seen as merely another good activity which, despite its goodness, does not contribute to the quantitative growth of the Church. Still, a "Never" vote toward dialogue may be too exclusive. Even in Italy where too often Christian workers are engaged in multifarious excellent works which are not productive in terms of converts in the churches, there may be instances when dialogue may indeed be indicated as the expedient form of witness.

A. R. Tippett, of the church growth school of thought, agrees in part with Beaver's argument that dialogue may indeed be indicated as the evangelistic necessity in today's world (Tippett 1969:47). But, in Tippett's judgment, that method may be employed for gaining a commitment to Christ on the part of the partner in dialogue. Also he insists that dialogue need not displace monological, authoritative proclamation of the Word of God.

> I see no reason why an evangelist, a teacher or witness should not use the dialogical approach in his evangelism, teaching or testifying, but the preacher and the apostle must reserve the right to make a monological proclamation as a word from the Lord (Tippett 1969:48).

Evangelists in Italy desiring to employ the dialogical approach must bear in mind the post-Vatican II objectives of the Catholic Church. Hans Kung, perhaps the most enlightened spokesman for the renewal of the Catholic Church, says that renewal is for the purpose of reunion. Catholics and Protestants must keep themselves open towards each other and meet each other in brotherly love.

The meetin of Catholic and Protestant is not a compromise. Differences are not to be soft-pedalled, nor the truth played down. It means self-searching, self-criticism, and self-reform on both sides (Kung 1964:144).

> If Catholics carry out Catholic reform and Protestants carry out Protestant reform, both according to that Gospel image, then, because the gospel of Christ is but one, reunion need not remain a utopian dream. Reunion will then be neither a Protestant "return" nor a Catholic "capitulation", but a brotherly approach from both sides...(Kung 1964:145).

The evangelist contemplating dialogue should bear in mind that the Catholic objective is reunion. But how soon can mutual understanding come when Kung himself deplores "the often more than questionable missionary methods of some of the American sects" (1964:151). A decision as to whether or not to become involved in dialogue must consider such attitudes in light of theultimate goal. In the words of Jack Shepherd, "Dialogue with the people of other faiths is appropriate if it does not involve relinquishing the missionary intention of persuasion" (Shepherd 1968:128). To be fair to Kung we must ask if his reluctance is the methods of evangelizing used by some or the evangelizing (proselytizing) itself.

Priorities. The question of dialogue is a question of priority. What should come first, evangelism, dialogue, or church planting? What is the ultimate goal in mission work? How can that goal be best accomplished? These all are questions of priority. Energy may be expended in the wrong way with few results.

Benedetto Croce, the Italian philosopher, illustrates the problem when he points out some reasons for the failure of Protestantism in Italy. He says that Protestant reform was powerless in Italy as an historical movement which tried "to repeat itself artificially out of due time." He sees this as the weakness of Protestantism in the 19th century too:

> The same weakness marked the many efforts which, aided by the Bible societies, more particularly in the decade following 1860, tried to establish throughout Italy either the evangelical churches of other countries, or the Waldensian Church which flourished in a corner of the Alps. That which the sixteenth century failed to accomplish could not be achieved in the nineteenth: but apart from this such efforts were unsuccessful owing to the warring energy and intellectual force of the churches, differing and disunited and all more or less deeply impregnated with modern rationalism, so much so that they were often allied with freemasonry, which was then being revived in Italy, with members being in many cases masons (Croce 1929:66).

Weaknesses pointed out by Croce, as well as others, may still be found in Evangelism in Italy today. In the chapters which follow I shall attempt suggestions relevant to the present challenges for Church and Mission Agencies in Italy today.

18

The Relevant Church

THEOLOGY

Italian Evangelicalism has produced no original theological expression of recent vintage. The writings of Americans and other Europeans have been translated. Possibly because they were imported rather than domestic these have not enjoyed wide acceptance. The very presence of foreign theological words may militate against indigenous development. Ideally even an immature Church should be developing some original articulation of theology. Peter Wagner make this one of the marks of the relevant Church (1970).

Denominational destinctives. Theology should be developed that is relevant to the people. It should not be imported. Church distinctives should fit the environment rather than carry over from the sending Church (Wagner 1970b). The Italian Church that is a near carbon copy of the American Church is probably not relevant to its own culture.

"Church-planters should expect that indigenous churches themselves will produce a multiplicity of structures and leadership patterns" (Tippett 1969:151). Missionaries may need to let some of their traditions go. They may have to content themselves with teaching the Bible minus their own cultural over-hang.

(1) Name. One tradition which missionaries in Italy possibly should be willing to sacrifice is the denominational name. It has rich significance for the missionary, but may be devoid of meaning to the Italian. McGavran says this about American or European missionaries:

> They think of their younger Churches as Episcopal, Free Methodist, Disciple, or Friends. They forget that Churches

> which have arisen through any given mode of growth are much more like each other than like their founding denominations...A Lutheran Church in India, which arises by gathering in famine orphans and occasional converts, will resemble a Baptist Church there which arose in the same way much more than it will the Lutheran Church of Germany or Minnesota (1970:74).

Luzzi a good many years ago lamented over the fragmented Evangelical testimony in Italy. His feeling that names like Methodist, Baptist, Brethren were meaningless to the Italians is expressed by many today. To speak of "Churches" seems foreign to those accustomed to the idea "that the true Church is one" (Luzzi 1913:237). Luzzi wished that foreign workers had said,

> We want to bring the Gospel to Italy; but we will not transplant...our names and our ecclesiastical organizations; we will not make a kaleidoscopic reproduction of our religious denominationalism in Italy. We shall work there not a Methodist, Episcopalian,...or as Baptists, or as Plymouth Brethren, but simply as evangelists, as missionaries. We shall give Christ and the Gospel back to Italy; and the Church shall have but one name: that of the Evangelical Church of Italy...(1913:238).

Luzzi's wish may have been naive, but expresses the fact that Italians fail to appreciate the heritage of our names imported from without. Denominational labels such as "Baptist" may have a rich, historical significance to the missionary, but not to the Italian. Missionaries who are uncompromising Baptists (or Nazarenes or anything else) can still teach the truth as they are convinced it should be taught without tacking the label on the Italian Church. Which is more important: to be Baptistic, or the have the name? Custom may vary in individual cases. The point is flexibility. The purpose is an Italian Church, not an American or German or English one.

(2) Government. More difficult than surrendering the name would be dropping a particular form of church government. Baptists and Independents believe in a democratic form of government. It is a system which has proved itself in England and in New England. Democracy, however, is new to Italians. They are not yet convinced that it will work for the State, let alone for the Church. Decisions are not made individually so much as in groups. But that is not necessarily democracy. In Italy each group has an authority figure. It is not surprising that the same persons will ask over and over, "But who is the head of your Church?" There must be some chief, other than Christ. Church government by autocratic rule may

not be congregational, but it is congenial to Italy. Rules of conduct, formal organization, and church constitutions, all of which may seem important to an American, may be unnecessary baggage to Italian Church life.

(3) Indigeneity. Perhaps the discussion of the indigenous Church should take place at this level rather than around the three "selfs". That is the opinion of William Smalley who writes in *Practical Anthropology* on "Cultural Implications of an Indigenous Church" (1958:51-65). Ingredients of an indignous Church, to Smalley, include merely society and the Holy Spirit. He defines the indigenous Church as a group of believers living out their life in the patterns of the local society, for whom any transformation of that society comes out of their felt needs under the guidance of the Holy Spirit and the Scriptures. Such a Church may be different from that known by the missionaries. Yet here is the indigenous principle. The Gospel, being supracultural, fits into each culture in a different mold. The missionary should be a source rather than an obstacle. Social change should come from the group. The Church is to decide concerning the use of wine despite the feelings of the missionary and his constituency. The non-Italian missionary cannot expect to start an Italian Church. By preaching and winning he can plant something that may grow into an Italian Church. Indigenous churches will result from the interaction of the Italians.

Our American denominations have been the result of a great deal of indigenous "American" expression. We must now be willing to allow the indigenous expression of the Church in the Italian culture. We should be very hesitant about imposing American concepts and patterns such as constitutions, committees, conferences. To do so may be to short-circuit the indigenous Church. Instead of "indigenizing" our plans and practices, we should be discovering what it means to be Italian. As Nida points out, Churches may have the characteristics which the missionaries feel they must have to be indigenous and still not really fit within their own society (1960:221). Perhaps certain Italian Churches are best when they insist that women must cover their heads and that men and women must be seated separately in services. Other practices which commend themselves particularly suited to the Italian setting include frequent communion (at least every Sunday), feet washing (the Pope does it at least once a year), baptism by immersion, and the love feast. These should all be considered in developing a culturally relevant Evangelical Church that is distinctly Italian. Substitutes for Catholic festivals, holidays, and rites should be developed. The ministry of healing should not be neglected. Services of prayer and anointing for the sick as well as of exorcism seem to commend themselves.

Relevant doctrines. An anthropologically sound Church develops those doctrines which are most meaningful to its situations. In addition to the standard doctrines found in a systematic theology, a number of areas need special emphases.

(1) Idolatry. Protestants in Italy feel particularly strongly about idolatry. Polemics are often engaged in at this point. To my knowledge, however, a well-thought out contemporary theology dealing with idolatry has yet to be produced.

(2) Eschatology and angelology. Animistic tendencies found in Italy demand that demonology be carefully developed by an Italian theologian familiar with spiritism as it is practiced in Italy today. A clear exposition of life after death is likewise needed by converts from Catholicism and superstition. Eschatology that is relevant will not concern itself with the tribulation but with Satan and the after-life.

(3) Salvation. The concept of Grace is extremely important for the Catholic convert. But for the Italian it is equally essential that he realize his salvation as a victory over death and the Devil. Tippett speaks of this as power encounter.

> The works of the devil have to be destroyed. Sinful man is bound. Christ came to unloose him. In the verse from John's letter the phrase may be translated "in order that he might unloosen" or "untie"...implying a new state of freedom. In the words of Jesus cited above we have a neat play on the encounter of powers. I have given you (perfect tense) power-with-authority...over the power...of the enemy (Tippett 1969:89).

The power of Pentecostalism is found no doubt at least in part in its preaching of such a power encounter as part of the conversion experience. Other points of theology should be developed in terms of the needs in Italy rather than of those of Switzerland, Germany and England.

SELFHOOD

The Italian Church to be a truly indigenous Church must have a full sense of selfhood. Tippett states this doctrine in six marks of the indigenous Church (1969:133-136).

(1) Self-image. The Church sees itself as the Church of Christ locally. Pentecostals in Italy have achieved a strong identity. They feel that they are the true Body of

Christ in Italy. The Brethren too seem to have achieved a similar sense. The same is certainly true of the Churches of Christ.

(2) Self-functioning. The Church achieves organic growth through the participation of its members. It does not rely on mission-paid personnel, but provides for "its own worship services, Bible study groups, prayer meetings, and classes for Christian education (Tippett 1969:134).

(3) Self-determining. The Church is not controlled by the mission, directly of indirectly. "The only authority a missionary retains in a truly indigenous Church is the authority of the office to which the nationals appoint him" (Tippett 1969:134). Has any Church in Italy presently related to any mission organization become self-determining?

(4) Self-supporting. The Evangelicals of Italy have tended to rely on outside aid for some of their projects and institutions. Even the venerable Waldensians have, understandably, been the recipients of aid. Amazingly the poor and persecuted Pentecostals seem to have come farther than the rest in complete self-support.

(5) Self-propagating. Pentecostals are engaged in spontaneous expansion. The Brethren likewise engage in projects of evangelism. At least one Italian serves as a missionary in Africa under the Sudan Interior Mission. No Italian organization exists for fulfilling the Great Commission. Wasdensian missionary efforts of the past were devoted to Italian colonies.

(6) Self-giving. If institutions such as orphanages are a measure, then most Italian Churches are self-giving. If it means the direct involvement by local congregations in deeds of mercy it may still be judged a self-giving Church.

In each case the Italian Church should be judged by Italian standards according to Italian culture.

HYMNOLOGY

A Church that feels itself to be The Church will generally express its faith and aspirations in singing. Indigeneity should express itself at this point. The theology of a people should be reflected in its hymnology. Both theology and hymnology should be Biblically and culturally sound. The hymnology should complement the theology. In actuality hymnology may reveal the lack of theological indigeneity. Tippett states that in the Western Solomons "the Christian hymns have been the dominant formative for popular belief" (1967:286). Tippett relates that the weakest point in the hymnody (Holy Spirit) proved also the most vulnerable point for a major deviation.

A glance at the contemporary state of Italian hymnody reveals some disarray. The old *Innario Cristiano* in use by most denominations is not a fully balanced collection. Unfortunately it omits Brethren hymns. The Brethren hymnal, on the other hand, is poorly arranged. It is not theological but "doctrinal", emphasizing Brethren peculiarities. *Alleluia* is an interesting collection largely of translations by Enrico Paschetto who, unfortunately, will not share them for general publication. The Pentecostal hymnals are the poorest of all: ver foreign, poor translations, no theological classifications, very one-sided with American Gospel songs. *Celebriamo Il Signore* is a poor attempt to satisfy all in a limited collection containing too many American choruses and too few traditional Italian hymns. It introduces a few new songs, but it is an American attempt.

The greatest problem is that missionaries fail to appreciate Italian hymnody (which they do not know, learn, like, or use) and substitute choruses and Gospel songs, sometimes in poor translations.

A contemporary hymn idiom has yet to be developed. This is important for the life of the Church and for its theology.

> Hymn collections are so formative in developing the character of an emerging Christian community that they should be systematically planned from the start and not grow haphazardly (Tippett 1967:291).

When hymnology is weak in certain areas, systematic enrichment should be encouraged. Chorus and Gospel singing has a definite place in warm-hearted Italian evangelicalism. The acceptance and use of "O Che Beato" (Heaven Came Down) bears witness to this fact. It is regretable that the little collections of songs and choruses that spring up do not produce much that is original to fill in the weaker areas. A planned program of translation of singable hymns from a theological perspective could serve to enrich the religious life of believers and strengthen the theology and worship of the Church. The program should be Italian. Budding musicians should be cultivated and encouraged to write for the honor of Christ and the Evangelical Church.

MATURITY

A relevant Church is a mature Church. Maturity, however, is difficult to measure. It has to do with that intangable, inner growth, as well as with numerical increase. Those two elements do not necessarily go together. All I can do, therefore, is suggest a few areas which seem to suggest maturity.

A growing Church. Mere church planting is inadequate. Needen are churches that will multiply and grow. Enns, studying the Churches of Argentina, makes an interesting comparison of Churches typed according to religious temperament. His classifications seem applicable in Italy. Type one Churches are described as dogmatic, fanatical, reactionary. He includes here the Pentecostals and Adventist who account for over half the Protestants of the country. Type two are the traditional conservatives -- those of strong convictions, but moderate, conservative. The third class consists of Churches that are tolerant, liberal, progressive - such as the Lutherans and Methodist (Enns 1967:230). It is obvious that the first group gets the most growth, the last, least. Pentecostals, Adventists, the Churches of Christ, and possibly the Brethren fit the first category in Italy. The Waldenses, Methodists and Baptists of the third group are largely static. In between are most of the Mission oriented groups and the Missions themselves. The conservatives should be making better gains.

The example of church growth in Argentina given by Enns of his own group includes four features worthy of contemplation in terms of Italy.

> What have been the characteristics of the Conservative Baptists whose churches, although young, show remarkable growth? Probably the most outstanding feature of their work is the extensive evangelistic itineration, always seeking to establish new churches....
> A second feature...has be the missionaries' rigid dedication to the classic expression of the indigenous principle of no financial subsidies. This principle created unusually difficult circumstances for the small groups of Christians in the cities where facilities for meetings were available only at exorbidantly high costs in rent... Approximately half of the total 50 churches have been able to purchase property and are building their own meeting places.
> A third characteristic of this work has been their emphasis on lay leadership. The baptisms and serving of the Lord's Supper are administered by these unordained laymen.

> The preaching is also largely their responsibility and privilege. These men are the pastors of the churches.... Another feature...is the emphasis on training broadly. Every church is conceived of as a Bible School with emphasis on public Bible study and individual correspondence type courses...Through this emphasis on study in the local church, several have felt the need for further studies in the Bible Institute. (Enns 1967:136-137).

Church growth principles. Since the goal is the rapid growth of the Church which results from winning large numbers from the world to Christ as Savior and Lord, the highest priority is to bear in mind and act upon principles which make for good growth. The modern apostle of church growth si Donald McGavran whose many writings relate to this subject. To one of his articles we turn for a summary of church growth principles in six points (cGavran 1966b:770-771).

(1) "Increase evangelism everywhere", especially among growing churches.

(2) "Multiply unpaid leaders among the new converts". Train them to go and communicate Christ to relatives, neighbors, and fellow workers.

(3) Take full advantage of the insights offered through anthropology, sociology, and psychology.

(4) "Evangelize responsive populations to the utmost". Missionaries should go not merely to "work among" a responsive population, but to multiply churches. They should be trained in how to multiply ever more churches in that kind of receptive people.

(5) Strive for multi-individual decisions. Without lessening the emphasis on individual salvation, seek the joint decision of many persons within the society at one time.

(6) "Carry on extensive research in church growth."

Christian social action. Italian Evangelicalism seems in great need of a strong theology of church growth. Traditional denominations have shifted from a clear evangelistic emphasis to ecumenical and social concerns. Evangelism is either eliminated or redefined. At this point Italy shares a common problem with Latin America where the older denominations have largely stopped growing. Peter Wagner describes the Church worker of the non-growing denomination:

> Finding little satisfaction in throwing himself entirely into unfruitful evangelism or church extension, he looks for another exciting cause, such as the revolution, into which he can divert his energies (1970:69).

Social action and ecumenical endeavor have been substituted for the winning of the lost. The old denominations have lost their first love.

It is not that social concern should be forgotten. The Evangelicals of Italy should be concerned over the evils which exist. However it is a concern of the Church, not of the missions. Missionaries are guests in the country. As McGavran states, "It should not be mission policy to foment rebellions among the masses and thus help them to achieve political, economic, and cultural goals" (1970:257). The Church, however, is in the midst, and cannot avoid the struggle. The problem is balance. It is not "either-or" but "both-and". As Wagner says, "The issue is how to balance the evangelistic, soul-saving ministry over against the social activities of the church" (1970:103). The liberals have gone off on one side, over-emphasizing social action and denying the Gospel. Fundamentalists have sttod so firmly on the other end that they have denied the power of the Gospel. Social action must not become a substitute for the Gospel or for evangelism. But it is a needed expression of true Christianity.

The greatest task of the Church is the preaching of the Gospel. As Wagner states, this announcing of the "kerygma" is to yet another end:

> The objective, according to the Great Commission, is to 'make disciples' and 'baptize them,' which indicates that they should become members of the Church (1970:105).

In the Church those who have been won enjoy "koinonia" or Christian fellowship. Fellowship, however, is not passive. "Koinonia serves to prepare believers to take their places in the centrifugal movement of kerygma" (Wagner 1970:105). In other words, the Church comes together in order to go out for Christian service and for further evangelism. The Church gathers in order to scatter. Christian service as part of the scattering is not the same as evangelism. Nor is it necessarily for the purpose of evangelism. It is the expression of Christian love. "It seems that, biblically speaking, loving one's neighbor should not be considered as a means to an end. Love carries no price tag" (Wagner 1970:107).

How is Christian social action to be expressed adequately by the relatively small Evangelical Church in Italy?

The answer would seem to be in the multiplication of churches. McGavran says:

> When churches multiply in a non-Christian population, they will bring Gods purposes for His children to bear on the particular part of the social order which they can influence (1970:258).

Church growth is the solution. McGavran gives several illustrations showing how Christians, when they became numerous enough, were able to effect changes in their society:

> Not only will individual Christians take part in such social action, but again and again whole congregations and denominations, as in the days of Abolition and Prohibition, will act for righteousness (1970:258).

Many of the evils in Italian life could probably be corrected if there were enough Christians to influence change in the laws, the end of corruption, etc. The Evangelicals are generally respected as honest law-abiding people. The multiplication of churches means the multiplication of Evangelical Christians which means an increased influence for good in Italy. "There should be no tension between mission and the advocates of social action" (McGavran 1970:258).

Aggressive plans for the rapid multiplication of churches should have priority in mission effort today. This calls for a strong theology of church growth.

God wills, not the "Christianizing of the social order" but the discipling of men. Mission is defined narrowly by McGavran as:

> An enterprise devoted to proclaiming the Good News of Jesus Christ, and to persuading men to become His disciples and dependable members of His Church (1970:34).

Not proclamation, but persuasion. Evangelism is not really evangelism until it wins. Growth of the Church is part of God's will. "Todays' paramount task", says McGavran, "is to multiply churches in the increasing numbers of receptive peoples of the earth" (1970:63).

In practicality this means that Italian Churches and Missions need to discover those areas most responsive to the Evangelical message and then take steps to see that growing churches are planted there. The examples of others should be studied. Latin America speaks to Italy. Pentecostal successes should be analyzed by all.

For theology it implies that the Scriptures should be searched for the revelation that God wills the expansion of His Church, that His Spirit empowers and bestows gifts for the growth and ongoing of the Church, that He wills in fact the winning of large segments of population to Himself. A Biblical search for a theology of evangelism and for ecclesiology by Italians may uncover Biblical patterns and norms which are much closer to Italian culture than are the imported plans and theories of American and European missionaries.

A maturing Church, then, will find ways to express its faith in society. A culturally relevant and Biblically sound plan for Christian social action will not, however, displace evangelism as the supreme task of the Church. Christians are to be involved in society. The Church is to spread the even of the Gospel by winning responsive segments of society to obedience in Christ. Church growth is the primary goal.

SOCIAL PROBLEMS

The role of the Church in social action has been touched upon as a necessary expression of Christian love. Social problems are a Christian concern. Although service is not equated with evangelism, it is part of Christian witness.

Anthropologically social problems are the concern of the Church, not of the Mission. The Church works from within the culture, as part of Italian society. The Mission comes from without the culture and at best can only advocate a degree of change. Making an effort at change the total program of the Mission would be a mistake, for change must come from within. The outsider may encourage change, but he should expect that when change comes it may be quite different from the original model. The solution to Italy's political woes, for instance, is not in adopting the American system. The solution must be Italian. This bears on church growth, for if missionaries advocate a change which if adopted makes the Italian convert appear a quasi-American, the result is ostracism and isolation and a stunted church growth. That is, individuals may be called out of the Italian society, but large groups will not follow. The Evangelical Church will appear non-Italian, and what Italian could be expected to be attracted to that? Possibly it would appeal to the rejects of society, but hardly to the masses of ordinary people. Perhaps this is one reason much missionary effort has brought scant results. I once heard an Aversa Evangelical testify of her accepting the Gospel as "listening to what the Americans had to say"!

Anthropologist Barnett charges that missionaries are sometimes the aggressive preservers "of the traditions of their homelands" (1953:310). Are we missionaries sometimes unwittingly guilty of trying to make converts over into our image? If so we are stepping out of our proper role. Church growth will not take place.

The missionary should remember his role to be that of advocate, not innovator. Tippett says, "The people themselves are the acceptors or rejectors of the advocated innovation" (1967:86). In Italian society and in the Church it should be kept in mind that "the converts and not the missionaries are the real innovators" (Tippett 1967:87). Change may be advocated in two areas: in the Church and in the world or society in general. In the former the individual missionary should exercise restraint. In the second the mission must exercise caution. The Church, not the missionary, can institute change. Society can be acted upon from within, by Christians and the Church, not by the mission.

The type of advocacy in the realm of the mission's responsibility is evangelism, persuading men to follow Christ. Social action is the responsibility of the Church, the brotherhood of believers. A number of the pressing issues in Italy today which effect the growth of the Church are as follows.

(1) The Political Problem. Communism is not the number one political problem. It is the Italian government itself, corrupt and bureaucratic. Politicians and the bureaucracy are denounced by nearly everyone. The government seems helpless in the face of crippling strikes and demonstrations. Office holders abuse their position for personal gain, while the ordinary person suffers. These people, with a grievance, express their protest by voting Communist (Fromm 1969:69). This claim by an Italian sociologist is corroborated by my own observation.

(2) The Economic Problem. In the South unemployment is widespread especially among young men. Poverty is extreme and common. A sociologist claimed that an economic revolution is taking place, but that the government has been unable to handle it. Schools, homes, hospitals are inadequate despite "dynamic industrial expansion" (Fromm 1969:70).

The economic miracle is related to the influx of rural people from the impoverished South to the cities. Rome has increased from one million to three. Turin from 400,000 to over a million. In Turin and Milan the miracle has been happening. To such cities as well as to Naples and Bari the workers have come. "In a little over 10 years, 6 million people...(Fromm

1969:70).

(3) Urbanization. The influx of people is said to be a major element in the unrest of the cities where it is causing a social explosion. The political and economic situations are tied up in this move to the cities. Here is a people in a state of unrest.

The Italian situation is not unique. Urbanization is upon most of the world to some degree. It has many ramifications for the Church. How can men be discipled to Christ in the secular city? One part of the world that seems somewhat parallel to Italy is Latin America. From the context of Brazil a churchman writes concerning a Church that can be relevant in the urban setting.

> The religious group that seems better adjusted structurally to the new situation si the Pentecostal. Its leaders are intuitively aware of the anomic conditions of those who come to the metropolis pressed by well-known problems and uprooted from their rural milieu. They offer immediate answers to these people's expectations and anxieties: a sense of belonging to a community of fellow-sufferers, new values to reshape the meaning of life and a useful God (Sapezian 1969:154-155).

Sapezian then criticizes the Pentecostals for "otherworldliness". In other words he sees them as properly structured but actually quite useless. One wonders if such criticism is not untrue of a growing church. By its very growth it demonstrates its virility in changing men's lives. Pentecostals in Italy have become the largest non-Catholic Church and are growing among these very people.

Urbanization is a continuing fact of life. Five years ago it was reported that less than one fourth of the population was in the countryside, and that about a fifth lived in the largest cities, with the remainder in the smaller cities and villages (Salvadori 1965:5). The rural percentage is probably lower today and the larger city proportion considerably more. Some areas have reached a population density of 2,000 per square mile.

(4) Emigration. Not all relocation was toward the cities. Many emigrated overseas. Emigration from Italy has taken place in large numbers throughout the century sporadically. In the post-War years emigration overseas averaged 42,000 annually, much lower than before the war (Dickinson 1955:9). Around the turn of the century entire areas are said to have been practically depopulated as the desperate condi-

tions forced the inhabitants to leave. By December 31, 1924, an official Italian government report shows that 8,385,739 Italians were resident in North and South America (De Michesis 1926:264-265).

The immigrant was open to new ideas. "For him imigration meant being born again....Such emigrants were very receptive to evangelical propaganda" (Cassin 1959:166). In the New World Protestant efforts to evangelize the Italians met with degrees of success and failure not known to us today. There are hints, however, that they were effective. A Catholic publication in Milwaukee is reported to have estimated in 1913 that a million Italians had already been lost to the Church. Many had simply abandoned all faith, "but an impressive minority go over to the various evangelical denominations, forming Italian congregations even in many small communities of the country (Foerster 1924:398).

Luigi Francescon was one who left his native Udine in 1890 for the United States. There he was converted, and in 1909 left Chicago with a Pentecostal friend to witness in Argentina among relatives and friends there. This was the beginning of Pentecostal work among the Italians of Argentina. Francescon's great work, however, was to be in Brazil where he arrived in 1910. The result of his ministry in Parana and San Paolo was the Brazilian Pentecostal denomination known as the Congregacao Crista which today numbers around a half million members. Today the founder is retired in Chicago where he has begun another church among his Italians in that city (Read 1965:25).

Thousands of emigrants did not remain abroad. For various reasons they returned to the *patria*. Among the returnees were converts to the Evangelical faith who, upon return, arrived at the evangelization of the Catholic masses. In the years of confusion following World War I, the converts and the missionaries toured the South making new converts -- Adventists, Pentecostals, Brethren, Baptists (Cassin 1959:167).

One who returned in 1908 was converted in an Italian Pentecostal Church in Chicago. He was instrumental in beginning several small communities in Calabria, the Abruzzi, and Rome. Response was especially good in Sicily and the South "where economic and social unrest associated with the poverty of those areas afforded fertil soil to a movement which here as elsewhere won adherents chiefly among the under-privileged and from lower educational and economic levels" (Latourette 1969:371-372). The work of Lombardi and his fellow returnees was effective and lasting. The Assemblies of God today form the largest denomination in Italy.

Historically migration has been important for the spread of the Gospel among Italians -- in Brazil, Argentina, Chicago, Sicily. Anthropologically the pattern of response indicates the significance of racial, linguistic, family, and cultural ties. McGavran's comment seems pertinent:

> It must be emphasized that in San Paulo, during the years 1910 to 1962 the Methodists, Baptists, Lutherans, and Presbyterians were strong. Only a very small number of the responsive Italians, however, became Evangelicals in these well established, Portuguese speaking denominations, each with notable mission schools and colleges buttressing it. Among other reasons, unquestionably one was this, that to become Evangelicals in any of these four Churches, Italians would have to cross linguistic and class barriers and leave their own community (McGavran 1970:206).

Migration (as opposed to emigration) still takes place today. Some emigration is still going on, mainly to Australia, South America, and Canada. Much more migration takes place within Italy. There is also a good deal of temporary emigration to other European countries for work. This sociological phenomenon is significant for church growth. Not only can the Church speak to this problem, but this is an opportunity for effectively offering the Hope of the Gospel. People in flux tend to be responsive. This has been proven concerning the emigrant. Barriers have been broken: he can respond.

Today potential is high. An indication is seen in the returning laborers who have been contacted either by Jehovahs' Witnesses or Christians. I have met more than one person who was completely open to the Gospel following the initial contact in Switzerland or Germany.

More than meeting the returning worker, there is a need to follow the migrant within the country. Italy is a heterogeneous society. Southerners are a different race from Northerners. Language, customs, attitudes differ widely. Therefore the Calabrian or the Sicilian or the Neopolitan migrating to Milan for work will not become a Milanese. His loyalties are to the South -- to his family which is Southern. His associations in the North will still be Southern. Uprooted, he is ripe for the Gospel. He will not, however, be very easily reached by the Northern Italian Church. Family closeness may well be the bridge for this man's salvation. Acceptance of the Gospel when it comes through Southern Italian channels will be in the form of innovation from within due to advocacy from within. In other words, to follow their people who move to the industrial North. Instead of referring them to Northern Churches this should be taken as an opportunity for Church extension in the new settlement by the Churches and missions of the South.

(5) Amoral familism. A fascinating sociological study of a typical poverty stricken village of Calabria is entitled *The Moral Basis of a Backward Society*. The term "amoral familism", used to characterize the Southern peasant, is described by the author as a rule of life:

> "Maximize the material, short-run advantage of the nuclear family; assume that all others will do likewise." One whose behavior is consistent with this rule will be called an "amoral familist"...(one who follows the rule is without morality only in relation to persons outside the family -- in relation to family members, he applies standards of right and wrong; one who has no family is of course an "amoral industrialist")....(Banfield 1958: 85).

The problem of the *Mezzogiorno* (Southern Italy) is old and complex. Programs for improvement, such as the *Cassa del Mezzogiorno* (fund for the South), have not been very effective. Charges of corruption are frequently heard. Excessive bureaucracy in Rome is said to eat up the funds before they reach their designation. The South is a demoralized society. Corruption is expected. It is assumed that officials will be thieves. All of this is related to what Banfield calls "amoral familism" which may be a major reason for the failure of programs and plans to alleviate the problems of the South.

The Southerner follows a philosophy of "each family for itself, and each one for his family". The private citizen takes no interest in public problems. They are no concern of his. Officials are paid to concern themselves with public affairs, and they are the only onew who will do so. Such concern on the part of a private individual would be considered "abnormal and even improper" (Banfield 1958:87). Office holders, on the other hand, have no personal identification with their duties, and will do only what is necessary to keep their positions or earn promotions. There is no sense of mission on the part of educated and professional people. (Banfield 1958:91).

It follows that in such a society there are neither leaders nor followers (Banfield 1958:91). The weak will favor "a regime which will maintain order with a strong hand" (Banfield 1958:96). This perhaps explains the popular support for the Fascist regime. I have heard many remember nostalgically the law and order days of Mussolini. Discontent with the ineffective present government stems from this fact. When the possibility of a coupe is discussed, it is generally with a view toward a "strong" central government. In other words the desire is for an authority to make the decisions for everyone. Democracy has not yet proven itself in Italy where the strong-man concept prevails.

(6) Mafia. Southern Italians are not generally concerned about obedience to the law. A desire for imposed order is not connected to respect for the law. "In a society of amoral familists, the law will be disregarded where there is no reason to fear punishment" (Banfield 1958:92). The Mafia is not a surprising development in this environment. In fact as an extended web relationship of family units, the Mafia seems quite a natural organization. The fact that it is illegal is superflous.

> The Mafia is an outgrowth of centuries of misery and despair, injustice and disappointment in one's fellow man generated by a loss of confidence in oneself as a man (Schachter 1965:65-66).

The Mafia is the product of a demoralized society. It is the perfect expression of Banfield's "amoral familism", maximizing the material, immediate advantage of the nuclear family and assuming that all others will do the same. Its immensity accounts for its power. Its durability comes from its secretive nature which is insured by the fact that it is a family organization. The various extended families composing its membership are related to each other through marriage.

In operation the Mafia may do "favors" for the peasant or for the padrone. The recipient is then bound to the Mafia for life. It is a logical Italian outcome. I have been informed that a similar system prevails outside of Sicily, reaching into the offices of the central government in Rome. The system of recommendations for securing jobs is based on precisely the same principle of securing and dispensing favors.

Those who study the situation in the Mezzogiorno are of a mind that there must be change. Change, however, seems unlikely. Greatly needed are broader self-interests, the development of some leaders, a tolerance toward organization, a new attitude toward work and more public services. Sociologists are generally pessimistic toward the outcome.

(7) Illiteracy. Banfield in his research of the municipal records of a typical town in the province of Potenza

in the year 1954 found that of the persons 21 years of age and over 48.9% had less than an elementary school education (in other words, were illiterate). 47.9% had completed the fifth grade, and only 1.2% had gone through Middle school (6-8 grades), and 2% had gone on to complete university training (Banfield 1958:179). Banfield's finding are presented in figure 28.

Figure 29 illustrates further the degree of illiteracy according to class in the same town in 1951. The age group 10-39 is covered.

Illiteracy has been widespread. The situation has been improving since the time of Banfield's work. Banfield's sample from 1951 showed an average of 29% illiteracy for all classes in the 10-39 age bracket for that one village. It is assumed that "Montegrano" was truely typical as reported. More recently it has been reported that one fifth of the population is illiterate in South Italy (Schachter 1965:77). That is a small improvement. It may be questioned whether the problem will be decreased very rapidly. For "while the Italian constitution prescribes that every child must go to school through the age of fourteen, a substantial number of people ignore the dictum" (Schachter 1965:77). My own observation concurs. Again the phenomenon of amoral familism takes over: who is to enforce the law?

(8) A way out. Students of the situation are gloomy in outlook. Needed change seems very dima dn distant. Banfield shares this pessimism, but he does suggest one possible effective agent of change: Protestant missionary activity!

> The change in outlook that is needed might conceivably come as the by-product of Protestant missionary activity. There is little prospect, however, that Protestants will be permitted to proselyte in southern Italy (Banfield 1958:171).

Banfield need not have been so pessimistic as to the possibility of Protestant activity. It may be that he was simply unaware of such activity in various parts of the South. At any rate he was wrong. Pentecostals and others have been active, and evangelistic efforts have brought change and hope into the lives of many. Mission activity has been quite acceptable when coming through the Italian people themselves. It has also been most effective under such circumstances.

Another dynamic at work changing the patterns of the South is urbanization. Nida suggests that this is where change

(figure 28)

AMOUNT OF EDUCATION
(HIGHEST GRADE COMPLETED),
PERSONS 21 YEARS OF AGE AND OVER,
*MONTEGRANO, 1954

less than elementary		elementary school (5 grades)		middle school (grades 6-8)		university		all	
No.	%	No.	%	No.	%	No.	%	No.	%
(males) 299	32.7	568	62.1	21	2.3	27	2.9	915	100
(females) 681	62.4	393	36.0	3	.3	14	1.3	1091	100
(all) 980	48.9	961	47.9	24	1.2	41	2.0	2006	100

*(Montegrano is a fictional name)

Source: Banfield, 1958: 179

FIGURE 28

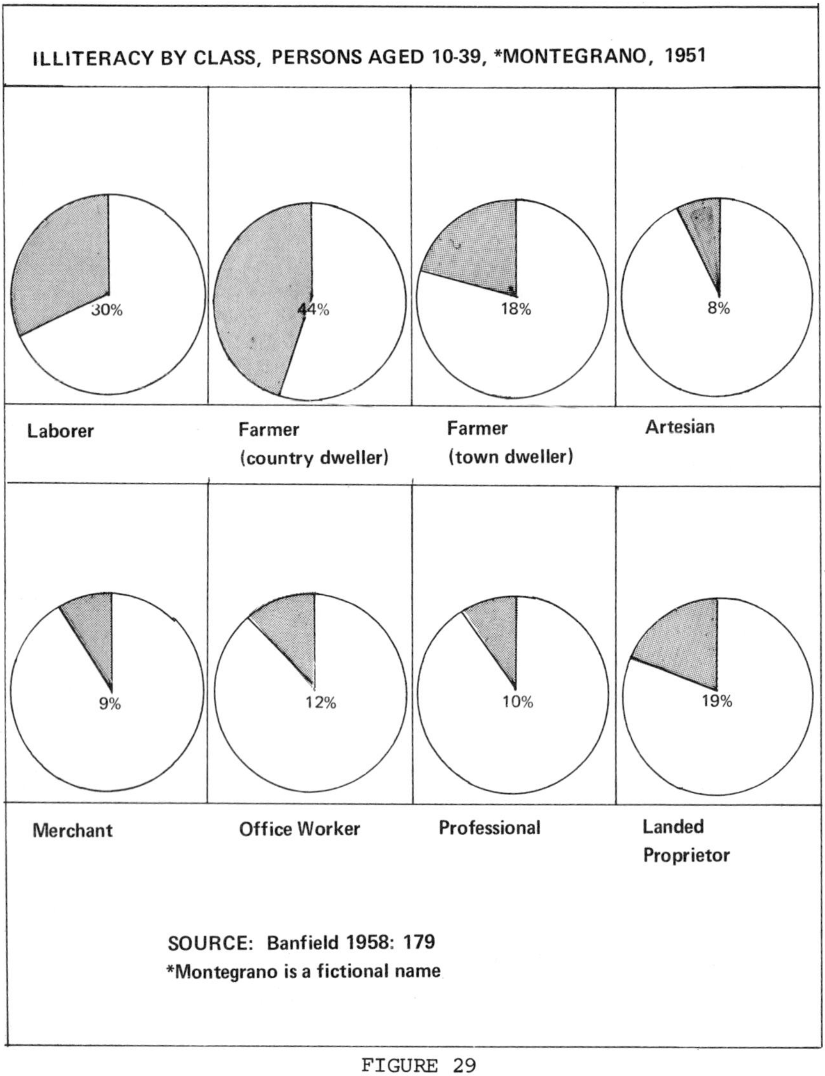
ILLITERACY BY CLASS, PERSONS AGED 10-39, *MONTEGRANO, 1951
30%
44%
18%
8%
Laborer
Farmer (country dweller)
Farmer (town dweller)
Artesian
9%
12%
10%
19%
Merchant
Office Worker
Professional
Landed Proprietor
SOURCE: Banfield 1958: 179
*Montegrano is a fictional name

FIGURE 29

really takes place. For such people are on the rise. "It is in this group that one usually finds a number of highly intellegent rebels who are determined to change their world" (Nida 1965:189). These individuals, if Nida is correct, would be the key persons to be evangelized. They are the keys to the larger group only, however, if they are still in contact with the masses from which they are arising. If they are unattached rebels, bohemians, they may prove a dead-end street (this fact apparently eludes Nida). Careful evaluation should be made at this point before setting a strategy for evangelism. A plan based on reaching the wrong strategy will prove abortive.

LAY MINISTRY

The Problem. A perpetual problem for church planting and evangelism is a dirth of workers. The starting of new churches, among the mission groups, has been largely in the hands of foreign missionaries who continue to function as the spiritual leaders of the developing groups of believers. That has been the pattern, for instance, of the Conservative Baptists. Therefore starting new churches only compounds the problem as it ties the available workers (missionaries) down even more.

An attempted solution is to hire nationals to serve as pastors of the churches that have bben started or to actually begin the new church groups. This is inefficient. It merely broadens the base a little. Instead of a fairly fixed number of missionaries to serve a certain number of churches, you have a slightly larger number of missionaries and nationals to serve an enlarged by still limited number of churches. Church growth is limited to the number of workers available.

A further complication is added in that all of these workers must be supported. Expansion is further restricted to the availability of funds. National workers assumed have in some instances had to deputate among the churches of Italy to raise support, much in the fashion of missionary support in North America.

The problem is more than a shortage of personnel. It is partly the result of following a traditional Protestant pattern for the ministry. In Europe and in North America it is customary for churches to support a full-time professional pastor. It is natural for missionaries coming out of a background where this system is widely employed, apparently successfully, to duplicate it. The practice of the traditional Protestant Churches of Italy is the same. Churches are cared for by full-time, seminary trained pastors.

The question is whether the traditional system is best for church growth in Italy. A certain amount of growth is possible, ceratinly. But growth will be limited to the number of professionals available. Therefore the traditional pattern must be questioned. It is not conducive to growth. Another pattern should be found. The development of a lya ministry is one pattern which commends itself as a solution.

Discovering Resources. Merle Davis years ago recognized this need.

> Unless the latent energy and motivations of a congregation are aroused, the powers of a majority of the members may never be discovered nor harnessed to the progress of a church. Ironically enough, an active deterrent to lay activity in a younger church may be the energy of a missionary or national pastor. The missionary or pastor finds awaiting him in a church many challenging tasks which need immediate attention. It is difficult to see how he can relate his laymen to them. He himself has been trained to do these things...(Davis 1947:134).

The missionary or the pastor must be willing to step out of the way. This requires humility. He must acknowledge that the Holy Spirit has given His gifts to all of the Church. The pastor or missionary does not possess all the gifts. They have been given sovereignly by the Spirit to each member of the Body. In every little community of believers the gifts are present. Even the most simple believer has been give some gift. Taken together these gifts are sufficient for the ongoing of the Church. This must be true of each local group of believers, when they are truly a gathering of believers. If this be so, the missionary or professional pastor should be able to step out of the local group and still see the group progress. It takes faith to dare to step out. Where a pattern of dependency has been set, time will be needed to educate and then allow dormant gifts to begin to function. This step must be taken, however, to begin to uncover the resources for growth.

Here is an endless supply (at least so long as there is evangelism). The laity in some cases is a virtually untapped resource. Every congregation, be it of 5 or 50, contains potential leadership. The present imposed leadership must acknowledge this fact before the power can be released.

The changing Roman Catholic Church recognizes the importance of the laity. Pope Paul in introducing the "Decree on the Apostolate of the Laity" at Vatican II spoke of the "spontaneous and fruitful...activity" of the laity of the early Church, and declared: "Our own times require of the laity no less zeal" (Abbott 1966:489-490). "The Layman's Call to the Apostolate" rang clear. Speaking of the teaching and ruling duty of the apostles, the Pope declared the "diversity of service but unity of purpose" in the Church (Abbott 1966:491).

> But the laity, too, share in the priestly, prophetic, and royal office of Christ and therefore have their own role to play in the mission of the whole People of God in the Church and in the world.
> They exercise a genuine apostolate by their activity on behalf of penetrating and perfecting the temporal sphere of things through the spirit of the gospel. In this way, their temporal activity can openly bear witness to Christ and promote the salvation of men.

The lay apostolate, declared the Pope, includes the announcing of Christ by words as well as the witness of the life. The activity of the laity is so essential to the Church within local communities "that without it the apostolate of the pastors is generally unable to achieve its full effectiveness" (Abbott 1966:500).

Sudden awareness of the importance of the laity by the Roman Catholic Church may surprise many Protestants. The priesthood of all believers is a cardinal distinctive of Protestantism. One would expect to find vast lay participation in Protestant Churches. However such participation is all too often absent in the worship and life of Protestant Churches. This lack is tragic among the Protestants of Italy. Two glorious exceptions as we have seen, are found in the Brethren and the Pentecostals. The former is by nature a "lay" movement in that it has no clergy, although it might be argued that the recognized elders constitute a clergy. Pentecostals by stressing the absolute necessity of witnessing gain the active participation of believers. Little groups of Pentecostals meeting in homes crop up spontaneously. The dynamic of both movements seems to lie largely in its active utilization of the laity.

Arno Enns testifies that the "effective use of the laymen in all aspects of the ministry" is the outstanding feature of the Plymouth Brethren in Argentina where they have become the largest Protestant Church (1967:189).

> ...The fact that there was no mission organization greatly aided the development of this movement. The missionaries did not form or participate in some power

structure that stood over-against the churches and their emerging leaders. They became members of these churches and participated as equals with their Argentine brethren (Enns 1967:190).

Financial help, when given for buildings, was without strings attached. Loyalty was strictly spiritual, not to any outside organization.

Much the same can no doubt be said for Brethren missionary activity in Italy. By its nature the Brethren movement utilizes laymen. Other Evangelical bodies who desire to be effectively evangelistic would do well to emulate this characteristic.

Supplementing the Clergy. The rediscovery of an active role forthe laity is to enable expansion. The need is not so much to discover new candidates for the ministry as to activate the existing evangelical communities. In Latin America when lay leaders already have pastoral and other responsibilities, "the need is not to find and train potential leaders but to train leaders who are already functioning" (Read, Monterosso, and Johnson 1969:333). This need exists in Italy as well, particularly among Pentecostals. For the mission oriented groups, however, there is a need simply to recognize and help equip the passive lay members of the Body.

The rold of the professional clergy (foreign missionary or ordained national) must then shift to that of instructor or trainer. While still engaging in active evangelism, he must be freed to direct local congregations in their self-expression of worship and evangelism. In place of "doing it all himself" he must step back and allow the body of believers full responsibility.

Psychologically this may be difficult for pastors and missionaries who have known a different pattern. It involves a different view of the ministry. Rather than a ministry of the Church. At first the new responsibilities may seem bewildering or overwhelming to laymen who have been mostly recipients. Nevertheless they may discover a new means of grace in meaningful service.

North American laymen have commonly been assigned an inferior role. Today that is changing. Laymen are expressing a "desire to share in the ministry", to be involved in what was once considered "the minister's job". Witnessing, visiting the sick, participating actively in Sunday services: "If the layman cannot perform these jobs, he is being deprived of true

Protestant Christian participation" (Raines 1961:104).

The Church belongs to laymen as much as to clergymen. A person working cross-culturally especially should acknowledge this fact. The Church is "of the people". It is their Church, not the foreigner's, not the mission's. Therefore they should be expected to minister in that Church. A "Church" ministry demands the full participation of all. Clerical distinctions must be forgotten. Southern Baptist missiologist, Calvin Cuy, states it clearly. "...the pastor should be an assistant layman, rather than the layman an assistant pastor" (1965a:209).

Professional leaders have the possibility of multiplying their effectiveness by training lay leaders. Melvin Hodges writes from the rich background of personal experience in effectively planting churches. His denomination has become the largest evangelical Church in a number of Latin American countries and in Italy. To the evangelical Church as a whole he declares, "We are missing a tremendous opportunity for the Kingdom by failing to develop a lay ministry" (1965b:121). Hodges speaks of a pattern which is reproducable indefinitely. The new convert can witness (and is expected to do so). Older Christians help the newer. The pastor assists the deacon, and the missionary the pastors, etc. Might this not be the secret of Pentecostal success? Certainly the believer need not have full knowledge before he begins to witness. To some extent this is true also of teachers. "One who teaches needs to be only one step ahead of those who are taught" (Hodges 1965b: 121).

Role of the Lay Leaders. Corporate and personal witness by the laity is extremely important.

The development of leaders is also essential. Without them the Evangelical Church of Italy will not break out of its rut into a vital, growing force. The gifts of the Spirit must be uncovered. This can be done through action.

(1) According to Roland Allen. Roland Allen in *The Ministry of the Spirit* has a whole section on the "Case for Voluntary Clergy" (1965:135-190). To Allen voluntary clergy are ordained men who "earn their living by the work of their hands or of their heads in the common market, and serve as clergy without stipend or fee of any kind" (1965:147). The "stipendiary system" he sees as suitable "for some settled churches of some periods". But "for expansion, for the establishment of new churches, it is the greatest possible hindrance" (1965:137). Allen feels that no group of Christians, however small, need be without ministers or without the sacraments,

for in the New Testament "the church is never remote from its members. Where the members of the church were, there was the church" (1965:169).

Nor does Allen find the solution to pastoral care in a "circuit" ministry. Circuit riders are by nature remote. Dependance of such a system produces undesirable results. "Infrequent services, irregular services, teach men to do without any" (1965:168). The Church, to Allen, must be a society, a fellowship, in which men live. The solution is, of course, to ordain a local lay leader. Allen does find a place for iteneration in the person of the missionary who, as as "wandering evangelist or teacher" is to convert the indifferent and encourage the Christians (1965:163). That is in contrast to the common practice in Italy of missionaries centralizing in the larger cities adn concentrating on the care of one or two small flocks.

(2) Illustrated from Indonesia. An example of mobilization of lay leaders comes from the Batak Lutherans of Indonesia. Because its effective solution to an acute shortage of pastors through lay involvement led to church extension their example is cited as meaningful to Italy.

> The congregations are clustered into resorts, similar to presbyteries, with a pastor and perhaps an assistant pastor in charge. The pastor meets each week with his elders for a study session in which they exegete and discuss the gospel lesson for the following Sunday. The elders appointed to preach then prepare their own sermons, based on this preparation (Kerr 1969:31).

An average of ten elders per congregation participates under this plan. Responsibility falls upon the laity. The result is a strong church. "Even if circumstances permitted them the luxury of a completely professionaly ministry, such a change would bleed life from the church" (Kerr 1969:32). Under indigenous lay leadership a program of church extension is underway.

> The Bataks come close to the ideal vision of the church in which the theologically trained professional becomes a resource person and educator, preparing lay people to do the day-by-day job of making Christ known to the community (Kerr 1969:35).

The Batak lay leaders remained laymen. They were not ordained, could not administer sacraments.

Merle Davis several years ago reported that this was

the typical plan.

> In most fields the Church has organized its scattered membership into parishes or circuits under the supervision of a trained minister, assisted by catechists or evangelists. As a rule these assistants are not ordained ministers. They teach, preach and render pastoral service but do not administer the sacraments. The minister in charge may have ten or even thirty such churches for which he is responsible (1939:120).

It appears common, then, for laymen to preach and teach as well as to witness. In Italy the non-Brethren and non-Pentecostal bodies appear to have been hesitant to go even that far. Perhaps this accounts in the past for the lack of significant growth. Correction should be made, releasing the layment to their work.

A further possible corrective would be the ordination of lay leaders who prove themselves in the pastoral and evangelistic roles. The wisdom of Roland Allen concurs. Churches should be able to extend themselves indefinitely under their own leadership including a ministry that would freely administer the ordinances.

(3) Illustrated from the Solomons. Failure to develop an indigenous ministry can obstruct the growth of the Church. That is what happened in Methodist work in the Solomon Islands. Tippett relates that the Methodists failed to develop her own ministry. "Each year Synod looked to New Britain for help rather than to her own resources" (1967:72). The Church did not grow organically. Though the Church had grown over four decades through converts from paganism, Tippett feels they should have done better. Until the time of the Pacific War, Methodists failed to take up all the opportunities.

> ...The members of Synod remained convinced that hundreds of open doors could really be handled only by more highly trained men. In other Oceanic areas where raw converts were sent out into frontier situations, to tell what great things the Lord had done for them, there was phenomenal growth -- conversion, quality and organic -- and some of these areas are today among the strongest churches of the Pacific (Tippett 1967:76).

Oceania is much different from Italy. Open doors in Italy have perhaps been fewer and harder to recognize. It is my personal conviction, however, that in recent years we have failed to respond to a number of opportunities. Missionaries were too over-worked. Trained nationals were not available. We have failed to tap the resources of "raw converts" who could tell what Jesus Christ has done for them. Waiting for better trained men, the potent testimony of newly transformed persons was forgotten. Italy does not necessarily need additional seminary or Bible School trained men to evangelize her masses. She does need humble witnesses to simply go to the people.

Values of Lay System. A ministry of the Church demands the ministering of each member of the Body. Mobilization requires the recognition of gifted laymen as the pastors and leaders of the Church.

(1) The first benefit to be derived from establishing such as a system is growth. One of the fastest growing Churches in the world utilizes its laity. Nearly thirty years ago (and before the tremendous recent growth) Merle Davis named as a source of the rapid expansion of the Evangelical Church in Brazil the fact that it is a layman's Church. Specifically it is a "man's church" in a male oriented society. Both for evangelism and for finances the leadership, time, and talents of the laymen were relied upon (Davis 1943: 79-80). For Brazil, at least, the practice was healthy, if we may judge in terms of numberical increase.

Writing for the totally different context of Liberia, a Lutheran missionary does not discount the role of ordained ministers ("professionals"). They have been "an important factor in the rapid growth of the Church" when placed in an expanding area to shepherd new converts (Wold 1968:105). But the growth of the Church in isolated areas where there is no pastor shows that "an even more important factor... is that the pattern of church planting be understood and carried out by village evangelists" (Wold 1968:105). The Lutheran Church of Liberia had some 200 of these lay evangelists.

(2) The second feature to recommend itself about a lay system for the ministry, is that it is an indefinitely reproduceable pattern. McGavran makes this a *sine qua non* for polity in emerging churches (1970:264,274). The system is reproduceable infinitely for two reasons. (1) It does not rest upon outside power (which may decline of change); it is not imposed from without, but rises from within. It is reproduceable because it is natural. (2) It creates no financial burden. Since lay ministers are self-supporting the Church need never lack for leaders because it cannot pay them. Poverty is a major problem in Italy as in many other fields. Most churches will never rise to the place of

being able to support a pastor. The imposition of leaders upon these churches becomes a kind of patternalism, linked directly or indirectly with the foreign missionary, his country, or his board.

(3) The third value of a system of lay pastors is related to the proceeding and has to do with communism. Communist influence in Italy is not conducive to a paid ministry. Hostility can be expected to be strong toward a church that is foreign dominated. A ministry that is partially supported by foreign funds (especially American funds) will come under suspicion. A lay ministry does not meet with these objections.

Recommendations. Several specific plans recommend themselves for the development of the ministry of the laity in the churches and groups of Italy.

(1) Devolve a "work" into small groups. Instead of attempting to "build-up" attendance at a large central meeting hall, break down into several house churches. If there is a church of 50, let it become 5 churches of 10, or ten churches of five. This is multiplication by division. It recognizes the basic family units which seem an important factor for Italian evangelism. It should be easier for ten churches of five, or 5 churches of ten to double, than for the more settled congregation of fifty to grow.

(2) Place responsibility for these little churches in the hads of the laity. Obviously a pastor or missionary cannot personally assume the care of all these groups. He should not. This calls for utilizing the elders. In some cases these elders must be found. No doubt many will be the heads of households where the new groups will meet. Two factors are involved: recognition of lay leaders, and utilization of lay leaders for regular services.

(3) Certain leaders must be deployed to key, central areas to instruct the laymen who teach and preach and lead the little house churches. Missionaries should be chosen with care for this teaching responsibility. It would be preferable to have qualified Italians in this role. These overseers must go to the provinces as well as to the cities. The placement of the right leader in the center of each cluster of churches is the key to making this plan succeed.

(4) Weekly meetings of instruction for the lay leaders are essential. These sessions would consist of exegesis and sermon preparation as well as some discussion of problems and blessings.

(5) Lay leaders who display the proper gifts and who rise as natural leaders in the churches should be ordained.

(6) Divide the territory surrounding local communities of believers and assign as specific areas of responsibility to local churches for church extension and to overseers for administration.

(7) Expand by opening new house churches in the homes of isolated believers and studies in the homes of sympathizers. This responsibility should be in the hands of the local lay leaders and should utilize laymen rather than the overseer.

(8) Teams of laymen, pastors, evangelists, and missionaries may be sent to open new churches in more distant areas. Or individual church planters may be deployed for this task.

Perhaps it would be helpful to illustrate how this could be carried out in Campania Region by the Conservative Baptists. Campania is divided into 5 provinces. Conservative Baptists now work in three of these provinces. In Caserta Province there is one church in the capital, a chapel at Aversa, and a preaching point at Castel Volturno. To these may be added the closely related preaching point of Acerra which is across the border in Naples Province. A key leader, national or missionary, should be located somewhere in this area (probably not in the city of Caserta). He might be placed in some town which is ready for a new church ("readiness" being defined as the availability of a home for developing a new house church). His chief responsibility would be to meet weekly with the lay leaders of the devolved groups. The leaders would correspond to the groups, probably two at Aversa, one in Acerra, six at Caserta, one in Castel Volturno. Naples Province contains a host of missionaries, most of them in the city of Naples, so it should be no problem to find one to serve as overseer. To the present only one church has been opened in Avellino province. The pastor of the church in the provincial capital would have to assist his own laymen as well as direct expansion into other cities. The provinces of Benevento and Salerno have not yet been entered. Leaders with proper evangelistic gifts should be relocated as missionaries to open new churches in these areas. The same system of delegating responsibility to lay leaders should be followed as new churches are formed.

Training Unpaid Leaders. A case for a lay ministry having been laid in the preceding division, it is logical now to consider the training of leaders. This subject may be discussed under four headings: who, why, what, and how.

Who? Melvin Hodges stresses the importance of training the entire Church rather that a few ministerial candidates. This eliminates gap between laity and clergy. It avoids creating a clerical elite, and recognizes that each member of the Body of Christ has a ministry. "The whole Church is an evangelizing organism". All are called to witness, although not everyone is called to be a preacher or teacher. The entire Church - an army of witnesses - should be mobilized. Jesus sent out the seventy as well as the twelve (Hodges 1965:120-121).

The key to training the whole Church is in training the new converts. Why wait? New Christians have enthusiasm, drive, and contacts among the unconverted. One of Dr. McGavran's principles of church growth is the multiplication of unpaid leaders among new converts, "training them to go out and communicate Christ to their unsaved relatives, neighbors, and fellow laborers" (McGavran 1966:770).

Why? The purpose of training is to create a multiplying Church. Laymen are the secret of growth when they are mobilized for continuous propagation of the Gospel. "Any form of clericalism, any limiting of evangelism to paid leaders, works heavily against church growth" (McGavran 1966:770). Even a receptive population does not insure growth. The layman, not the professional, must be the evangelist.

What? Obviously the kind of training in view here is not that of the standard seminary or Bible school. In "The Case for Voluntary Clergy" Roland Allen stresses the apostolic training which is mostly "spiritual and practical" rather than merely intellectual. Our conventional training through institutions is comparatively superficial. The practical and spiritual emphasis is basic and vital (Allen 1965:145).

Beginning with the total membership, instruction should relate to the role of each believer in spreading the Gospel. Bradshaw mangifies Dr. McGavran's convictions thus: "Ordinary Christians should be trained to understand the dynamics of church growth that are in force about them" (Bradshaw 1969:31).

A more intense education should be given recognized leaders. (Note that again it is not ministerial candidates, but functioning leaders who are given further training to make them better equipped leaders. That is the role of the Assemblies of God Bible Institutes in Rome). Again Bradshaw concisely states the McGavran thesis.

> It should be added that pastors and future pastors and laymen in leadership should be educated to see homogeneous units, social stratification and extended family relationships as channels along which the Gospel can flow (Bradshaw 1969:31).

The web of family relationships has been proven a channel for the Gospel among Italians. These dynamics should be in the minds of all Evangelical leaders.

How? The training of leaders requires a plan. It does not happen by accident. The system should not extract the individual from his society, but should serve to integrate him into his church's evangelistic effort. His training, then, should be organized. However, as McGavran points out, mere organization accomplishes little. The proof is in a deepening Christian experience which "gets ordinary Christians gladly bearing witness to what Christ has done for them and persuading their fellows to become disciples of Christ" (McGavran 1966:770).

Bradshaw suggests the use of graphs in reporting evangelistic progress as a means of imparting missionary zeal. A plan of evangelism could be presented utilizing maps and charts.

> A map could show where there are villages or city blocks with a concentration of Christian families which might become a nucleus for a new house church. The map could spot unreached areas marking in where individuals or households have yielded allegiance to Christ. The number of churches, established and new, could be graphically displayed. Quarter by quarter bar graphs of baptisms from each church would keep the people alert as to progress or slackening in their evangelism. (Bradshaw 1969:31).

Recognition given publicly to laymen instrumental in shepherding a given number of persons into the Church would serve to stimulate. Evangelistic teams of gifted laymen might tell in other churches how their relatives had been won to Christ (Bradshaw 1969:31). That is practical, spiritual training; it is not book-learning.

These suggestions are offered as opening a way toward a lay Church which will be relevant, growing and maturing.

19

The Relevant Mission

THE MISSIONARY QUESTION

Is there a place for the missionary in Italy today? The evangelistic task is gigantic, and on this basis it is assumed that missionaries are needed. At the same time it is a mistake to assume that evangelism must be in the hands of foreign workers. It is also the task of the Italian Church.

Beaver from a different perspective makes a case for the need of missionaries from Asia and Africa in Western lands, "since large segments of the population do not respond to the evangelism of the churches in their midst" (Beaver 1968:92). If that be true, it ought to be even less objectionable for American and British missionaries to go to Italy. Beaver feels that Christians from India might be effective witnesses to our poor and our intellectuals. Furthermore he insists on the missionary responsibility of the Churches of Asia, Africa, Oceania, and Latin America. They are not excused from sending missionaries (Beaver 1968:92-93).

This raises the question as to whether such missionaries might not be more suitable for the Italian situation. North Americans find it difficult to adapt to the Italian cultural milieu. Latin Americans might much more fully identify with the masses of Italy. Possibly missions should consider seeking volunteers from sister Churches in Latin America to serve in Italy. Missionaries are needed to work with Italians and Italian Churches in the task of evangelism.

RELEVANT MEN

Cross-Pollination. Dayton Roberts states, "We discovered that the Latin American has a distinct advantage over the North American in communication to Asians and Europeans" (1967:75-76). Roberts speaks from the experience of speaking about Evangelism in Depth in the Orient and in Europe. His statement gives an example of what is meant by "cross-pollination", which is an attempt to escape the Americanization which colors much mission-centered evangelism.

Italy's closeness culturally to Latin America would seem to indicate that missionaries and evangelists from the rapidly growing Churches of Latin America should possibly be called to spread revival in Italy. Italian immigrants in Brazil and Argentina especially suggest themselves since they still have family ties in Italy. The birth and growth of the Pentecostal movement in Italy illustrates this potential.

Nearer at hand are the countries of Europe. Operation Mobilization has effectively utilized young people from many nearby, less-American countries for evangelism in Italy. Under the direction of an Italian, the internationals have proven their worth when working with and through the local church. Many of the young people come from cultures nearer the Italian than do North American missionaries.

Cross-pollination might take place with evangelistic teams from other Latin countries of Europe where something exciting has been happening. At least the possibility of supplementing present forces in Italy with evangelists from France, Spain or Portugal should be considered.

Exchanging of teams has taken place in other parts of the world. A missionary reports that such a team from Indonesia brought a breath of revival when visiting Pakistan. Italy could profit from fresh life to supplement sagging missionary evangelism.

Cultural problems are fewer for the Latin going to Italy than for the North American. More important, acceptance is easier on the part of Italians. The North American missionary, despite his best efforts, is suspect simply because he is an American. I have been introduced by Italians to their friends as "Canadian", apparently because they felt my United States citizenship might be embarrassing. It is very easy for an Italian who is bombarded with propaganda to believe that the missionary may be an agent of

American "imperialism". It is assumed the U.S. Government pays the missionary's salary. Therefore it is logical to suppose he is in Italy in the interests of the United States. Furthermore Italians "know" that all Americans are "rich"!

Christians from South America, Spain and Portugal do not have these problems. They are accepted as people like themselves--poor, exploited, and Latin.

Anthropologically trained missionaries. Robert Moffatt of 18th century African missionary history fame, lauded for many virtues, is also castigated for his lack of anthropological insights.

> In spite of his love for the Africans, he had little interest in the background of their thoughts, and left behind no treasure of anthropological observations. He underestimated their religious traditions, and introduced unaltered the fervent evangelical Christianity of his own tradition without considering the possibilities of its adaptation to an African world. His methods were always and increasingly patriarchal (Neill 1966:313).

This failure on the part of American and British missionaries in Italy is more subtle. Missionaries moving from one section of Western civilization to another easily assume that patterns in the home culture are totally acceptable to the second. Application of anthropological concepts could correct much misguided zeal.

Anthropology as a field of knowledge may be divided into physical and cultural anthropology. The latter is particularly relevant for the missionary. Keesing's Cultural Anthropology: The Science of Custom (1963) is the basis for the definition and descriptions which follow.

Cultural anthropology may be defined as that segment of "man'study" which describes and seeks general understandings about human customs or "cultural behavior." As a field of knowledge anthropology describes man as physical, cultural, and social. Anthropologists collaborate with other groups of scholars, such as historians and sociologists, to produce a Holistic viewpoint. Cultural anthropology concentrates on four aspects: prehistoric archaeology, linguistics, ethnology (factual description and historical analysis of culture), and social anthropology (scientific generalizations about culture, society, and personality).

The new missionary's first task should be to observe the new culture. He does this best my participation rather than from the "ivory tower" of classroom or textbook. As observant and participant the new missionary is applying the research method of cultural anthropology. He learns the language. He becomes "at home" in the culture and with its people. He eats their food, drinks what they drink, attends funerals and social functions, visits in their homes. He lives with the people and becomes, gradually a specialist in that one culture. The missionary is a modified cultural anthropologist. In his work he utilizes the science of applied anthropology.

The need for the insights of anthropology is demonstrated by ethnocentricism (own-group centeredness i.e., "the American way is best"). Several examples of ethnocentrism exist. Missionaries tend to reflect American values in hymnology. A feeling is sometimes expressed that American missionaries coming after the War should have compiled their own hymnal, "to eliminate the confusion in Italian hymnody." Some individuals have complained that tunes have been altered ("A Mighty Fortress") or that bad tunes have been adopted ("Red River Valley"). The fact is that "Red River Valley" has no "bad" connotation to the Italian. Luther's "altered" tune very likely is more near the original than is the American version. In both cases the missionary needs to appreciate the Italian way. Unfortunately missionaries tend to neglect hymns of Italian composition coming out of the Evangelical resurgence of a hundred years ago, and instead translate the recent songs of John Peterson into Italian.

Ethnocentrism effects the style of religious services conducted by missionaries: announcements and offering are part of the ritual preceding the sermon, and communion is offered once a month rather than every Sunday. More seriously it determines that the type of ministry will be in the image of the missionary -- professionally trained and paid. This may seem to fit the European pattern, but is possibly the result of the background of the missionaries. A highly-trained, full-time ministry may seem desirous, but is hardly practical for struggling, tiny, beginning, groups of believers. The pattern of the foreigner's own educational background may be seen in the curriculum of schools and training programs initiated by these missionaries.

Missionaries have failed to leave America and England behind, and have inflicted Italian churches with foreign ways. Tippett (1960) makes the point that new missionaries are unprepared, and that early years of service should be a continuation of learning. Formal education has prepared the missionary to deal with the educated, but not the animistic. Many who belong to the lower classes which comprise 75% of the population of Italy hold beliefs which could be described as animistic. Yet have many missionaries really given thought to the problems of communicating the Gospel to people with superstitious (animistic) beliefs? The animist, says Tippett, must overcome his animism at his own level. Conversion must be at the level of the receiver, not that of the communicator. The missionary who is oblivious to the existence of animistic practices (the horoscope) in the cities of his homeland is not yet prepared to confront the spiritist in Italian society. Italian Evangelical believers once described to me the local gobblins, witches, and people who at night were transformed into animals with magical power. I assuredthem that this was superstition and that such beings do not exist. Very likely I was wrong. My denial may have had the effect of driving these beliefs "beneath the surface". Much better would it have been to have proclaimed the power of Christ as having defeated all principalities and powers.

Anthropology as an aid to missionary endeavor is feared by some as denoting human evolution. Fehderau (1961) points out, however, that it is cultural anthropology which interests the missionary. Some missionaries fail to consider that different peoples have different systems of learned behavior. In our own culture allowance is made when speaking to different age groups. That is common sense. But this is even more true in a cross-cultural situation, and here anthropology can help. People must understand if they are to believe. Does this eliminate the Holy Spirit? No! But we must not distort the message by our blundering promotion of an assumed "Christian cultural heritage." We must adapt the message (not change it) to the audience. Matthew and Luke did so in writing for Jewish and Greek minds respectively (Fehderau 1961).

Specialization. The purpose of anthropological training is not to create specialists in anthropology, but to aid in the accomplishment of the primary task. Missionaries, unfortunately, tend to specialize in everything except church-planting evangelism. In a survey recently done, of the 59 missionaries working in Rome, few were involved in direct evangelism, and few churches were in the process of being planted. This is not to deprecate the good work being done.

The problem is departmentalization. As a specialist a missionary has a certain responsibility which becomes his area of concern. The limited funds available are coveted by each missionary for the projects in his department. Wold saw this in Liberia where the institution invariably took precedence over evangelistic work (Wold 1968:103). Institutionalism in Italy is sometimes in the more subtle forms of literature, radio, and building programs.

Protestant Lay Order. Professional missionaries, whatever their specialization, tend to become absorbed in the non-productive mechanics of running the mission. This is one factor which leads me to suggest the need for a new breed of missionary, the layman. The present seminary-trained, ordained, professional is not obsolete. He is still needed. The problem is that the professionals tend to all become "chiefs" concentrated in a few centers.

The need is for "Indians" to get out and do the basic work. An Order of Protestant Laymen might supply this need by getting out into the provinces and away from the present centralization in a few cities. Such an organization might also supply the supporting activities that could release the "professionals" for evangelism.

The Order could be named something like "Militant Men for Missions". It would complement the present societies and their workers, and would not compete with them for funds or position. Organized, directed, and financed by laymen, it would place qualified lay people where needed and support them for variable terms of service.

Such an agency would recruit untapped manpower for missionary service. Many persons are unable to go out under present short-term voluntary programs that demand self-support. Some do not at present qualify for regular-full-time missionary appointment. Such appointment usually is for life. Requirements often include ordination and Seminary or Bible School training. Lay persons who do not meet these specifications could render valuable service in secretarial, administrative, musical, teaching, and other positions. In some instances they might require only sustenance support for the years on the field.

Evangelistic workers might also be supplied by the Order. For instance, qualified single workers might be recruited for service in the provinces of Italy where inadequate educational opportunities militate against the residence of missionary families.

RELEVANT PLANS

Effective missionary work does not just happen. It requires planning and the execution of plans. A comprehensive plan should cover the placement of personnel, goals, areas of ministry, and methodology.

Deployment of workers. The kinds of missionaries needed have been discussed. Their placement should complement their gifts. Placement should make the best use of available time, means and men. Good placement is good stewardship. Missionary anthropologist Luzbetak stresses the importance of logistics. "Missionaries, like soldiers, must be placed in the most strategic positions, not in the most agreeable ones" (Luzbetak 1970:119).

Two tendencies in Italy may be mentioned. One is a complete inattention to logistics: missionaries go wherever they choose and change assignments whenever they choose, and a lack of continuity is the result. The other tendency is that of deploying workers to the wrong places. For instance, it is sometimes argued that Christian workers should leave the South and go work in the neglected North. The argument betrays simplistic thinking. Which "North" is in mind? There are more Protestants in Piedmont than in any other region of Italy! On the other side, some of the "neglected" areas of the North have proven resistant to the Gospel. The German area of Bolzano, Alto-Adige, which has probably fewer Protestants than any comparable part of the country, is simply not receptive. It would therefore be poor stewardship to invest heavily in manpower and money there. The same may be said of many large cities. The point is to go to the responsive people. In the North the responsive ones are probably the colonies of Southern immigrants surrounding the industrial centers.

Church Growth Research in Latin America (CGRILA) uncovered a similar situation in South America.

> Some of the newer missions consider the localities having the fewest evangelicals as the best place to start churches. The fallacy in relying on this supposition as the sole criterion is that the area may have the smallest percentage of Evangelicals because it is the poorest site for mission -- it is the most resistant to the Gospel. If missions would choose areas where Evangelicals have already won large numbers they

might do better (Read, Monterosso, and Johnson 1969:306).

It seems to me that the same applies in Italy. With the millions of unreached, there is little need of sheep-stealing or unhealthy competition. But Conservative Baptists, for instance, might indeed do well to follow the Pentecostals in those areas where they have thrived in the South, and there plant additional churches to reach additional peoples.

Goals. A good plan includes goals which are specific. Methods should be studied and applied that will best help achieve the goals.

"Primary goals are: converts won and churches established. All others are secondary, either ministering to these or growing out of them" (Guy 1965:139). Unless stated, the obvious is easily forgotten.

At a missionary conference a missionary engaged in Bible translation was asked how he reconciled that work with the priority of evangelism. He replied that translation is evangelism. Granted that Scripture translation is essential, it still is hardly evangelism. To call it so is to confuse the issue. Translation does not in itself win men to Christ nor plant churches. This discipling of men in Christian communities is the main goal, to which translation and other activities, though an aid, must remain subordinate.

Areas of ministry. The meaning and purpose of mission is discipling. A program may be measured in terms of its productivity. A large number of missionaries and mission organizations seem to be fairly ineffective in terms of visible results (i.e. church growth). Likewise some Churches are failing to attract many new people. The fault may in part be in a mistaken emphasis on services provided for the churches by the missions, services which in themselves are good but which do not effectively evangelize. It is important to evaluate in terms of productivity those areas of ministry in which mission agencies are engaged.

(1) Institutions. The dangers of institutionalism have been mentioned already. But let us repeat some of them. Churches tend to devote disproportionate amounts of personnel and money to institutions which often become a substitute for evangelism rather than an aid to church planting. Six pitfalls that institutions can present to a mission are enumerated by Westlund (1968:231-234). (1) Requirements are difficult to control because personnel may have to be transferred to keep the institution going, and finances cannot be

cut here. (2) Spiritual surveillance is difficult. (The institution is not the church, and compromise may seem permissable as well as necessary). (3) Super-nationals are created. (4) Christian leaders are not generally produced. (Potential ones have in some cases been spoiled, in others dismissed). (5) Institutions tend to become top-heavy. (6) Institutions are failing to help build the Church in proportion to the investments in them. (The evangelism budget may be cut, but not the institutional budget. Evangelistic workers may be placed in the institution, but it is rare for the institutional worker to abandon that post for evangelistic work).

Westlund offers seven questions helpful in evaluating our institutions:

(1) Does it maintain a vibrant Christian witness?
(2) Does it help build a strong Church?
(3) Could it be merged with another?
(4) Could the government take it over?
(5) Would we be willing to close it?
(6) Could the national church take it over?
(7) Can the cost be justified? Westlund 1968: 234-236).

If we must answer "no" to either 1,2,6, or 7, it seems to me we have gotten the cart before the horse and need to reevaluate. Some of our projects are less obvious than institutions such as schools and book stores, but nevertheless present the same dangers to the basic purposes of mission as do the institutions.

(2) Publications. On the one hand in Italy there seem to be too many Protestant publications of a certain kind. A great deal of energy is expended in producing little papers that have little impact. At the same time, we have too few. There seems to be a need for a quality publication of the right kind, one that is not necessarily sectarian or polemical but which is a real evangelical voice. Such a paper would forget the missionary issues and the problems confronting American and Northern European Churches, and would deal with Italian ones. It would serve the Italian Church.

(3) Student ministry. The college and university system of Italy is a neglected field consisting of 29 institutions with thousands of students. Five years ago the enrollments in the seven largest universities were as follows:

(Crow 1965:362).

Rome	34,000
Naples	26,000
Milan	23,000
Bologna	12,000
Bari	12,000
Palermo	10,000
Turin	9,000

Evangelicals maintain slight contact with the first three through InterVarsity workers at Rome, through missionary Hurvey Woodson at Milan, and through the Conservative Baptist Foreign Missionary Society's Student Center at Naples. Operation Mobilization, during 1969, aimed their campaign at the university students.

Students, by and large, seem neglected. Yet they are a responsive segment of society. The question is how much effort should and could be devoted properly to this area of ministry. For responsive though they may be, student work alone will not necessarily produce or build churches. On the Italian scene the Church, to endure and expand, must touch the basic unit of society, the family. Student work in isolation does not do this.

The solution probably lies in the direction of the student ministry that is closely church-related. Responsiveness can then be harnassed to open closed doors and produce growth.

(4) Sunday School and children's work. Italian Sunday Schools are insignificant. Therefore it is probably opportune that a number of evangelicals are cooperating to produce major Sunday School literature in Italy. The Sunday School can be utilized for qualitative growth of the churches.

We should not, however, make the mistake of conceiving of the Sunday School as the vehicle for evangelism that it is in the United States. The teaching ministry should be geared for the development of those already in the Church. Establishment of branch Sunday Schools can become the means for extending the Church, true. But the function of the Sunday School is basically that of instruction - that is, growth in depth, not breadth. Attempted evangelism via Sunday School has been abortive in Italy. This is the Experience also in Brazil where the Church leaders hoped to attract the parents through the children in the Sunday Schools. Instead the churches lost many from the Sunday School and failed to touch the unconverted (Tyson 1965:95).

Tyson's objection to the claims of those who hope to win the parents through evangelizing their children was that it was wrong to make the approach through the child. Rather in Brazil, he said, the evangelistic approach to the family should be through the man.

In Italy the approach should normally be through the family as a unit. The mother figure is strong, especially where religion is involved, and the mother is central in the family. "In some societies," says Nida, "and in certain restricted circumstances, children can be very useful in providing an entrance to the family, but by and large porportionately too much time has been spent on children rather than on the total family group" (Nida 1965:183). This judgment seems applicable to Sunday School work and to other efforts centering mainly in children. A child-centered ministry can be misconstrued as taking an unfair advantage of their youth in the absence of their parents. The accusation can be avoided by working closely with the families and through the churches.

(5) Radio. Quite different from Sunday School and children's work, is radio activity. Wonderful testimonies have been received by those connected with this ministry of persons listening under unusual circumstances and in places where Christian workers could not go. Mass media is enthusiastically welcomed as a means of communicating the message.

Nida, however, cautions us. "We seem to think that the wider the audience, the more valuable the message" (Nida 1960:177). The tendency with mass media is to make the message more and more generalized so as to fit more people. Nida does not minimize the importance of radio which can be very helpful. Its problem is in being impersonal, detached, and easy to turn off. The Gospel is not a product to be sold. It is a message of life, very personal, and "the message of life must be carried primarily by life" (Nida 1960:177).

Is radio, then, a waste of time? Or to put it another way, "Does Gospel Radio Grow Churches?" (McGavran 1965b:97). McGavran feels that more study needs to be done on this point. He has come to several conclusions of his own.

First, radio is a means for sowing the word more widely than could be done by word of mouth. Furthermore, broadcasting of the Gospel over radio helps create a favorable image of Christianity. Third, if it leads listeners to become responsible members of Christ's Church, it does contribute to the discipling of the nations. Fourth, there must be churches for the people to join or radio will contribute little to church growth. This means, fifth, that Gospel radio should be asking, "How can we reach more and lead more or those reached to become responsible members of Christ's Church?" The founding of new churches may be part of the answer (McGavran 1965b:98).

One of the most powerful Protestant stations in the world is RVOG, in Addis Ababa, with a planned technical coverage of half the world's population. The concern expressed by the direction is that the station remain "a means of evangelism rather than a church institution" (Aske 1967:355). Yet it is only a means. The churches, not the station, do the evangelism. Programs are produced by the churches in the area where they are heard (Aske 1967:359). Direct conversions have been reported, but the more important role is that of "climate-creation" (Aske 1967:363). The effects were described as revolutionary for Near East churches that had led a closed existence, speaking to their own few inside small buildings. But now the churches were speaking to the world! (Aske 1967: 363). The most important issue was whether the churches would take up all aspects of audience relation work: advertising the broadcasts, "giving personal attention to listener mail, directing each interested hearer into the local congregation, and there receiving him with the love of Christ (Aske 1967:364).

Can those broadcasting over Monte Carlo, and those hoping to conduct future broadcasts within Italy, make radio an effective tool of church growth?

These are some of the points to consider concerning some of the areas of missionary ministry.

Methods. Strategy for evangelism involves methods. Choosing the right ones (those both effective and meaningful in the Italian culture) requires study. A survey made by the Missions Advanced Research and Communication Center reveals that much more research should be done of most mission fields to discover "what is happening, what needs to be done, and what methods would be the most applicable to the particular situation" (MARC 1967:9).

The Annual Christian Workers Conference in Italy seems to suggest itself as a starting place for discussing the prospect of research and for discovering the tools available for information gathering. More than for fellowship and inspiration, the Conference itself could be utilized for sharing the wealth of pertinent information that must be held by the many evangelical workers in Italy. The Evangelical bodies might consider the possibility of forming a research center to aid in evangelism through the utilization of modern scientific achievements. Why is it that certain groups (Pentecostals) are growing while most others are making little progress? Which segments of the population are receptive to the Gospel? What methods are most effective in reaching them? The present study is an effort to come to some conclusions as to these questions. A scientific research, possibly utilizing a computer, would probably give very clear directions in a number of these areas.

A system approach to evangelism should not be feared as negating the place of the Holy Spirit any more than the printing press may have been feared as destroying the sacredness of the Bible. The invention of printing was the means of making the Scriptures widely available to ordinary people. Likewise modern science can be the vehicle for bringing salvation to the Gospel-ready peoples of Italy.

In the meantime this study in an effort to aid the Evangelical missions of Italy to a more fruitful evangelism. Methods are varied and many. The goal is the persuasion of Italians to become committed followers of Jesus Christ in His Church. I will now comment on certain points which seem to bear on the establishment of growing Italian Evangelical churches.

(1) Subsidy. The question of subsidy is an emotional issue when discussed among missionaries. It is unfortunate that the discussion of the indigenous church often revolves around this very issue. True, support is one of the classic "three selfs." However, it is possible to have a church which might conceivably be self-governing, self-propagating, and self-supporting but which still not "indigenous". An indigenous Church is one which is of the indigenes. That is, it is Italian in its nature -- not an Italianized church transplanted from Britain or America. Tippett"s marks of the indigenous Church included six selfs. Therefore it is unfortunate that the question of finances has been blown up out of proportion.

The issue is not the use or non-use of foreign funds. The missionary himself is not indigenous and is supported from abroad. It is a question of how funds should be used. On the one hand a refusal to use foreign money may mean that nothing gets done. One the other hand dependance on non-Italian sources results in an immature Church and one which remains non-indigenous and incapable of self-direction. It is tied to a pattern which is not infinitely reproducable. This second alternative means a stunted Church. The first alternative (no foreign funds) may, however, mean no growth at all.

The solution seems to be in a judicious use of whatever funds are available for moderate "priming of the pump". Examples of pump-priming might be the payment from the mission treasury of the initial expenses for preparing a meeting hall, or publicity for evangelistic campaigns, of salaries for evangelists and church planters for a limited period of time. The danger is that what is intended to be temporary may become a permanent pattern. Therefore a definite, carefully thought-out, specific plan should be formulated ahead of time. The items included should be such that they can be terminated painlessly, and they should be operations that will result in church growth. There is no point in sending an evangelist out to "get decisions" if there is no plan for conserving the results in local churches. A highly publicized campaign is of little value if it is not geared to producing increased church membership.

A problem with mission-planned and financed programs of church extension or evangelism is that they tend to be "American" or "British" in style. This sets an unfortunate pattern from the begining, and is contrary to the definition of the indigenous Church as a Church belonging to and being of the people in its nature. The American or Northern European style of Church (or of evangelism) is beyond the means of the little Italian congregations. Writing from years of experience in a field with a vast economic depression, an American missionary writes concerning the role of the mission and money:

> Western missions have established Churches along the lines of their own fixed notions about the ministry, organization, and methods of raising money, which in many cases are, in fact, beyond the ability of the people to support. To operate this Western kind of Church, it becomes necessary to depend upon foreign resources. Under such a system the successful missionary is not the one who teaches good stewardship practices to his people but rather the one who learns how to promote a project and obtain funds, from whatever source, to run it (Wold 1968:186).

An anthropologically sound approach to support is one which is not planned on the basis of an American or Northern European economy, but which is locally relevant -- it draws on Italian resources and meets local needs. "The growth of a young Church", says Tippett, "should be oriented to the economic pattern" (1967:185). Anthropologist Tippett goes on to suggest that when self-support is presented as part of the follow-up of the conversion experience the problem of paternalism practically never arises.

It has been suggested that one way to avoid paternalism is to establish a central budget to pay Italian Church workers and other expenses of a developing Church. This is only one step removed, and is little improvement since the mission remains the chief contributor.

Missions working in Italy have seen very small church growth. They are understandably tempted to subsidize Italian workers as the only means to develop a Church. Nida admits that this has been the procedure of most mission boards, but that it produces enormous problems and is not congenial to effective church growth. It means that eventually the mission will be forced to cut-off support, provoking resentment. The Southern Baptists in Italy have experienced the difficulties involved in this procedure. Instead of the Mission first supporting a worker full-time, then part-time, and eventually withdrawing all support, it might be better to allow the Church to gradually assume such a worker as they feel the need and are able to support him on local economy.

Subsidies for nationals may result in the immediate growth of a program, but will probably not pay off subsequently. Velocity is not the same as momentum. Subsidy may result in initial velocity. That velocity is not terribly meaningful, however, if that remains the rate for the duration of the life of the Church. Lack of subsidy may mean a much slower beginning. But when the Church which is not tied to foreign funds is subsequently able to carry out its own mission of evangelism the result is momentum (the snowball which gets larger and rolls faster and faster down the hill).

> On the whole, the first type of support -- fully paid salaries from foreign funds -- should never be undertaken if the mission is truly concerned with effective church growth; for nothing so stifles local enthusiasm and leadership as foreign-paid ministers (Nida 1965:185).

Missions should take care to not impose a dependent pattern. Dangers in regard to subsidizing workers should also apply to the programs of the developing Churches -- literature, Christian education, etc. Pump-priming, while legitmate, should be engaged in with caution. It should be engaged in. But let the members of the missions involved do so with their eyes open. Let there be planning and much beforehand discussion. There is a need for direction and a clear understanding of the issues involved. The formulation of a code of action is necessary ahead of time, not in the midst of battle.

(2) Mass evangelism. The problem of foreign style in evangelism and church extension has been alluded to. This problem, it seems to me, is present in a subtle way in many programs of mass evangelism. Nida puts it bluntly.

> In a day of mass communication and demographic thinking, it is customary to think primarily in terms of the masses and to evaluate the impact of the message in terms of listening - minutes or viewer-minutes. But the Gospel is neither soap nor breakfast food, and response is not calculable in terms of audience size (1965:179).

To put it another way, piazza meetings which blare "the Gospel" over loudspeakers to the crowds and the repeated mass distribution of literature through the streets are probably a waste of energy and money since they do not win people as disciples of Jesus. An exclusive reliance on evangelistic crusades to win people is probably equally a mistake. This mania for mass means of evangelism is a product of American cultural over-hang. Methods directed toward the masses are in error because they overlook the nature of the individuals who make up the masses. In America mass evangelism is logical because the individual acts as an individual. His decision is a personal decision. He can make it without consultation with others. The American represents an individualistic society.

Italian society is a little different. The individual does not normally act alone. Decisions are made in consultation with family members. Mass evangelism is generally geared to the individual as an individual and not to the context of the family unit. If Italian society is family centered evangelism should be directed toward the family unit. Mass evangelism tends to violate this principle. In fact, any form of evangelism which tends to draw the person out of or away from the basic sociological unit is inappropriate. It is poor anthropology, and it is bad methodology. Church life which centers in something other than the unit's members and their relation to God and society at large is a distorted church life. A Church which is a heterogeneous congregation of little-related individuals violates both Scripture and the Italian pattern. It results from a sort of cultural imperialism on the part of missionaries. The American or British way is not necessarily the best way. Nor is it the Italian way, and it is certainly not the New Testament way. Church history in Acts reveals a pattern which is much nearer the Italian way of life than the American or Northern European.

Mass evangelism was not excluded by the Apostles, but neither was it employed exclusively. At Pentecost mass evangelism was the effective, Spirit-directed tool. Subsequently this technique was interspersed with extensive face-to-face evangelism. Nida affirms the need for a balanced approach.

> While recognizing the limitations of mass techniques, however, it is important not to exclude mass evangelism as a legitimate approach to the problem of church growth. Although the end results of large mass meetings are seldom proportionate to the energy expended, the real answer to this problem appears to be, not to choose between mass and personal evangelism (or communication), but to employ both (1965:179-180).

(3) Follow-Up. Mass evangelism is often criticized for its failure to have effective follow-up. It may be questioned whether evangelism without follow-up is really evangelism. Certainly it is not effective evangelism.

A better term might be "follow-through". The implication is that there must be incorporation into the life of the Evangelical community. Being Christian involves a life. The Christian life is nurtured in the corporate life of the Church. Decision brings commitment. That is conversion. It is not "easy believism".

Evangelism which disregards this phase is ineffective. It may be quite negative, amounting to an "innoculation" against the Gospel. It is questionable whether an evangelistic program should be engaged in unless it includes a plan for after-care.

McGavran calls this phase of evangelism "folding". The folding ministry is as important as the "finding". God wants His lost sheep found, and the found sheep He wants secured in the fold. Folding involves the instruction and nurture of the Church and may follow baptism. It is an essential part of the task.

The tragedy of an evangelistic effort without church-planting is illustrated by the account of Italy's first tent campaign in June, 1958, in the central Italy small town of Marsciano. The Greater Europe Mission reports that the several hundred who attended nightly meetings formed the largest crowds that had ever attended evangelistic meetings in Italy. The campaign produced 19 converts. Eleven years later a missionary returned to Marsciano to search for remaining fruit from those meetings. It was found that some had died and that others had been frightened by the local priests.

> Four converts are still faithfully attending an evangelical church in a nearby city, where they are now living. The church planting effort in Marsciano had been a failure. There had been no missionary or Italian pastor to stay after the tent meetings to shepherd the little flock (Greater Europe Mission 1969:16).

New converts must not be abandoned. "The first two or three days after their decision are the most important in their lives. The next two or three weeks are also important" (Wold 1968:209). It is not enough to merely instruct them to come to a class at a fixed time the following week. Wold suggests a full week of instructional classes immediately following the evangelistic campaign and preceding the baptism of converts. Believers are thus incorporated quickly into the life of the church. Instruction continues through participation, classes and the visits of leaders in the homes. Wold's plan is worthy of adaptation for Italy.

Baptismal postponement seems characteristic of Italian Evangelicals. It is my impression that baptism is delayed usually by several months from the time of initial decision. The Conservative Baptists, for instance, have no rule but this seems to be the practice. Serious thought should be given to the advisability of changing this practice. There is no Scriptural precedent for it. Not only did Peter baptize Jewish converts immediately on the day of Pentecost, but also Gentile converts at Caesarea. Paul baptized the household of the Philippian jailor the night of their conversion. While the centurion may have had previous instruction which had led him to become a "God-fearer" and was prepared for baptism, the jailor most certainly did not. Baptism was a rite of incorporation into the Christian community where they were to be nurtured. Where no Christian community existed, it was the rite which initiated such a community in the house of the new believers.

It is not strange that McGavran speaks of post-baptismal care, enumerating eight elements giving quality to the Churches. Since his treatment of people-movement Churches is applicable to the kind of Church that arises in Italy when the family homogeneous unit is recognized, these elements are mentioned here. (1) Regular worship involving Bible study and teaching in the home and community; (2) A meeting place, either as house churches or in a rented hall; (3) Liturgical worship using memorized Scripture passages, hymns, the Apostle's Creed; (4) Lay training; (5) The provision of a body of essential Christian knowledge; (6) Strengthening of family ties; (7) Day-school education of children; (8) Teaching illiterate Christians to read the Bible and hymnbooks. (McGavran 1970:326-327).

The recognition of follow-through as part of the discipling process gives greater incentive to evangelism as it eliminates much of the problem of losing converts before baptism. It restores the Church to its proper place as the fold.

(4) Nationalization. A missionary's goal is sometimes said to be to work himself out of a job. By this it is intended that the work which he begins will be turned over to the nationals. The procedure is more easily stated than carried out. It usually involves a structure which is mission centered and controlled. The purpose of turning over control is thought to be the emergence of the indigenous Church. I suspect that missionaries hope that nationalization of their work will bring the expansion of the Church that they themselves had failed to see. It could be that we have put the cart before the horse. Melvin Hodges criticizes the typical procedure.

> Probably the most common mistake in mission administration today is to organize the work from the top down, rather than from the grass roots up. We usually start in a field with a missionary organization. We place missionaries in key places of responsibility. We hope that in some way our principles and administration will seep down to the pastors and then to the converts, and thus everyone will eventually find his proper place in the organization. What we really do is to stifle the initiative of native converts. What chance of expressing his power of individual action does a convert or native pastor have with capable, energetic Americans in charge? They have a thousand pro-

> motional plans for the work, which they carry out according to American methods rather (than) along lines that nationals can follow. How can a national hope to fill a position of importance and responsibility? Men with better training are already occupying the principal places (Hodges 1965a:218-219).

Hodges' alternative is the planting of local churches that are indigenous or self-sufficient from the start. The basic unit is stressed in this way. Expansion is foremost. Evangelism is done through forming new converts into little churches. Organization, when it comes, is to facilitate the task of evangelism. Emphasizing the local church puts the indigenous believers in the forefront. Organization is not imposed from without but arises from within, to meet a felt need. The kind of structure which if formed may be quite different from the parent (i.e. that of the missionary). But it is true to native culture.

An example of an imposed scheme is the nationalization plan followed by the Conservative Baptists. Basically the plan calls for the organization of the Mission into a Field Conference. As evangelism produces churches, Italian church leaders are to be asked to serve on joint committees with the missionaries. Step by step, the plan is to turn over the organization to these pastors and Church leaders until the entire operation is in their hands. The Church would then be considered nationalized, and the Mission would be free to move on.

Several criticisms may be leveled against this plan. It expends much time and energy attending to organizational details which could be time spent in evangelism. In other words evangelism is relegated to second place and is neglected.

The plan is paternalistic. It centers in and is imposed by the foreigner. The Mission is central, not the Italian Church. Missionaries are in control and appear to "condescend" to invite Italians to join.

Committee work is itself contrary to the Italian way. Organizational flare is an American trait. To structure the Church this way is to give it a foreign flavor. This is the basic objection.

Committee work may be part of the program, but possible Italian ways of running the Church should be considered.

Missionaries all too easily become bogged down with the machinery. Italians are more apt to forget about the machine. Which is more important, to run the machine or to multiply churches? If neglect of organizational work allows more time for evangelism, the latter seems desirable. The more natural Italian approach would probably be to leave administration to one or two capable individuals and let them handle it. This fits the strong-man concept. It also is logical in Southern Italian society which lacks both followers and leaders. Therefore it seems wise to allow the developing Church to take its own course. Imposing an American-type structure almost certainly will create problems.

Roland Allen evaluated well the problem of the joint-work committee scheme.

> The nationals who sit on these committees are all men who have been trained in western habits of thought; and the money upon which the committees depend to carry on their work is almost wholly derived from a foreign source. The committee is an institution of foreign creation... Thus, from the point of view from which we are now considering them, it makes no difference whether the committee is wholly foreign or composed almost entirely of nationals. The work is foreign and must be conducted to the satisfaction of foreigners (Allen 1965:96).

The executing of such a planned program of "nationalization" seems to work against the indigeneity of the Church. Instead of concern to develop an Italian Church, Italians are being made over into the image of missionary administrators. Instead of an Italian Church being planted, an Italianized American Church is being transplanted. Nationalization of this sort is not the same as indigenization. The indigenous Church is not produced by nationalizing a foreign type of committee.

The problem is complicated by the fact that missionary church planting in Italy has been a slow process. Experience has shown that it takes as much as two terms for a missionary to start and get a church on its feet. During this period the missionary acts as pastor, preacher, priest, and evangelist. When he leaves a national must fill the spot as pastor. Can a national do so? He is expected to be a "professional", full-time pastor in much the same role as the missionary. "Nationalization" in this case means a difficult transition for both pastor and the church.

For the missionary this kind of church planting can be frustrating. He is forced to be everything in one situation for a long term. The church which develops cannot help imbibing the foreign influence, and the decontamination process called nationalization becomes necessary.

An evil derives for the missionary too from a nationalization scheme. Italians are found to fill the committees and this is hailed as progress. One of the goals of the Mission is being fulfilled. The result may be self-deception. There may be no numerical increase. The Church could be static. Everyone is rejoicing over "progress" which could actually deter the true organic indigenous growth of the Church. Instead of increased Italianization the Church may be experiencing greater Americanization. The missionary fails to see this because he is confused by having the wrong goal. Nationalization of this type neglects both the quality and quantity growth of the Church.

Business-like organization is the typically American way of running the Church. Italians too have a concern for organization, but they tend to mean something different by the word. To them it is more likely a function which is not an end in itself. Italians are very capable business people although they do not operate in our American fashion. Surely they are capable of running their Church effectively in an Italian way.

Those evangelistic groups which seem most effective in Italy do not bother a great deal about organizational matters. Both the Brethren and the Pentecostals owe thier existence to influences from outside the country, but they are considered very Italian. They are "indigenous" and have spread as Italian Churches. They possess Italian characteristics not found in their sister Churches in England and America. They have innovated.

Methodology, then should be consistent with the goal of mission, which is the production of a vital Italian Church.

Action. Recognizing the prime task is essential. Paper plans, however, despite their excellence, are of little value unless acted upon. Yet this is precisely where excellent plans sometimes fail. Calvin Guy, apparently from the setting of a week in which missionaries have been planning their next year's work, makes a very revealing evaluation. "Budgets, salary scales, repairs, rents, and scholarship take hours. While the bulk of their planning ought to concern the spiritual thrust, most of it deals with matters material and mechanical" (Guy 1965:146).

Guy, after having discussed the matter of time with a number of missionaries, suggests that the average missionary spends no more than two weeks out of the year in the spiritual ministry of praying, preaching, training, etc. (Guy 1965:147). This, it would seem, is our major obstacle. We are too busy with the wrong things.

A RELEVANT MESSAGE

Christ is the Message at the heart of the Gospel. This message must be conveyed. Its communication is the reason for missions. A relevant mission is one which communicates Christ effectively across cultures. The central message never changes although its cultural framework does. In Italy the message must be announced in relevant terms which vary from substratum to substratum.

Communication. "The major difficulties in communication result largely from the fact that we take communication for granted." Thus Nida begins the first chapter of his book on the cross-cultural communication of the faith (1960). Missions revolves around communicating Christianity which is a way of life encoded in the Bible. Speech, writing, emotions, the senses are parts of a host of ways of communication. Communication is not limited to the conveyance of information. The essence of Christianity is new life in Christ. The issue is the effective communication of new life.

Words alone are inadequate to impart life. The message must be couched in relevant terms. In human experience the incarnation is the supreme example of relevant communication. God communicated Himself to man by taking a body and living among men as a man. The Bible is the inspired source for this revelation. The message and its communication must not be taken for granted. It seems obvious that most people would not understand that message as originally written. The Greek of the New Testament and the Hebrew of the Old must be translated. That is one step toward relevance and communication. There are also others, a selected number of which are to be considered briefly here. The Gospel is more than information: it is Good News which brings new life. This is what the successful bearer of the Gospel does: he carries the Good News of new life in such a way that the Holy Spirit is able to impart that life to the receiver. Samuel Moffett speaks of evangelism as purposeful preaching with power. It is planned and it produces results --people are persuaded to believe and obey Jesus Christ (Moffett n.d.:9). That is actual communication.

Communication is two-way. The source as well as the receiver is involved. The messenger must be acceptable to his audience. The receptor must be in a position to accept. The roles of participants must be understood in terms of the society. Communicators need to be aware of the dynamics of the situation.

In Italy individuals may respond as individuals, but experience shows that church growth takes place better when persons respond as part of the family. Therefore Nida's judgment stands that, "if people can respond only as families, the challenge must be to families" (1960:178).

Nevertheless certain individuals may become the means for the entrance of the Gospel even as others may impede. "Target" individuals should be chosen with care. Nida points out that persons who are the censors of information are not good candidates for spreading the faith to others because of their negative role. At the opposite end of the spectrum are persons who act primarily as receivers and readily accept the message. But as the former sit in judgment rather than broadcast the message, the latter are unable to disseminate it. For effective growth the Good News should be directed to the opinion makers, "to the creators and purveyors of information" in the mainstream of the society (Nida 1965:183-184).

An incident from personal experience illustrates the power both of the censor and of the opinion maker. For several months I had conducted a Bible study in an Italian village. Interest varied, but at times seemed high. Many visited sporadically, but others were regular attendants. Potential seemed high for establishing a church. One week interest seemed to have reached a peak, centered in a woman who had never attended before. That was the last such meeting in that village. I was politely invited to not return. Someone had exercised negative influence which prohibited even the very interested from carrying on. This seems a case of the censor circumventing communication. My analysis seems substantiated by the fact that the earlier Bible studies had been well received by another family who had opened their courtyard to the neighborhood. The head of that family was an effective advocate of the missionary's message. Had he remained in the community a church would no doubt have developed. Its demise followed his departure and the appearance of this woman.

The role of this Italian advocate indicates the need for study of methods of communication in Italian societies. Much peasantry of the South may be regarded as a face-to-face society. The missionary needs to learn the structure of such a society, and then follow appropriate principles for communication (Nida 1960:110). (1) Personal friendship is the basis for effective communication. The missionary should develop friendly contacts rather than spend his time in administrative detail or in the mass distribution of literature. This principle suggests that a person's influence will be somewhat limited. Industrial studies have shown that one person may develop intimate ties, or a personal relationship, with about 200 persons. (2) Persons who can effectively pass on communication to members of their families should be the objects of the initial approach. Possible advocates of change in Italy may be students and local gossips as well as their American relatives. (3) It takes time for new ideas to be diffused within the group. Time must be allowed for the advocates, recipients, censors, and innovators of the society to interact. (4) The challenge must be addressed to those socially capable of deciding concerning a change of belief and action. Certainly these are not children. In Italian society they are the family heads. Women hold a great deal of religious influence and should not be disregarded.

Communication methods need to be adjusted to fit the subcultural mosaic. The mass media easily fall into a trap of appealing to one limited subgroup while failing to influence society at large (Luzbetak 1970:122). Radio programs and literature may reach the elite but miss the masses. The professionals may be attracted by an approach while repels the peasants. "Each subsociety has its own way of life and underlying assumptions, values, and goals, and unless the communication is geared accordingly it will fail to inform, convince, and persuade" (Luzbetak 1970:122). Mass evangelism may fail to communicate because it is a shotgun approach which scatters broadly without specific aim. As it generalizes to suit all it may fail to zero in on any specific segment of the mosaic.

Communication to be effective considers also the difference in viewpoint between the missionary and the Italian. The one is Protestant, the other Catholic in background. The social and theological outlook of Latin society is dominated by the principles of miracle, mystery and authority. The missionary sometimes fails to realize what an extensive adjustment from this view is called for by his preaching (Nida 1970:53). The approach to morality is culturally different. Catholics and Protestants belong to different subcultures within the same country and do not speak the same cultural language (Luzbetak

1970:121).

The Protestant finds authoritative communication in the Bible. But for the Catholic it comes from Church tradition and the Pope. Proceeding to teach the Bible, the Missionary fails to appreciate the vast differences in the connotations of his Italian hearers. Grace now is the unmerited favor of God rather than an earned "blessing". Works are no longer preached as meritorious; yet works are insisted upon as the demonstration of faith. This is for the Italian a new frame of reference. The work of Christ takes on a new meaning. The Church is no longer a place to obtain merits for salvation, but is the company of believers. This reorientation should be kept in mind by the communicator.

What is our communication? Nida summarizes it as "primarily sowing the seed, not transplanting churches" (1960: 221). McGavran would probably object to the terminology used, but would certainly agree that we must not reproduce our own cultural patterns. Nida no doubt means, too, that seed sowing is meaningless unless it brings forth fruit. There must be harvest. Real communication of the Gospel does plant the seed of the Word in such a way as to bring a valuable yield. As McGavran says, "Evangelism is accomplished communication" (1964:2). It means the multiplication of converts in expanding, multiplying Evangelical Churches. The Protestant Movement in Italy must be a contemporary reality as well as a fact of past history.

Masses and nominals. To accomplish its end, communication of the Gospel must be directed in a meaningful way to people who will respond. It is my contention that this in Italy means evangelizing the masses of lower class people who are only nominally Roman Catholic. Meaningful communication involves accommodation, not of changeless truth, but of the messenger to his audience.

The lower classes make up most of the population of Italy. Exact numbers are difficult to obtain. Banfield in his study of the South concludes that typically only 10 per cent belong to the upper classes. The upper class person does no manual labor, has had more education, and usually enjoys a higher living standard. Peasants make up the bulk, or about two thirds of the population. This is the lowest status in the social structure, with the exception of the Gypsies who have no status at all. Another 10 per cent are artisans and merchants (Banfield 1958:69-70). While the upper class controls most of the wealth, the lower classes contain most of the people. Priests automatically are entitled "Don", which distinguishes them as "gentlemen" or members of the upper classes (Banfield 1958:70). Nevertheless priests are recruited from the lower classes, probably the only sure way to break the class barrier. Peasants are unable to escape the degrading attitudes attached to their relationship to the soil. It is rare for a peasant to become a professional (Banfield 1958:75). Although status is not fixed, to change social classes is not easy - there are too many associations, such as relatives, that cannot be changed.

Foreign missionaries tend to come from a middle class background. Thus they are attracted to professional people, from a background that seems similar to their own (Read, Monterroso, Johnson 1969:230). The problem with this is that it is doubtful whether a middle class really exists in Italy. What may seem middle class to the missionary may be looked upon as upper class by most of the people. Italy consists of the haves and the have-nots. Class change is possible, but the one who climbs out of the lower classes may find himself part of the "haves". Besides it is difficult to change classes. A fortunate one may become a merchant or a government clerk. Marriage is also a way out (Banfield 1958:73). Such persons may have attained "Middle Class" status as we look at it, but in terms of Southern Italian society is probably still tied to his lower class people.

The lower classes are where most of the people are. It is logical for missionaries to work with them for there can be found the responsive peoples. Among the lower classes there is great potential for church growth. As McGavran states, "remembering that our Lord came to save sinners, one must presume that the more sinners saved the better pleased He is." Again, "it seems reasonable to believe that if a hundred thousand Christians are good, two hundred thousand are better" (McGavran 1962:9). The Pentecostals have been growing among these kinds of people, and McGavran's reasoning seems applicable to their strategy. If a hundred thousand Pentecostals are good in Italy, then two hundred thousand should be even better.

"Nations cannot be Christianized without significant growth in the number of Christians" (McGavran 1962:8). The conversion of one per cent of the people is inadequate, according to McGavran. In Italy about a third of one per cent of the population has membership in the Evangelical Churches. The ineffectiveness of the missions may possibly be traced to their inattention to discipling the masses of poor people.

The traditional Protestant approach to the middle classes may have to change (Nida 1960:106). "In the battle between the classes and the masses, the masses are going to win. The future belongs to the common man" (McGavran 1962: 40). The Church must evangelize the multitudes of nominals and semi-nominals of the classes who will respond. The Church must not close itself off as a company of the elite.

Emphasis on the Bible must take into consideration the illiteracy of many. Ability to read is not a prerequisite for conversion or church membership (Wold 1968:57). Heavy use of literature in evangelism implies literacy and tends to eliminate many illiterates and semi-illiterates. Thus we inadvertently minister to the classes and exclude the masses. Radio evangelism likewise appeals to the same audience, the literate - urging the people to "write in". Those who write in are students and priests and the educated, the "elite" and those on the way "up".

A solution seems to be in extensive evangelistic iteneration among the poorer classes and the establishment of lower class churches. The best approach would seem to be through the families, not the use of mass evangelism. Mass media is not required simply because of masses of people. Persecution too may be avoided through private encounter and persuasion (Nida 1960:111-112). The churches founded can then be family churches (even house churches), thus presenting and strengthening the basic unit in Italy society.

Pastors of thse churches should be from among these people, even though they be ignorant and unlearned. "Such pastors from among the people, earnest Christians but little educated, may be *sine qua non* for growth among the masses" (McGavran 1962:39). Rapid church growth can probably only take place when the Churches and Missions of Italy turn to the oppressed peoples who are ready for a change. Nominal Catholics, they may respond to a message of life, bringing hope and meaning to a drab existence.

Catholic Holy Clubs and staunch Roman Catholics. The nominal masses may be described as "Gospel-ready", at least to a degree. Missionaries frequently contact persons of a different type who may also respond to the Gospel message. However, despite a commitment of their lives to Jesus Christ, these persons are not ready to leave the Roman Catholic Church. They have been changed, but for various reasons they choose to remain Catholics. It may be family pressure, fear of losing one's position, or simply a sense of loyalty to the Catholic religion. Or it may be that suitable Churches are not available for them to join. This situation occurs most likely among professional people. The proper solution might be the formation of a different type of church for them to join. But this may not be possible in some circumstances. The missionary can force neither the individual, the ecclisiastical hierarchy, nor the other members of the mission.

What is suggested here, therefore, is an expedient for such situations with such persons. It is not advocated as a rule. For the Masses, Churches should be formed along a "Pentecostal" style, even if they are Baptist and Independent Churches! But for these professionals who do not fit in the Church of the masses, thought should be given to forming some sort of "Holy Clubs" within the Roman Church. Methodists were originally groups of "Holy" people within the Church of England - the idea is not a novelty! In due time the persons in the "Clubs" may choose to leave and form churches of their own or to join other churches. Or may be forced out. But in order to nurture "converts" who choose to remain in the Roman Church, some sort of organism should be set up. The Holy Club would serve as a cell movement within the Catholic Church. Spiritually-minded persons would be sought out by members of the cell and would find that spiritual communion not normally available to him.

Perhaps I am suggesting a type of house church where these people would have regular Bible study and spiritual fellowship. However it would not be called a "church" if the participants are also attending mass.

Evangelicals within the Catholic Church have been found at various times in Italy's history. Some of them have had a profound influence there. Nevertheless the more famous of them came to encounter insurmountable difficulty within the Church.

Let it be noted that what is advocated is not a turn in emphasis. It is a special measure for extraordinary circumstances -- one hopefully temporary. Mission and Church emphasis should continue to be on planting growing churches among the responsive masses.

But the formation of Holy Clubs suggests certain other possible developments. The Italian Church needs to be more Italian. One reason some new converts do not join Protestant Churches is that they do not feel at home in those that exist. The contrast between the Catholic Church and the Protestant ones is too drastic for them, perhaps.

The pentecostal-Baptist churches advocated for the masses make the Protestant-Catholic differences very distinct. They provide substitutes for Catholic practices. Differentiation becomes very important to rivals. Barnett points out that the early Christians rejected many Jewish rites and substituted baptism, the Trinity, communion, Sunday, and the cross. Protestantism has done the same toward Catholicism.

> Protestantism has not only rejected many features of the Catholic Church but has gone on to develop tenents and rituals of its own, such as predestination, unitarianism, and revival meetings. Christian missionaries of all sects make a deliberate effort to prevent a confusion of their faith with local native religious, and in so doing they are often innovative (Barnett 1953:73).

But there is always the nagging suspicion that some practices of the Catholic Church were eliminated merely as a means of differentiation rather than because of theology. This seems true, for instance, of Pentecostalism in some respects, and Brethrenism in others. But in the case of Roman Catholic Christianity, as in Wesley's day with the Anglican Church, it may be necessary to restudy what is the gospel, and allow Catholicism where converts are not in opposition to it or even favor it. My suggestion of Clubs is to reverse this process of deliberate differentiation. Italian converts may need "Catholic"-type Churches. The Club allows opportunity to "hold" the Catholic who has found new life until he finds a church which fulfills his desire for Catholic religious forms yet evangelical fervor and spirit.

Missionaries must be flexible. It is wrong to rigidly impose an un-Italian system of worship and belief. Belief must be Biblical, but worship should also be Italian. Surely the point of missionary work is to reaffirm the Gospel in every possible way.

The Catholic Church herself is beginning to rediscover this flexibility of form. In the days of extensive Catholic missions it was proposed that missionaries would adapt to local customs. This was not necessarily a compromise of the message. It was accommodation. The Sacred Congregation for the Propagation of the Faith, founded in 1662 by Pope Gregory XV, in 1659 sent out instructions to its vicars apostolic which included the following:

> Do not regard it as your task, and do not bring any pressure to bear on the people, to change their manners, customs, and uses, unless they are contrary to religion and sound morals. What could be more absurd than to transport France, Spain, Italy, or some other European country to

> China? Do not introduce all that to them, but only the faith...It is the nature of men to love and treasure above everything else their own country and that which belongs to it. In consequence there is no stronger cause for alienation and hate than an attack on local customs, especially when they go back to a venerable antiquity... Do not draw invidious contrasts between the customs of the people and those of Europe; do your utmost to adapt yourselves to them (Neill 1966:179).

Can we not say the same for our work today? Italians need Italian Churches, not Italianized American, German, and English ones. Can we not let the Italians introduce their own changes? Then change is not imposed by outsiders. To illustrate, our refusal to allow even a simple cross in our meeting halls is a stumbling-block to some Catholics. Yet the cross is a symbol for all Christians, not just Roman Catholics.

Again the Catholic Church provides the negative example. Pope Benedict XIV in 1742 swept away all "Jesuit accommodations". Offending China in the process apparently did not matter. It meant that Catholic Christianity was to be "Roman" wherever found. "Rome had ruled that Roman practice, exactly as it was at Rome, was to be in every detail the law for the missions" (Neill 1966:194). This "foreign" orientation was to govern Catholic missions for two hundred years. It was a tragic blow.

The Holy Club cell movement would be left in the hands of Italians. It must not be missionary oriented or directed. Planned spontaneity seems the word. I am not suggesting that we abadon our present programs of evangelizing and church planting. Rather I believe we should increase them. But I am calling for flexibility. We should study the kind of church we are planting and developing. Different situations call for different solutions. We should consider diversity in this area too.

Experimentation with this idea should bear in mind the characteristics of the New Catholicism. The Foccolari Movement with its Bible emphasis seems worthy of investigation in relation to the present proposal. How "Evangelical" is this Catholic ecumenical group? My own acquaintance with the Foccolari is limited. However I have the impression that emphsis of the Movement is on Christ and the Bible. At the University for Foreigners at Perugia I observed what I considered a very effective piece of evangelism on the part of the

Foccolari Center of Assisi. The film, "The Gospel According to Saint Matthew", was shown at the University to the international students. Interested persons were extended an invitation to discuss Jesus Christ with Center members and to visit the Center for study and meditation. The tone of that particular meeting was certainly evangelistic, and while I do not know the doctrinal emphasis of the Movement, it appeared on that occassion quite "Protestant".

A relevant mission is one that dares to be all things for all men in order to win some to the Savior.

Bibliography

ABBOTT, Walter M.
1966 The Documents of Vatican II. London, Geoffrey Chapman. (Translated by Msgr. Joseph Gallagher from the original Latin).

ALLEN, Roland
1965 The Ministry of the Spirit. Grand Rapids, Michigan, William B. Eerdmans Publishing Co.

ASKE, Sigurd
1967 "Radio Voice of the Gospel," International Review of Missions, LVI: 355-364.

BANFIELD, Edward C.
1958 The Moral Basis of a Backward Society. Glencoe, Illinois, The Free Press, University of Chicago.

BARNETT, H. G.
1953 Innovation: The Basis of Cultural Change. New York, McGraw-Hill Book Co. Inc.

BARRON, Louis ed.
1963 Europe. Vol 3 of Worldmark Encyclopedia of the Nations. New York, Harper & Row.

BARZINI, Luigi
1967 The Italians. New York, Atheneum.

1968 "Italy: The Fragile State," Foreign Affairs An American Quarterly Review, 46, 3: 562-574

BEAVER, Robert Pierce
1968 The Missionary Between the Times. Garden City, New York, Doubleday and Company Inc.

BINGLE, E. J., and GRUBB, Kenneth G. eds.
1952 World Christian Handbook. London, World Dominion.

1957 World Christian Handbook. London, World Dominion.

BLACKMER, D. L. M.
1968 Unity in Diversity: Italian Communism and the Communist World. Cambridge, Massachusetts, MIT Press

BLUNT, John James
1823 Vestiges of Ancient Manners and Customs, Discoverable in Modern Italy and Sicily. London, John Murray, Albemarle-Street.

BODENSIECK, Julius, ed
1965 "Italy," The Encyclopedia of the Lutheran Church, Vol. II. Minneapolis, Augsburgh Publishing House.

BRADSHAW, Malcolm R.
1969 Church Growth through Evangelism-in-Depth.. South Pasadena, William Carey Library.

BROOKS, Cyril H.
1969 "Joint Protestant-Catholic Translation: Should We or Shouldn't We?" Evangelical Missions Quarterly, 5; 3: 170-179.

BRUNK, George
1969 "Mennonite Church in Italy," A Report given at Christian Workers' Conference, Naples, Italy.

BURGALASSI, Silvano
1967 Italiani in Chiesa, Analisi Sociologica del Comportamento Religioso. Brescia, Morcelliana.

1968 Il Comportamento Religioso degli Italiani. Firenze, Vallecchi Editore.

CAMMETT, John M.
1967 Antonio Gramsci and the Origins of Italian Communism. Stanford, California, Stanford University Press.

CAPPELLETTI, Mauro, MERRYMAN, John H. and PERILLO, Joseph M.
1967 The Italian Legal System, An Introduction. Stanford, California, Stanford University Press.

CARRINGTON, Hereward
1909 Eusapia Palladino and Her Phenomena. New York, B. W. Dodge and Company.

CASSIN, Elena
1959 San Nicandro. London, Cohen & West. (Translated by Douglas West from the original French.)

CBFMS
1969 Minutes of the Evangelism Committee of the Conservative Baptist Mission in Italy, September 23, 1969.

CHURCH, Frederic C.
1932 The Italian Reformers, 1534-1564. New York Columbia University Press.

CHURCH GROWTH BULLETIN
1965 Vols, I & II. Pasadena, California, School of World Mission and Institute of Church Growth.

CHURCHES OF CHRIST
1969 Christian Chronicle XXVI 46. Austin, Texas, Sweet Publishing Co.

CLARK, Francis E. and CLARK, Harriet A.
1909 The Gospel in Latin Lands. New York, The MacMillan Company.

COAD, F. Roy
1968 A History of the Brethren Movement. Grand Rapids, Michigan, William B. Erdmans Publishing Co.

COCHRANE, Thomas, ed.
1953 "The Colporteur in Italy," World Dominion, XXXI, 6: 334.

COMBA, Ernesto
1930 Storia dei Valdesi. Torre Pellice, Libreria Claudiana.

CONSIGLIO FEDERALE DELLE CHIESE EVANGELICHE IN ITALIA
1967 Cristianesimo Evangelico, 1967-68 Annuario. Torino, Editrice Claudiana.

COOK, Harold R.
1967 Highlights of Christian Missions. Chicago, Moody Press.

COXILL, H. Wakelin, and GRUBB, Kenneth G. eds.
1962 World Christian Handbook. London, World Dominion.

1968 World Christian Handbook. London, Lutterworth Press

CRIVELLI, P. Camillo
1936 I Protestanti in Italia (Specialmente nei Secoli XIX e XX), I. Isola del Liri, Soc. Tip. A. Macioce e Pisani.

1938 I Protestanti in Italia (Specialmente nei secoli XIX e XX), II. Isola del Liri, Soc. Tip. A. Macioce e Pisani.

CROCE, Benedetto
1929 A History of Italy 1971-1915. Oxford, Claredon Press. (Translated by Cecilia M. Ady from the Original Italian.)

CROW, John A.
1965 Italy, A Journey through Time. New York, Harper & Row.

DAVIS, J. Merle
1939 The Economic and Social Environment of the Younger Churches. London, The Edinburgh House Press.

1943 How the Church Grows in Brazil. New York, International Missionary Council.

1947 New Buildings on Old Foundations. New York, International Missionary Council.

DE MICHELIS, Giuseppe
1926 L'Emigrazione Italiana Negli Anni 1924 E 1925. Commissario Generale dell'Emigrazione.

DICKINSON, Robert E.
1955 The Population Problem of Southern Italy. Syracuse University Press.

DOUGLAS, J. D.
1962 "Italy," Christianity Today, VI, 20: 12.

DURANT, Will
1953 The Renaissance. Part V in The Story of Civilization. New York, Simon & Schuster.

1957 The Reformation. Part VI in The Story of Civilization. New York, Simon & Schuster.

ELWORTHY, Frederick T.
1958 The Evil Eye. New York, The Julian Press Inc.

ENNS, Arno W.
1967 "Profiles of Argentine Church Growth." An unpublished M.A. thesis, School of World Mission and Institute of Church Growth, Fuller Theological Seminary.

EVANS, Robert P.
1962 "Missionary Situation in Europe," Christianity Today, VI, 6:15-16.

1963a "Can Europeans Evangelize the Continent?" United Evangelical Action, 22; 2: 65f.

1963b "Europe - Darkening Continent," Eternity, 14: 8-10ff.

1963c Let Europe Hear. Chicago, Moody Press.

1965 "Europe - Mission Field Under Camouflage," Moody Monthly, 65: 9: 18-20f.

FEHDERAU, Herald W.
1961 "Missionary Endeavor and Anthropology," Practical Anthropology, 8: 221-223

FLEMING, Louis B.
1969 "Italy Divorce Law Seen No Family Threat," Los Angeles Times, December 7, 1969: 4-5.

FOERSTER, Robert F.
1924 The Italian Emigration of Our Times. Cambridge, Harvard University Press.

FOY, Felican A. ed.
1969 Catholic Almanac. Garden City, New York, Doubleday & Co., Inc. Distributor (or St. Anthony's Guild, Publisher, Paterson, New York).

FRAZER, Sir James G.
1935 The Golden Bough, A Study in Magic and Religion, Part IV, Adonis Attis Osiris Vol. II. New York The MacMillan Co.

FRIED, Robert C.
1963 The Italian Prefects. New Haven, Yale University Press.

FROMM, Joseph
1969 "Peace, Plenty and Problems: That's Europe," U.S. News and World Report, LXVII; 24: 68-72

FULLER, Roy
1969 "Church of the Nazarene." A Report given at Christian Workers' Conference, Naples, Italy.

GEBHART, Emile
n.d. Mystics and Heretics in Italy. New York, Alfred A. Knopf.

GIBBS, Joe Edward
1958 "Mission Work of the Churches of Christ in Italy 1949-1957." An unpublished M.A. Thesis, Harding College, Memphis, Tennessee.

GODDARD, Burton L. ed.
1967 The Encyclopedia of Modern Christian Missions. Camden, New Jersey, Thomas Nelson & Sons.

GREATER EUROPE MISSION
1969 Greater Europe Mission Reporter, Vol XII; 3. Wheaton, Illinois.

GUICCIARDINI, Francesco
1969 The History of Italy. New York, The MacMillan Company. (Translated by Sidney Alexander from the original Italian edition of 1561).

GUY, Robert Calvin
1965a "Directed Conversation" in D.A. McGavran (ed.)

1965b "Elimination the Underbrush" in D.A. McGavran (ed.)

HALPERIN, Samuel W.
1939 Italy and the Vatican at War. Chicago, University of Chicago Press.

1937 The Separation of Church and State in Italian Thought from Cavour to Mussolini. Chicago, University of Chicago Press.

HARPER, Michael
1965 As at the Beginning; the Twentieth Century Pentecostal Revival. London, Hodder & Stoughton.

HERDER, H. and WALEY, D. P.
1963 A Short History of Italy, Cambridge, University Press.

HODGES, Melvin L.
1965a "Administering for Church Growth" in D.A. McGarvan (ed.).

1965b "Developing Basic Units of Indigenous Churches" In D.A. McGavran (ed.).

1968 "A Pentecostals' View of Mission Strategy," International Review of Missions, LVII; 227: 304-310.

HOLT, Ivan Lee and CLARK, Elmer T.
1956 The World Methodist Movement. Nashville, Tennessee, The Upper Room.

HORNER, Norman A. ed.
1968 Protestant Crosscurrents in Mission. Nashville and New York, Abingdon Press.

HUGHES, Philip
1952 A History of the Church; Volume Two, The Church and the World the Church Created. London, Sheed and Ward.

HYDE, A. B.
1888 The Story of Methodism. Springfield, Massachusetts, Willey and Company.

IRONSIDE, H. A.
1942 A Historical Sketch of the Brethren Movement. Grand Rapids, Michigan, Zondervan Publishing House.

JAHIER, Augusto
1924 Riformatori e Riformati Italiani dei Secoli XV XVI. Firenze, Societa' Editrice Claudiana.

JALLA, Giovanni
1914 Storia della Riforma in Piemonte. Firenze, Libreria Claudiana.

JAMES, E. O.
1959 The Cult of the Mother-Goddess. London, Thames and Hudson.

JEMELO, Arthro C.
1960 Church and State in Italy, 1850-1950. Oxford Basil Blackwell. (Translated by David Moore from the original Italian.)

JOHNSON, Harmon A.
1969 "Authority Over the Spirits: Brazilian Spiritism and Evangelical Church Growth." An unpublished M.A. thesis, School of World Mission and Institute of Church Growth, Fuller Theological Seminary.

JONES, Robert
1970 Personal letter to author, February 9.

KANE, J. Herbert
1965 "Europe's Missions at a Glance," Moody Monthly, 65: 9: 21-22.

KEESING, Felix
1963 Cultural Anthropology: The Science of Custom. New York, Holt, Rinehart and Winston.

KELLER, Adolf
1936 Church and State on the European Continent. London, The Epworth Press.

KERR, John S.
1969 "Laymen: the Secret of Strength," World Encounter, 7; 2: 30-35.

KESSLER, J. B. A.
1963 "Hindrances to Church Growth," International Review of Missions, LVII; 227: 298-303.

KUNG, Hans
1964 The Council and Reunion. London, Sheed & Ward.

1965 The Changing Church. London, Sheed & Ward.

Kung, Hans ed.
1969 The Future of Ecumenism. Vol. 44 of Concilium, Theology in the Age of Renewal. New York Paulist Press.

LATOURETTE, Kenneth Scott
1941 The Great Century, A.D. 1800-A.D. 1914, Europe and the United States of America. Vol. IV of A History of the Expansion of Christianity. New York, Harper and Brothers.

1959 The Nineteenth Century in Europe. Vol. II of Christianity in a Revolutionary Age. New York, Harper and Brothers.

1969 The Twentieth Century in Europe. Vol. IV of Christianity in a Revolutionary Age. Grand Rapids, Michigan, Zondervan Publishing House.

LELAND, Charles G.
1899 Aradia or the Gospel of the Witches. London, David Nutt.

LENTI, Libero
1962 "Italy," Chicago, Encyclopedia Brittanica. Vol. 12

LESSA, William A. and VOGT, Evon Z. eds.
1965 Reader in Comparative Religion. New York, Harper and Row.

LUZBETAK, Louis J.
1970 The Church and Cultures. Techny, Illinois, Divine Word Publications.

LUZZI, Giovanni
1913 The Struggle for Christian Truth in Italy. New York, Fleming H. Revell Co.

MALINOWSKI, Bronislaw
1965 "The Role of Magic and Religion," in Lessa and Vogt eds.

MAMMARELLA, Giuseppe
1966 Italy After Fascism, A. Political History 1943-1965. Notre Dame, University of Notre Dame Press.

MARC
L(¢& "Analysis of Missions Research." Monrovia, California, Missions Advanced Research and Communication Center.

McCRIE, Thomas
1842 History of the Progress and Suppression of the Reformation in Italy in the Sixteenth Century including a Sketch of the History of the Reformation in the Grisons. Philadelphia, Presbyterian Board of Publications.

McGAVRAN, Donald A.

1962 Church Growth in Jamacia. Lucknow, India, Lucknow Publishing House.

1964 "Principles of Church Growth," Church Growth Bulletin, I; 1: 1-3.

1966 "Church Plantings in Post-Christian Europe," Church Growth Bulletin, II; 3: 125-126.

1966b "Why Neglect Gospel-Ready Masses?" Christianity Today, X; 15: 769-771.

1970 Understanding Church Growth. Grand Rapids, Michigan, William B. Eerdmans Publishing Co.

McGAVRAN, Donald A. ed.

1965a Church Growth and Christian Mission. New York Harper and Row Publishers.

1965b "Does Gospel Radio Grow Churches?" Church Growth Bulletin, II; 1: 97-98.

McNAIR, Philip

1967 Peter Martyr in Italy. Oxford, At Clarendon Press.

MISCIATTELLI, Piero

1924 Fascisti e Cattolici. Milano, Casa Editrice Imperia del Partito Nazionale Fascista.

MISSIONARY RESEARCH LIBRARY

1968 North American Protestant Ministries Overseas Directory. 8th Edition. Monrovia, California, Missionary Research Library in cooperation with Missions Advanced Research and Communications Center.

MOFFETT, Samuel H.

n.d. The Biblical Background of Evangelism. Pittsburgh, Presbyterians United for Biblical Concerns.

MOLLAR, R. J.

1968 "New Step toward Unity: Federation of Italian Protestants," Christian Century; 85: 119-120.

MOORE, W. Dewey
1951 "Italy, the Land of the Book" in N. F. Weeks.

MUSSOLINI, Benito
1928 My Auto Biography. New York, Scribners.

NASSE, George N.
1964 The Italo Albanian Villages of Southern Italy. Washington, National Academy of Sciences.

NEILL, Stephen
1966 A History of Christian Missions. Vol. 6 in The Pelican History of the Church. Middlesex, England, Penguin Books.

NEUFELD, Don F. ed.
1966 "Italy," Seventh-Day Adventist Encyclopedia. Vol. 10 in Commentary Reference Series. Washington, Review & Herald Publishing Assn.

NICHOL, John Thomas
1966 Pentecostalism. New York, Harper & Row Publishers.

NIDA, Eugene A.
1957 "The Roman Catholic, Communist, and Protestant Approach to Social Structure," Practical Anthropology; 4: 209-219.

1960 Message and Mission. New York, Harper & Row Publishers.

1965 "Dynamics of Church Growth: in D. A. McGavran (ed)

O'HANLON, D. J.
1963 "Pentecostals and Pope John's New Pentecost," America, 108: 634-636.

OLIN, John C.
1969 The Catholic Reformation: Savonarola to Ignatius Loyola. New York, Harper and Row.

PECK, Royal L.
1966 "The Myth of Christian Italy," World Vision Magazine, 10; 5: 5-6f

1969 "Greater Europe Mission." A Report given at Christian Workers' Conference, Naples, Italy.

PERNA, Alfred J. Sr.
1970 Personal letter to author, February 10.

PETTAZZONI, Raffaele
1952 Italia Religiosa. Bari, Giuseppe Laterza e Figli.

RADIN, Paul
1935 The Italians of San Francisco, Their Adjustment and Acculturation. Abstract from the SERA Project 2-F2-98: Cultural Anthropology.

RAHNER, Karl
1966 The Church After the Council. New York, Herder and Herder

RAINES, Robert A.
1961 New Life in the Church. New York, Harper & Row.

READ, William R.
1965 New Patterns of Church Growth in Brazil. Grand Rapids, Michigan, William B. Eerdmans Publishing Company.

READ, William R., MONTERROSO, Victor M. and JOHNSON, Harmon A.
1969 Latin American Church Growth. Grand Rapids, Michigan, William B. Eerdmans Publishing Company.

ROBERTS, W. Dayton
1967 Revolution in Evangelism, The Story of Evangelism-In-Depth in Latin America. Chicago, Moody Press.

ROHRBAUGH, Ruth
1969 "By Whose Spirit," Conservative Baptist Impact, 26: 4: 3.

ROSE, Philip M.
1922 A Razor for a Goat. Toronto, University of Toronto Press.

ROSE, Philip M.
1922 The Italians in America. New York, George H. Doran Company.

RUSSO, Giovanni
1958 c L'Italia dei Poveri. Milano, Longanesi.

SALVADORI, Massimo
1965 Italy. Englewood Cliffs, New Jersey, Prentice-Hall, Inc.

SALVATION ARMY, THE
1968 The Salvation Army Year Book 1969. London, Salvationist Publishing and Supplies, Ltd.

SANTINI, Alceste, ARTISSI, Alvise & CAPEZZANT, Giorgio
1969 Minoranze Religiose in Italia. Roma, Edizioni Religioni Oggi.

SAPEZIAN, Aharon
1969 "Renewal in Mission - A Brazilian View," International Review of Mission, LVIII: 153-157.

SCHACHTER, Gustav
1965 The Italian South; Economic Development in Mediterranean Europe. New York, Random House

SEVENTH-DAY ADVENTIST
1918-1968 Statistical Report of Seventh-Day Adventist Conferences, Missions, and Institutions. Takoma Park, Washington D.C., General Conference of Seventh Day Adventists.

1948 Yearbook of the Seventh-Day Adventist Denomination. Washington, Review & Herald Publishing Assn.

1957 Yearbook of the Seventh-Day Adventist Denomination. Washington, Review & Herald Publishing Assn.

SHEPHERD, Jack F.
1968 "The Missionary Objective: Total World Evangelism," in N. A. Horner (ed.)

SILVERMAN, Sydel F.
1968 "Agricultural Organization, Social Structure, and Values in Italy: Amoral Familism Reconsidered," American Anthropologist, 70; 1: 1-20.

SMALLEY, William A.
1958 "Cultural Implications of an Indigenous Church," Practical Anthropology, 5; 2: 51-65.

SOUTHERN BAPTIST CONVENTION
1968 Annual of the Southern Baptist Convention 1968. Nashville, Executive Committee, Southern Baptist Convention.

SOUTHERN BAPTIST CONVENTION
1970 "Europe and the Middle East." An unpublished manuscript, The Foreign Mission Board, Richmond, Virginia.

SPAULDING, A. W.
1949 Christ's Last Legion. Washington, Review and Herald Publishing Association.

1962 Origin and History of Seventh-Day Adventists. Vol. 3. Washington, Review & Herald Pub. Assn.

SPINI, Giorgio
1956 Risorgimento e Protestanti. Rapoli, Edizioni Scientifiche Italiane.

STANDRIDGE, Maria Teresa
1968 "Italian Literature and the Foreign Missionary." A Paper presented at the 20th Annual Evangelical Workers' Conference, Rimini, Italy, December 31.

STEINER, Leonard
1957 "The Pentecostal Movement," World Domination, XXXV; 1: 51-54f.

TIPPETT, A. R.
1960 "Probing Missionary Inadequancies at the Popular Level," International Review of Missions, 49: 411-419.

1967 Solomon Islands Christianity. London, Lutterworth Press.

1969 Verdict Theology in Missionary Theory. Lincoln, Illinois, Lincoln Christian College Press.

TYSON, Brady
1965 "Three False Ideas About Church Growth," Church Growth Bulletin, II; 1: 95-97

VILLARI, Luigi
1926 "Italy," London, Encyclopedia Brittanica.

VINAY, Valdo
1965 Luigi Desanctis e il Movimento Evangelico fra gli Italiani durante il Risorgimento. Torino,

VINGIANI, Maria
1969 "Ecumenical Experiments in Italy" in H. Kung (ed.)

WAGNER, C. Peter
1970a Latin American Theology: Radical or Evangelical? Grand Rapids, William B. Eerdmans Publishing Co.

1970b "Toward a Mature and Relevant Church." Lecture delivered at School of World of Mission, Fuller Theological Seminary, Pasadena, California.

WEBB, Leicester C.
1958 Church and State in Italy 1947-1957. Melbourne University Press on behalf of the Australian National University.

WEEKS, Nan F. ed.
19511 Europe - Whither Bound? Nashville, Broadman.

WESTLUND, Lester P.
1968 "Avoiding the Dangers of Mission Institutions," Evangelical Missions Quarterly, 4; 4: 227-236.

WHITLOCK, Raymond C. and Lois S.
1969 "A Spectre is Haunting Europe..." A Paper presented at the 29th Annual Evangelical Worker's Conference, Rimini, Italy, January 1.

WHYTE, William F.
1955 Street Corner Society; the Social Structure of an Italian Slum. Chicago, University of Chicago Press.

WINEHOUSE, Irwin
1959 The Assemblies of God; A Popular Survey. New York, Vantage Press.

WOLD, Joseph Conrad
1968 God's Impatience in Liberia. Grand Rapids, William B. Eerdmans Publishing Company.

WOLF, Eric
1965 "The Virgin of Guadelupe: A Mexican National Symbol" in Lessa and Vogt (eds.)

WYLIE, Rev. J. A.
n.d. History of the Waldenses. London, Cassell, Petter, Galpin and Company.

YOUNG, W. H.
1949 The Italian Left; A Short History of Political Socialism in Italy. London & New York, Longmans, Green.

Index

William Carey Library

PUBLICATIONS

Africa

PEOPLES OF SOUTHWEST ETHIOPIA, by A. R. Tippett, Ph.D.

A recent, penetrating evaluation by a professional anthropologist of the cultural complexities faced by Peace Corps workers and missionaries in a rapidly changing intersection of African states.

1970: 320 pp, $3.95. ISBN 0-87808-103-8

PROFILE FOR VICTORY: NEW PROPOSALS FOR MISSIONS IN ZAMBIA, by Max Ward Randall.

"In a remarkably objective manner the author has analyzed contemporary political, social educational and religious trends, which demand a re-examination of traditional missionary methods and the creation of daring new strategies...his conclusions constitute a challenge for the future of Christian missions, not only in Zambia, but around the world."

1970: 224 pp, Cloth, $3.95. ISBN 0-87808-403-7

THE CHURCH OF THE UNITED BRETHREN OF CHRIST IN SIERRA LEONE, by Emmett D. Cox, Executive Secretary, United Brethren in Christ Board of Missions.

A readable account of the relevant historical, demographic and anthropological data as they relate to the development of the United Brethren in Christ Church in the Mende and Creole communities. Includes a reformation of objectives.

1970: 184 pp, $2.95. ISBN 0-87808-301-4

APPROACHING THE NUER OF AFRICA THROUGH THE OLD TESTAMENT, by Ernest A. McFall.

The author examines in detail the similarities between the Nuer and the Hebrews of the Old Testament and suggests a novel Christian approach that does not make initial use of the New Testament.

1970: 104 pp, 8 1/2 x 11, $1.95. ISBN 0-87808-310-3

Asia

TAIWAN: MAINLINE VERSUS INDEPENDENT CHURCH GROWTH, A STUDY IN CONTRASTS, by Allen J. Swanson.

A provocative comparison between the older, historical Protestant churches in Taiwan and the new indigenous Chinese churches; suggests staggering implications for missions everywhere that intend to promote the development of truly indigenous expressions of Christianity.

1970: 216 pp, $2.95. ISBN 0-87808-404-5

NEW PATTERNS FOR DISCIPLING HINDUS: THE NEXT STEP IN ANDHRA PRADESH, INDIA, by B.V. Subbamma.

Proposes the development of a Christian movement that is as well adapted culturally to the Hindu tradition as the present movement is to the Harijan tradition. Nothing could be more crucial for the future of 400 million Hindus in India today.

1970: 212 pp, $3.45. ISBN 0-87808-306-5

GOD'S MIRACLES: INDONESIAN CHURCH GROWTH, by Ebbie C. Smith, Th.D.

The fascinating details of the penetration of Christianity into the Indonesian archipelago make for intensely interesting reading, as the anthropological context and the growth of the Christian movement are highlighted.

1970: 224 pp, $3.45. ISBN 0-87808-302-2

NOTES ON CHRISTIAN OUTREACH IN A PHILIPPINE COMMUNITY, by Marvin K. Mayers, Ph.D.

The fresh observations of an anthropologist coming from the outside provide a valuable, however preliminary, check list of social and historical factors in the context of missionary endeavors in a Tagalog province.

1970: 71 pp, 8 1/2 x 11, $1.45. ISBN 0-87808-104-6

Latin America

THE PROTESTANT MOVEMENT IN BOLIVIA, by C. Peter Wagner.

An excitingly-told account of the gradual build-up and present vitality of Protestantism. A cogent analysis of the various subcultures and the organizations working most effectively, including a striking evaluation of Bolivia's momentous Evangelism-in-Depth year and the possibilities of Evangelism-in-Depth for other parts of the world.

1970: 264 pp, $3.95. ISBN 0-87808-402-9

LA SERPIENTE Y LA PALOMA, by Manuel Gaxiola.

The impressive success story of the Apostolic Church of Mexico, (an indigenous denomination that never had the help of any foreign missionary), told by a professional scholar now the director of research for that church. (Spanish)

1970: 200 pp, $2.95. ISBN 0-87808-802-4

THE EMERGENCE OF A MEXICAN CHURCH: THE ASSOCIATE REFORMED PRESBYTERIAN CHURCH OF MEXICO, by James Erskine Mitchell.

Tells the ninety-year story of the Associate Reformed Presbyterian Mission in Mexico, the trials and hardships as well as the bright side of the work. Eminently practical and helpful regarding the changing relationship of mission and church in the next decade.

1970: 184 pp, $2.95. ISBN 0-87808-303-0

FRIENDS IN CENTRAL AMERICA, by Paul C. Enyart.

This book describes the results of faithful and effective labors of the California Friends Yearly Meeting, giving an analysis of the growth of one of the most virile, national evangelical churches in Central America, comparing its growth to other evangelical churches in Guatemala, Honduras, and El Salvador.

1970: 224 pp, $3.45. ISBN 0-87808-405-3

Europe

THE CHALLENGE FOR EVANGELICAL MISSIONS TO EUROPE: A SCANDINAVIAN CASE STUDY, by Hilkka Malaska.

Graphically presents the state of Christianity in Scandinavia with an evaluation of the pros and cons and possible contributions that existing or additional Evangelical missions can make in Europe today.

1970: 192 pp, $2.95. ISBN 0-87808-308-1

THE PROTESTANT MOVEMENT IN ITALY: ITS PROGRESS, PROBLEMS, AND PROSPECTS, by Roger Hedlund.

A carefully wrought summary of preliminary data; perceptively develops issues faced by Evangelical Protestants in all Roman Catholic areas of Europe. Excellent graphs.

1970: 266 pp, $3.95. ISBN 0-87808-307-3

U.S.A.

THE YOUNG LIFE CAMPAIGN AND THE CHURCH, by Warren Simandle.

If 70 per cent of young people drop out of the church between the ages of 12 and 20, is there room for a nationwide Christian organization working on high school campuses? After a quarter of a century, what is the record of Young Life and how has its work with teens affected the church? *"A careful analysis based on a statistical survey; full of insight and challenging proposals for both Young Life and the church."*

1970: 216 pp, $3.45. ISBN 0-87808-304-9

THE RELIGIOUS DIMENSION IN SPANISH LOS ANGELES: A PROTESTANT CASE STUDY, by Clifton L. Holland.

A through analysis of the origin, development and present extent of this vital, often unnoticed element in Southern California.

1970: 304 pp, $3.95. ISBN 0-87808-309-X

General

THEOLOGICAL EDUCATION BY EXTENSION, edited by Ralph D. Winter, Ph.D.

A husky handbook on a new approach to the education of pastoral leadership for the church. Gives both theory and practice and the exciting historical development in Latin America of the *"Largest non-governmental voluntary educational development project in the world today."* Ted Ward, Prof. of Education, Michigan State University.

1969: 648 pp, Library Buckram $7.95, Kivar $4.95. ISBN 0-87808-101-1

THE CHURCH GROWTH BULLETIN, VOL. I-V, edited by Donald A. McGavran, Ph.D.

The first five years of issues of a now-famous bulletin which probes past foibles and present opportunities facing the 100,000 Protestant and Catholic missionaries in the world today. No periodical edited for this audience has a larger readership.

1969: 408 pp, Library Buckram $6.95, Kivar $4.45. ISBN 0-87808-701-X

ABOUT THE WILLIAM CAREY LIBRARY

William Carey is widely considered the "Father of Modern Missions" partly because many people think he was the first Protestant missionary. Even though there was a trickle of others before him, he deserves very special honor for many valiant accomplishments in his heroic career, but most particularly because of three things he did before he ever left England, things no one else in history before him had combined together:

1) he had an authentic, personal, evangelical passion to serve God and acknowledged this as obligating him to fulfill God's interests in the redemption of all men on the face of the earth.

2) he actually proposed a structure for the accomplishment of that aim - he did indeed, more than anyone else, set off the movement among Protestants for the creation of "voluntary societies" for foreign missions, and

3) he added to all of this a strategic literary and research achievement: shaky those statistics may have been, but he put together the very best possible estimate of the number of unreached peoples in every part of the globe, and summarized previous, relatively ineffective attempts to reach them. His burning conclusion was that existing efforts were not proportional to the opportunities and the scope of Christian obligation in Mission.

Today, a little over 150 years later, the situation is not wholly different. In the past five years, for example, experienced missionaries from all corners of the earth (53 countries) have brought to the Fuller School of World Mission and Institute of Church Growth well over 800 years of missionary experience. Twenty-six scholarly books have resulted from the research of faculty and students. The best statistics available have at times been shaky -though far superior to Carey's - but vision has been clear and the mandate is as urgent as ever. The printing press is still the right arm of Christians active in the Christian world mission.

The William Carey Library is a new publishing house dedicated to books related to this mission. There are many publishers, both secular and religious, that occasionally publish books of this kind. We believe there is no other devoted exclusively to the production and distribution of books for career missionaries and their home churches.